Election Campaigning

D1376570

JN
956
.K38
1995

Election Campaigning
The New Marketing of Politics

Dennis Kavanagh

BLACKWELL
Oxford UK & Cambridge USA

DAVID L. RICE LIBRARY
UNIVERSITY OF SOUTHERN INDIANA
EVANSVILLE, IN

31754377
AAW2794

Copyright © Dennis Kavanagh 1995

The right of Dennis Kavanagh to be identified as author of this work has been asserted in accordance with the Copyright, Designs and Patents Act 1988.

First published 1995

Blackwell Publishers Ltd
108 Cowley Road
Oxford OX4 1JF

Blackwell Publishers Inc.
238 Main Street
Cambridge, Massachusetts 02142
USA

All rights reserved. Except for the quotation of short passages for the purposes of criticism and review, no part of this publication may be reproduced, stored in a retrieval system, or transmitted, in any form or by any means, electronic, mechanical, photocopying, recording or otherwise, without the prior permission of the publisher.

Except in the United States of America, this book is sold subject to the condition that it shall not, by way of trade or otherwise, be lent, resold, hired out, or otherwise circulated without the publisher's prior consent in any form of binding or cover other than that in which it is published and without a similar condition including this condition being imposed on the subsequent purchaser.

British Library Cataloguing in Publication Data
A CIP catalogue record for this book is available from the British Library.

Library of Congress Cataloging-in-Publication Data
Kavanagh, Dennis.
    Election campaigning / Dennis Kavanagh.
      p. cm.
    Includes bibliographical references and index.
    ISBN 0–631–19809–1 (acid-free paper). – ISBN 0–631–19811–3 (pbk.: acid-free paper)
    1. Electioneering—Great Britain. 2. Communication in politics—Great Britain. 3. Advertising, Political—Great Britain.
    I. Title.
JN956.K38 1995
324.7′0941–dc20
                                  94–48275
                                      CIP

Typeset in 10 on 12pt Baskerville by Photoprint, Torquay, Devon
Printed in Great Britain by Hartnolls Limited, Bodmin, Cornwall

This book is printed on acid-free paper.

To Helen

CONTENTS

FIGURES

TABLES

PREFACE

For several years I have observed the people who shape the general election strategies of British political parties. They are a diverse group, including party politicians and officials as well as what I call the professional communicators – the opinion pollsters, consultants from advertising and public relations agencies, speechwriters and other advisers and helpers. This is a book about the communicators and their activities. The main focus is on the Conservative and Labour parties. I regret omitting the Liberal and the Nationalist parties but I decided that the two major parties were enough for one pair of hands.

Many debts have been incurred in writing this book. I am grateful to those practitioners, listed on pages 251–3, who agreed to be interviewed. Some of these interviews date back many years, to February 1974 when I began writing the Nuffield General Election Studies with David Butler. In a few cases I have cited from correspondence and notes of interviews which Butler and his co-authors conducted in earlier elections. Interviewing has been an essential source of data, partly because so little has yet been written about the activities of the professional communicators. The contrast with the amount of published material on campaigning in the United States is remarkable.

For reading some earlier versions of chapters I am grateful to Hugh Berrington, Jay Blumler, Ivor Crewe, James Douglas, Peter Morris and Colin Seymour-Ure. My secretary at Nottingham, April Pidgeon, has been her usual reliable and patient self in coping with my dictation and handwriting. Needless to say, I alone bear responsibility for the contents.

Dennis Kavanagh

ACKNOWLEDGEMENTS

We gratefully acknowledge permission from the following to reproduce copyright material: Conservative Central Office for reproduction of Conservative Party election posters and advertisements; The National Museum of Labour History for reproduction of Labour Party election posters and advertisements; Express Newspapers plc for cartoon by Cummings from the *Daily Express*, 1955; Macmillan Ltd for reproduction of collage from *The British General Election of 1951* by David Butler, published 1952; and for reproduction of front pages and headlines from the press: Ewan McNaughton Associates on behalf of The Telegraph plc – *Daily Telegraph*, 1951 © The Telegraph plc, London, 1995; Express Newspapers plc – *Daily Express*, 1951 and 1992; Guardian Newspapers Ltd – *Manchester Guardian*, 1951; Mirror Group Newspapers – *Daily Mirror*, 1951 and 1992 and *Daily Herald*, 1951; News Group Newspapers Ltd – the *Sun*, 1992; Solo Syndication Ltd on behalf of Associated Newspapers Ltd – *Daily Mail*, 1951 and 1992, *Daily Graphic/Sketch* and *News Chronicle*, 1951.

INTRODUCTION

Free competitive elections are inseparable from representative democracy. They are the only regular institutionalized opportunities which are available for citizens to decide who governs them. The few weeks of a general election campaign allow voters to hear politicians defend their records, criticize those of their opponents and propose policies for the future. A campaign opens the pores of a political system and an election provides the parties with the electorate's verdict on the past and preferences for the future. How politicians go about campaigning and the extent to which they provide an informed choice for voters is therefore an important subject of study.

Election campaigning in Britain is changing, largely as a response to new technology and the importation of the skills of professional communicators. The literature on voters is enormous, that on the campaign 'producers' tiny. This book is a study of these changes and the people who are behind them. Some participants and commentators welcome the communication changes, some deplore them, few are neutral. Prominent politicians admit that television has become the crucial medium for communicating with voters and feel that it is essential for them to employ the skills of advertising agencies, pollsters, public relations advisers and speechwriters. At the same time, however, they often resent their dependence on these technicians, and seem to recall some golden age of campaigning when they, the politicians, were more important and before public relations moved in. They accept the services of the pollsters and consultants but do not empathize with them. A study of US campaigning concluded that, 'most candidates know they want consultants and vaguely know consultants are "necessary" without quite understanding what consultants do' (Sabato 1981: xiv). Print and broadcast journalists, locked in a loveless embrace with politicians and campaign managers, have their own complaints. They often deplore the ruthless way in which party managers concentrate on image projection, photo-opportunities and soundbites, and criticize the growing stage-management and trivialization of the electoral process. Politicians in turn often complain that these features are a consequence of the style of media coverage. Commentators and campaigners blame each other.

This book explores the rise of the new campaign professionals and the reactions of the politicians to them. It shows how the parties have come to terms with the new techniques and assesses the influence of pollsters and advertising agencies on election campaigns. The use of the term 'Americanization' to describe the process acknowledges that many of the media-related activities and the reliance of politicians on professional communicators developed first in the United States and have been emulated in other countries (Butler and Ranney 1992; Mancini and Swanson 1995). The trends are no respecter of national boundaries; British and American experts in the new techniques have been prominent in the recent free elections in South Africa and Eastern Europe. The parties in those countries provided pictures and sound-bites for television's evening news programmes and commissioned polls and focus groups to research the concerns of 'floating' voters – just as in Britain and the United States. The influence does not, however, flow one way only. If the Conservative's negative tax campaigns against Labour in 1992 echoed the attacking advertising of the Bush Presidential campaign in 1988, the Bush strategy in the 1992 election borrowed in part from the Conservative themes of tax and leadership.

Modern campaigning involves three key groups of actors. Voters have been much studied. Although there have been disputes over alternative explanations we now know a good deal of what shapes electoral behaviour (Heath, Jowell and Curtice 1985, 1991; Rose and McAllister 1990). Campaigners are interested in this research because it helps them to understand the voter and to target their communications more effectively. An academic study of the aspirations of working-class voters in 1960 (Abrams and Rose) influenced the thinking of Labour leaders about electoral strategy. Later studies, which emphasized how voting behaviour is shaped by long-term forces, have also influenced campaign strategies. In 1992, three months before the general election began, both Labour and Conservative parties sought to set the agenda and open a decisive lead for themselves in the opinion polls. The election, they concluded, would be largely decided before the campaign officially began. Campaign managers in both the Labour and Conservative parties were influenced by an academic study, *How Voters Change: The 1987 British General Election Campaign in Perspective* (Miller et al. 1990). This showed how the key aggregate shifts in voting behaviour (to the Conservatives) had been achieved in the six months prior to the beginning of the 1987 election campaign. Political parties are now convinced of the need to fight long campaigns.

Although the literature on electoral behaviour is enormous, the voters are only one element in the campaign equation. The press and television journalists constitute a second group of actors. For long there has been a close relationship between British politicians and the press, both London and provincial. In the first half of the twentieth century the party leaders' attempts to manage the media did not go much beyond cultivating press proprietors, editors and lobby journalists, and the party publicists largely confined themselves to sending out press releases to favoured papers. The arrival of television, and the growing importance of its campaign coverage since 1959, has transformed the relationship between political parties and the media and between press and television. As long as the great majority of voters rely on the mass media for their knowledge and impressions of politics, then politicians depend on television and newspapers to communicate with voters. The campaign managers now adopt media-oriented publicity strategies. In a discussion of communications strategy in 1992 the Conservative party's 'War Book' stated, 'The most important target group is the media'.

Much debate centres on the role of the media in setting the election agenda, i.e. shaping the campaign's major issues and themes. Does media coverage largely reflect the parties' agenda or does it, as politicians often complain, initiate its own agenda? Posed in this way, however, the question is too simple. The politicians disagree among themselves about the main themes and issues, and the mass media, including different television channels, programmes, newspapers and magazines, are hardly homogeneous (e.g. Blumler et al. 1989; Seymour-Ure 1974, 1991; Semetko et al. 1990). The main television channels are subject to regulations about political and election coverage, governed by public service norms and expected to provide 'balanced' coverage of the parties. Newspapers are under no such restrictions and Labour leaders complain bitterly about the bias against their own party.

Finally, there are the politicians, campaign managers and advisers, the people whose job it is to influence the voters. The Nuffield College studies of general elections, starting with the 1945 election, have provided some information about the electoral thinking and calculations of British political leaders and campaign managers. (For the most recent study see Butler and Kavanagh 1992.) But the topic has been rather neglected, as is true of the thinking and operating procedures of politicians as a whole. Nearly thirty years ago, Richard Rose wrote *Influencing Voters* (1967) at a time when television, public relations and opinion polling were just beginning to have an impact. Rose was impressed by the lack of professionalism of campaigners in their efforts to influence voters.

There have been numerous studies of election campaigning and political marketing in the United States, starting with Stanley Kelley's seminal *Professional Public Relations and Political Power* (1956). For Britain there has been no follow-up to Rose although there is an inside account by a former Communications Director of the Conservative party (Bruce 1992) and a study of the (often tense) relationships between politicians and the television media by Michael Cockerell (1988). Nicholas O'Shaughnessy's *The Phenomenon of Political Marketing* (1990) has something on the British experience, but draws mainly on the United States. Campaign consultancy has become a major business in the United States and has undoubtedly transformed campaigning there. A sample of the book titles gives some idea of the significance often attributed to the consultants: *The New Kingmakers*, *The Political Image Merchants*, *The Political Persuaders*, *The Election Men: Professional Campaign Managers and American Democracy*, *The Rise of Political Consultants* and *Packaging the Presidency*. The consequences of the new trends for the quality of American politics and the health of democracy have caused concern (Jamieson 1992a, 1992b; Sabato 1981, 1992; Bennett 1992). They have been blamed for further weakening political parties, increasing the leverage of single-issue groups, facilitating the rise of politicians whose main merits are good looks or media skills, and encouraging leaders slavishly to follow public opinion. According to one writer

> Political consultants, answerable only to their client-candidates and independent of the political parties, have inflicted severe damage upon the party system and masterminded the modern triumph of personality cults over party politics in the United States. All the while they have gradually but steadily accumulated almost unchecked and unrivalled

power and influence in a system that is partly their handiwork. (Sabato 1981: 3)

Chapter 1 discusses how campaign communications have changed in the course of the century and how politicians have reacted to developments in political marketing. Essentially, the professionals ask the party representatives to define the party's 'message' which they will then try to communicate to voters, using the most effective available methods. To quote one Labour politician who has also been a publicist for the party, 'The professionals concentrate on the message, the electorate, and getting one to the other in a way that few politicians and officials do' (Mandelson interview). Because many of the methods were first developed in the United States and exist in a 'higher form' there, the main features of the 'professional' model are drawn chiefly from that country. The distinctiveness of each campaign makes generalizations risky but there are also many constants. Chapter 2 discusses such constant factors as the election rules – for example, about expenditure and access to broadcasting – and the forces for change among the electorate, structures of the parties, electoral themes and media.

Chapters 3 and 4 examine the role of the professional communicators in the Conservative and Labour election campaigns since 1959. Labour has blown hot and cold on the usefulness and propriety of involving such people and employing such techniques. Since 1959 it has often relied upon unpaid volunteers from the communications industry, who were highly organized in 1987 and 1992. The Conservatives experimented with different advertising agencies between 1959 and 1970 but have employed Saatchi & Saatchi for all general elections from 1979 to 1992. Chapters 3 and 4 explore the ways in which the parties have, sometimes reluctantly, used the skills of professional communicators in recent elections and describe the tensions which have often occurred between the two. There is a tension between, on the one hand, the Parliamentary and Cabinet system, political culture and broadcasting regulations in Britain, and on the other, the new forces of political marketing, largely American inspired.

Chapters 5 and 6 describe and analyse the work of opinion pollsters. Opinion polls now play such an important part in elections, not least for the mass media which report the findings, that it is difficult to envisage campaigns without them. Moreover, their messages about which party is ahead or which one is gaining (the election 'horse race'), or the comparative strengths and weaknesses of the parties' images, increasingly shape media coverage of the election. They also affect the morale of the politicians, the judgements of the commentators and, sometimes, even the decisions of campaign managers. Public polls have moved from providing a reading of the campaign to being a part of it. The consequences, for the professional standing of the pollster and for the calculations and morale of the politicians, have been the subject of much debate. Chapter 6 reviews the ways in which political parties have used their private polls to shape election strategies and the relationships between pollsters and politicians. It compares the very modest role of the private pollsters in Britain to their American counterparts. Chapter 7 presents an overview of the parties' use of the new communications in election campaigns, noting the similarities and differences. It also attempts to assess the claims made for and against the electoral effectiveness of these professionals, as well as their impact on the conduct of campaigns and on the parties. It considers finally, claims that the professionalization is part of a larger political agenda, in particular the downgrading of distinctive party ideologies.

In communicating with a mass electorate, politicians and campaign managers increasingly concentrate their communications on television. Campaign strategies are largely media strategies. One regularly hears at various party headquarters the refrain 'this election will be won or lost on television'. In Britain 99 per cent of homes have at least one set and most people derive their impressions of politics and politicians from television. Chapters 8 and 9 examine respectively the campaign roles of press and television and how the media has affected the behaviour of the campaign managers. In chapter 10 a comparison is made with campaigns in the United States and crucial differences in the political contexts of the two countries are emphasized. In Britain, the parties are stronger, the culture less populist and the broadcasting media more regulated and more 'closed' to the politicians than in the United States. There is a handful of campaign consultants in Britain compared to over 5,000 in the US. The British parties turn to advertising agencies whose commercial viability derives from their non-political business between elections. In Britain there is as yet no market for campaign consultancy.

Chapter 11 tries to draw together the discussion and analyses of the previous chapters and assesses the effectiveness of modern campaigning methods, the barriers to effectiveness and the consequences of the developments for the quality of British democracy. Although campaigning is changing, politicians in Britain are still creatures of habit and there remain many obstacles not only to the professionalization but also to the effectiveness of campaigning. Television and the techniques of political marketing have led to some similarities in campaigning in Britain and the United States, but differences in the countries' political institutions and cultures have prevented convergence. The importance of the communicators and consultants varies inversely according to the strength of the parties. Apart from the US they are significant in the emerging democracies in Asia, Latin America, South Africa and Eastern Europe. In Western Europe the prominence of the new methods and new parties in Italy in 1994 also reflect in large part the decay of the older parties. In Britain, the stronger party system means that the pollsters and experts on public relations and communications still have an insecure relationship with the politicians. In this respect British elections are still far from being Americanized.

1

NEW CAMPAIGN COMMUNICATIONS

Election campaigning adapts by employing the latest techniques and ideas in effective communications and persuasion. In this respect parties are like businesses seeking to promote their products: one seeks votes, the other sales. In the late nineteenth century the main forms of election publicity in Britain were leaflets, posters and manifestos, which were distributed in the constituencies by party workers. A party's case nationally was largely carried by leaders addressing mass meetings and reports of the speeches in the regional and national press. The creation of a mass electorate, as a result of the extensions of the suffrage in 1918 and 1928, stimulated the parties to use the newly invented cinema and radio. Stanley Baldwin in Britain and Franklin Roosevelt in the USA were among the first political leaders to make effective use of radio in the 1930s.

But most politicians were slow to adapt. On one day during the 1924 general election the Labour leader Ramsay MacDonald left Glasgow at 9 a.m. and in the course of the next 12 hours addressed large crowds in 16 constituencies. Needless to say he was exhausted at the end of the day by these methods of communicating with voters (Marquand 1977: 379). As recently as the 1955 general election campaign, the Prime Minister Sir Anthony Eden would spend Monday to Friday touring the country, staying overnight in provincial hotels, accompanied only by two or three aides. He would have a late-night telephone talk with the party Chairman, read the morning newspapers over breakfast and deliver a set speech each night. He had no need to plan mass-media campaigns or monitor the output of television and radio – which did not report the campaign – or comment on the opinion polls. He did not hold daily strategy meetings and gave very few press conferences or media interviews (Lindsey interview).

Technology has now made such methods of campaigning 'old style'. The new methods enable politicians to communicate with millions of voters via television or direct mail, rather than hundreds of voters face to face. A consequence has been the party leaders' growing use of short statements for television soundbites and a reduction in the number of major campaign speeches delivered or which are reported at length in the press. In recent general election campaigns Margaret Thatcher, John Major and Neil Kinnock each gave only a handful of set-piece speeches. Servicing the media is now a major operation and requires a great deal of advance preparation. In contrast to Eden, the party leaders are now accompanied by several aides, in regular touch with campaign managers by fax and mobile phones, and followed by buses containing scores of journalists. The new technologies have also given scope and influence to new campaign elites, recruited from public relations and advertising, with expertise in television, direct mail and opinion polls.

Labour and Conservative parties have differed in their use of professional communications, differences which in part derive from their contrasting political values and party structures. But the convergences between the parties now outweigh the differences and amount to a new professionalization of campaign communications. For the 1992 election the parties devoted more resources to advertising, public relations, opinion polling and marketing strategies than ever before. A typical judgement on the election's stage-managed media events and photo-opportunities was that it 'was the most orchestrated, sanitised and Americanised campaign Britain has ever seen' (Berry 1992: 565). More broadly, according to Bob Franklin, we now live in 'a media democracy in which politicians and policies are packaged for media marketing and public consumption' (1994: 23). According to two observers of the successful Presidential campaign of Mary Robinson in Ireland in 1990, 'The political campaign is analogous to the product development process and can be described and managed in the same way' (Butler and Collins 1993: 4). Similar trends are evident in business, local and central government, pressure groups and many organizations. Franklin (1994: 4) quotes a Conservative Cabinet minister in 1988, saying 'policies are like cornflakes, if they are not marketed they will not sell'. All want to improve their internal and external communications.

We would not expect parties to be different, for a general election is the largest of all exercises in persuasion.

Professionalization

The trends towards the professionalization of the parties' campaign communications have not been confined to Britain. They are increasingly found across many countries where competitive elections are held, and where the uses of computers, television, advertising and opinion polling are well developed. This globalization of the new methods is sometimes called an 'Americanization' of campaigning. In the United States, computers and television have revolutionized American campaign methods and facilitated the rise of a corps of campaign consultants, pollsters and media advisers who in turn have made politicians dependent on them and their services. The main features of the professional model are (Blumler, Kavanagh and Nossiter 1995):

1   *The importance of campaign communications.* This process includes the parties' recruitment of technical experts from the public relations, media and advertising industries to assist with campaign publicity, media presentation, opinion polling and advertisements. It is accompanied by an *ethos* of professionalism in which the parties emphasize the need for co-ordination, orchestration and discipline in their communications.

2   *An uprating of publicity priorities in campaigning, as the party actors devote more energy and resources to media strategy and tactics.* Much of a leading politician's campaign day – the morning press conference, afternoon walkabout and evening rally – is largely shaped by the requirements of the media and setting the media agenda is the main purpose of the communications strategy.

3   *The explanation of a party's election victory or defeat in terms of (1) and (2) above, i.e. publicity-related factors.* Poor communications or 'failing to get the message across' are often advanced as major reasons for a party's defeat.

4   *The adaptation of the campaign to the presumed format requirements of television.* These include the persistence of leader walkabouts, focus on the leader and organization of press conferences and events suitable for soundbites, photographs and film.

5   *The idea of electioneering as political marketing.* Parties commission public opinion polls to research the mood of voters and the results are used by parties to shape their campaign communications. Opinion polls are also used by the news media to report how the parties are doing or what Americans call the election 'horse race'.

6   *An increase in negative or attack campaigning.* Publicity concentrates at least as much time attacking the defects of opponents as presenting the merits of the sponsoring party. More campaign managers appear to believe that such communications are electorally more effective than positive appeals. The aggressive tone is strengthened as journalists present a more negative interpretation of the campaign, in the sense of reporting it in adversarial terms (Patterson 1993).

7   *The dilemma for political journalists in defining a role for themselves in an era of 'saturation' coverage and manipulative politicians and campaign advisers.* Faced with the parties' efforts to shape and even manipulate media coverage, journalists respond by commissioning opinion polls, concentrating on campaign gaffes, assuming a 'disdainful' style of coverage and presenting behind-the-scenes stories about the party's strategies and image-making efforts (Levy 1981; Semetko et al. 1990).

8   *The main gainers from the new political campaigning being the independent experts such as advertising personnel, media advisers and pollsters, most of whom are recruited from outside the parties.* Within the party machine those charged with responsibility for publicity and campaigning have moved up the pecking order ahead of other officials. The publicity chief is often, *de facto* or *de jure*, a formal or informal member of the strategy group formed around the leader; this will not usually be so for other officials. The losers have been old-style politicians and party officials, in so far as they have not absorbed the new techniques.

Resistance

The above trends emerged rapidly in British elections between 1959 and 1970 and have been consolidated since. But initially they faced hurdles. Before 1959 there was little polling and no political advertising during general election campaigns. Even when professional communicators were employed they were often kept at arms' length by party leaders. One reason was the general scepticism among senior politicians that such techniques, perhaps suitable for promoting goods and services, were effective for politics. They claimed that politics was different and that, as elected politicians, it was their job to understand and to lead public opinion. They were their own communicators via speeches reported in the press, and political statements of national importance were made in Parliament not to the media. Most politicians also probably regarded themselves as having a higher social status than people employed in advertising or the media. In 1950 a deferential television interviewer asked Prime Minister Attlee if he had anything he wished to say on the eve of the election campaign. Attlee replied 'No' and after an awkward pause that was the end of the interview!

There was also resistance from some officials employed in the parties' headquarters and from agents in the constituencies. During elections it was their task to report back on the voters' mood in the constituencies and to organize the distribution of party pamphlets and leaflets to the voters. The new methods and the new men were a threat, an invasion of their 'turf'.

There was, further, a perceived legal obstacle to importing the skills of the advertising industry. Party leaders assumed that political advertising during an election was illegal, because Section 63 of the Representation of the People Act provides that no person other than the candidate's duly authorized agent may incur election expenses. They feared that a display of national posters in a constituency might be regarded as an election expense and be chargeable to the local candidate. A court case (R v. Tronah Mines Ltd) in 1952, however, ruled that political advertising which did not mention specific candidates was not a breach of the law on expenses and opened the way for the use of nationwide posters in the campaign in the late 1950s. But parties remained uncertain about the legality of press advertising in the campaign and abstained from it until 1979. Since then the increase in such advertising has added substantially to the costs of elections, with the Conservatives for example spending nearly £4 million on press ads in the 1987 campaign. The rules governing access to the broadcasting media also limited the scope for political advertising – and therefore the use of money. Neither the BBC nor independent television allows party political advertising. According to a policy decision of the Independent Broadcasting Authority (IBA) 'No advertisement may be inserted by or on behalf of anybody the objects whereof are wholly or mainly of a political nature, and no advertisement may be directed towards any political end' (see Briggs 1970). Until recently, therefore, the scope for using the skills of the modern persuaders was restricted.

The most notable party use of an advertising agency and large-scale press advertising was by the Conservatives in the 1959 election and it produced much hostile comment. Labour politicians criticized the methods as 'Americanization', 'selling politics like soap powder' and some Conservatives also thought them vulgar. But the trends continued and by 1964 Labour followed suit. In the course of a review of a study of the 1964 election the Political Correspondent of *The Times* warned 'The real risk is that we are moving towards the day when market research, opinion poll findings, techniques of motivational persuasion and public relations, and even the analyses of political scientists would be crudely and cold bloodedly used to govern party strategies in government and out' (27 April 1965).

Projecting Party Images

Achieving a favourable image for the candidate or party is now a key objective of modern campaigning. Parties and candidates will have images freely provided by the mass media and by their political opponents. Hence the incentive to do it for themselves. A prerequisite for good political communications is to understand the thinking of the voters. As long ago as 1908 Graham Wallas, in his *Human Nature in Politics*, questioned the assumption that most people thought rationally about politics; he was more impressed by how emotional and prejudiced they were and by their susceptibility to propaganda and symbolic appeals. Voters carried in their heads simple images of the parties and politicians should address that fact. In Wallas's words: 'Something is required, simpler and more permanent, something which can be loved and trusted, and which can be recognised at successive elections as being the same thing that was loved and trusted before; and a party is such a thing' (1948: 83).

Walter Lippman's *Public Opinion* (1922) also refuted assumptions that voters were rational; he claimed that most people thought about public affairs in terms of stereotypes. Joseph Schumpeter was another who emphasized the scope which politicians had for crude persuasion and making irrational appeals, largely because most people found politics complex and remote compared to, say, making decisions about spending the household budget; they wanted simplicity. Schumpeter believed that voters were more interested in a party's image than its policies (Schumpeter 1976: 283). A more up-to-date statement about the importance of the politician's and party's image was made by a speechwriter for Richard Nixon, then seeking the Republican nomination for the Presidential election in 1968. In a memorandum to his campaign colleagues he stressed that the voters' approval of a candidate was not based on reality, but

is a product of the particular chemistry between the voter and the image of the candidate. *We have to be very clear on this point: that the response is to the image, not to the man* ... It's not what's *there* that counts. ... and this impression often depends more on the medium and its use than it does on the candidate himself. (McGinnis 1970: 174–5, original emphasis)

The new methods of political communications were pioneered in the United States. In 1933 the Californians Clem Whitaker and Leone Smith Baxter formed the first firm of campaign consultants, Campaigns Inc., providing the strategy and advertising for local candidates. Today their many successors can draw on computers, opinion polling, direct mail and diverse media outlets to plan more sophisticated and expensive campaigns. A significant development in political marketing via television advertising was the 1952 Presidential campaign of the Republican candidate, Dwight Eisenhower. His campaign team recruited from leading advertising agencies, commissioned Gallup to research the issues which concerned the voters and employed a Hollywood actor, Robert Montgomery, to improve Eisenhower's television performances. The candidate then made television and radio 'spot' commercials, lasting between 20 and 60 seconds, for transmission in key states. At the time half of American households already had television sets. The messages, in which Eisenhower expressed his concern about a particular issue and made a vague promise to improve things, were played repeatedly over the last few days of the campaign. Even greater influence was attributed to the medium in 1960 when John F. Kennedy impressed viewers in the first televised Presidential debates with Nixon.

Since then political marketing and the use of television in the United States have increased significantly in scale, sophistication and expense (Sabato 1981: ch. 4). The development of telephone canvassing and direct mail enables candidates and parties to write personalized letters to millions of 'target' voters for support and funds. Speeches are now made in specially staged locations to facilitate television coverage and in the hope of gaining an insert in a news broadcast, enabling candidates to speak to millions of voters in their living rooms. The 1968 Nixon Presidential campaign, designed to project a 'new Nixon', drew heavily on the skills of pollsters, advertising and public relations consultants and speechwriters, and marked a new stage in professionalization. Since then the Reagan, Bush and Clinton campaigns marked similar breakthroughs respectively in media management, negative advertising and research-based campaigning.

British parties have responded and are now expected to enter an election with what is called a communications strategy, just as a business does when it launches a new product. The professional communicators write planning papers well in advance of an election, stating the campaign's strategic objectives and proposing ways to realize them. The papers cover plans to set the political agenda, fight by-elections, increase or reduce the salience of particular issues and themes; they will also include suggestions for 'pacing' a campaign, timing initiatives, selecting themes and photo-opportunities for each campaign day, anticipating the election strategies of other parties and how these might be countered, as well as which research to commission, phrases and arguments to deploy for attack and defence and personalities to give prominence to. Posters and stage sets for the leaders' meetings are specifically designed to attract the 'free' coverage in the press and television news reports. Television coverage of the 'unveiling' of a single party poster is a virtually cost-free exercise and all parties ruthlessly exploited the format in 1992.

British party leaders delegate campaign arrangements to the head of the party organization. In the Conservative party this is the party Chairman, who heads Central Office and is usually a senior politician; for Labour, the General Secretary who runs the party headquarters. Each in turn will allocate a major responsibility to the party's communications director who, in contrast to other officials, is likely to have had public relations or media experience. The director will usually be the *de facto* client for the advertising and polling agencies and give approval to the proposals from the communications team. He or she is the link between party organization and the communications professionals.

Advertising agencies regularly ask or help their clients in business or politics to define their objectives. What do they stand for? How do they differ from their competitors? Why should people vote for them? In drawing up a strategy the essential questions they ask of the party managers, as of commercial clients, are:

What are we trying to say?
Whom are we trying to reach?
How should we reach them?

The policies are a matter for the politicians, and for the governing party they exist in the form of its record and its promises for the future; for the opposition parties in the form of their programmes. The target voters, usually potential converts or potential defectors, are identified on the basis of focus-group research and surveys. Once the strategy has been designed the agency plays a significant role in choosing the media mix for communicating the party's messages. In 1991 Saatchi & Saatchi proposed that the Conservative party should concentrate on increasing the salience of issues on which it was favourably regarded by voters (e.g. defence, tax and law and order) and improving its standing on issues which were more salient (e.g. health, unemployment). The politicians agreed (see pp. 68–9).

Harry Treleavan, a member of Richard Nixon's advertising team in the 1968 Presidential campaign, wrote about the need to develop the '*proposition* . . . the message we want to communicate', something that is more than a slogan or a theme (McGinniss 1970: 154). Communicators working for British parties listen to politicians, officials and researchers expounding the party's case and then use this information to propose themes for speeches, broadcasts and advertisements. Once the strategy emerges it will, as far as possible, be distilled to one or two pages. (For an example, see the Conservative strategy document for 1970 in the Appendix to chapter 3, pp. 75–6.)

Condensing a party's message to, say, one page, however, is not always easy. One difficulty, according to communicators, is that most politicians talk in a particular style and language. They are often evasive, invoke approved party symbols and myths and tend to be specific about benefits and vague about costs; they resort to generalizations and vagueness to avoid offending voters. Politicians may also remember that simple statements and slogans have often got political leaders into trouble. Chamberlain's 'peace for our time' (1938), Macmillan's 'never had it so good' (1957), Wilson's 'pound in your pocket' (1967), Heath's 'at a stroke' reduction in the rate of price rises (1970), Saatchi's 'Labour isn't working' poster (1978) and Callaghan's alleged 'Crisis? What crisis?' (1979), all soon came to haunt them.*

The fact that a government is unpopular, say, because of a poorly performing economy, divisions in Cabinet or outside events may also make it difficult for the party to answer the communicators' questions directly. Geoffrey Tucker, who has helped in various capacities with Conservative campaign communications, is struck by the sheer

---

* Callaghan did not use these words. It was the *Sun* newspaper's headline interpretation of his reply to a reporter's question on his return from Guadaloupe during widespread strikes.

variability of what is marketed in politics, compared to commerce: 'A can of coca-cola or a car does not change from day to day. But perceptions of a party, a government or a leader can shift dramatically not because they have changed but because of the impact of events. And we cannot control these' (interview). In 1963 the Conservative communicators felt themselves unable to project a positive message for the party because of the uncertainty over Harold Macmillan's leadership, scandals, by-election humiliations and economic problems. Labour's agency in 1983 had difficulty summarizing a positive case for such a divided party and for policies which many leaders found abhorrent. In 1991 the Conservative advertising agency Saatchi & Saatchi found that party managers took some time to define John Major's new Conservatism. According to Jeremy Sinclair,

> We had worked for Thatcher for many years and voters had a clear idea of what she stood for. We now wanted to know if the party clearly stood for lower taxes over more spending and the delay was in large part because the client did not yet know what he stood for. Politicians are bad, they don't have the discipline say, of the marketing department of Procter & Gamble. The job of advertising is to supply that discipline. What we want from a client is the objective or the proposition, what there is to support that proposition and what tone do they want to adopt. This produces three paragraphs and is the purpose of modern marketing. This simplicity comes as a surprise to many politicians. They want to go on and talk for ages. (Interview)

The typical politician's career background does not help. A party leader, or Conservative party Chairman or Labour General Secretary will usually have had less experience of acting as a client for an advertising or polling agency than will the managing director or marketing manager of a large company. The party leader or Conservative Chairman is plucked from the ranks of professional politicians, while most managers will have worked their way up the organization and, at each stage, probably been involved in decisions about marketing strategy. And few politicians before reaching the top have had to think in terms of preparing a communications strategy for the electorate as a whole. As they ascend the career ladder, politicians acquire skills in speaking to different audiences – local activists, fellow MPs, civil servants, party conferences and committees. But not until they become leaders do they regularly address the national electorate.

Why Communicators get Involved

It is understandable why a major party or ambitious candidate recruits a pollster, an advertising agency and volunteers from the public relations and communications industry. But parties can be difficult clients and not all advertising or polling agencies are willing to handle a party's account. Politics is controversial; a party's account may divide the agency's workforce and, particularly if the party is Labour, other clients of the agency may be offended. The pressures at election time are intense and even if the agency is large the demands may overload it or force it to neglect its other clients. Working for a political party is also high risk; mistakes are magnified and covered by the media, losing politicians are usually ungrateful, agencies are not expected to answer back and there is a dreadful finality about being on the losing side on polling day.

Yet many agencies and pollsters eagerly court political parties. The Conservatives, in particular, have had no shortage of applicants. Many are inspired by the record of Saatchi & Saatchi, whose turnover and profits before tax grew ten-fold and six-fold respectively in the first five years after taking the Conservative account in 1978. But that growth record was not sustained and a commercial boost is far from assured. An advertising agency will agree a programme of work and a budget with a party, covering fees for services and expenses of staff; in addition it will collect the standard 15 per cent commission for placing press advertisements, as well as costs for additional services. The financial rewards are modest, compared with what can be earned from commercial clients and payments from a party are often irregular and delayed; some Saatchi executives claim that the party has often undercharged for services and that, at best, the agency has broken even on the Conservative account. In 1992 the Saatchi election budget was some £5 million, and the account was still being paid off 24 months after the election by a Conservative party heavily in debt. In contrast, commercial clients usually settle accounts promptly. Communicators who have worked on a paid basis for Labour in the past have also complained about the difficulties in extracting payment from the party.

Most of the many rewards for the communicators are therefore less tangible. There is also the prospect of political honours (e.g. Labour's Lord Lyons and Lord Lovell-Davis, as well as the Conservatives' Sir Tim Bell, Sir Ronald Millar and Sir Gordon Reece). They certainly acquire more visibility; handling a party account guarantees massive publicity for the agency or pollster. Communicators who have worked on an election campaign often look back on it as the most exciting period in their career. It provides an opportunity to meet a Prime Minister or other senior political figures (compared to the middle-level executives that they usually deal with), to help elect a government and to influence the way in which a country is governed. There is also the challenge that comes from the opportunity to write ads which are guaranteed wide publicity. Even professional communicators who have found working on an election campaign a bruising experience and the politicians ungrateful, usually still regard it as a highlight in their professional careers.

Full-time employees for the political parties do not always take easily to the arrival of the communicators. They are aware that most pollsters and advertising directors are highly paid, have careers and sources of income apart from their work for the party and enjoy privileged access to key party figures. They may also feel that the communicators' jobs are not on the line, in the way that their own are. As a group the communicators have little time for the labyrinthine committees so beloved of parties, particularly Labour.

There are analogies between an agency selling the merits of a political party or leader to voters and, say, a bar of chocolate to customers. (Indeed in 1981 the Conservatives recruited an executive from the American Mars chocolate company to head a new marketing department in Central Office and to promote direct mail.) In both cases the task is to formulate a communications strategy and then implement it. A profits-oriented firm or business wants to know what customers want and how to sell it to them. The communicator builds on the existing brand loyalty of customers or voters, tries to meet the dislikes and wishes of potential purchasers or supporters and selectively reviews the strengths and weaknesses of rival brands or parties. Voters are like customers and the party has to respond to their concerns and establish its own 'brand' image to distinguish itself from rivals.

Communications specialists are reluctant to state that selling parties is like selling a bar of soap because they know that politicians resent the analogy. But they also make clear that many of the disciplines involved in selling the two are similar. This is not surprising, for they have gained most of their experience in the commercial field and draw on it when employed by the political parties. A political scientist, Adrian Sackman, defends the relevance of a political marketing approach 'which views the political party as a "player" in the political market, exploiting the techniques of audience research and persuasion in a similar way to actions of a commercial firm operating in a competitive market' (Sackman 1994: 466).

In spite of similarities between promoting a product and promoting a party, differences remain. Publicists and pollsters who have worked in both fields claim that nothing in product promotion compares with the pressure of an election campaign – the need for speed, the intense scrutiny of the media, the public interest and the finality of the verdict on election day. In commerce there may be many rival brands but in an election campaign there is a more clearly defined opponent – be it a party or a candidate. John Bartle, a managing director of the BBH agency which does not handle party campaigns, reflected: 'There is no repertoire in politics. If you are advertising chocolate, people can buy two or three brands or change from day to day. But in politics you can vote for only one party. That is why you have to believe strongly what you are promoting in politics' (interview).

Targeting Voters

Experts in political communications, like their counterparts in commerce, talk about targeting specific groups. They broadly divide voters and constituencies into 'ours' and 'theirs'. In a competitive two-party system the crucial voters are those who are weakly attached or not attached to a party. The purpose of the opinion polling and qualitative research is to enable the party's strategists to identify the characteristics and concerns of these voters and then address them. Target voters may be variously defined by geographical location, life style, values or attitudes, demography, e.g. age, sex or social class, and so on. Another approach is to define the targets in terms of constituencies, particularly the marginal seats, the results in which decide most general elections. Apart, however, from some clustering in a few regions marginal seats are found across the country and the social characteristics of voters in such seats are pretty similar to those found elsewhere.

But some experts doubt the effectiveness of targeting, for commercial experience suggests that if the sales of a product increase they usually do so across social groups. It is also difficult to target voters precisely in a national campaign. The *Guardian* readership, for example, is largely middle class but the paper and the great majority of its readers do not support the Conservative party; the *Sun* has a largely working-class readership and is read by many Labour voters but is hostile to the party. Martin Harrop's warning is apposite: 'Target voters should therefore be identified by attitudes to parties rather than to policies and, when this is done, they turn out to be much like everyone else. It is therefore no surprise that the campaign that works for target voters works for other groups as well' (Harrop 1990: 283). At constituency level, the development of computers and information technology does provide the opportunities for making targeted appeals to voters. Local parties can use telephone canvassing, direct-mail appeals for funds and support and leaflets to different socio-demographic groups. As yet, however, Britain still lags behind the United States in using these techniques and the strict laws on local campaign expenditure mean that they will be more widely used before the campaign is officially declared and limits on expenditure operate.

Conclusion

The ways in which a more professional communications approach has been adopted by the Conservative and Labour parties are considered in succeeding chapters. The development has had the effects of promoting among campaign managers a greater interest in studying the mood of the electorate; an increased awareness of 'key' voters and determination to target campaign messages at them; a concentration on and greater repetition of arguments and phrases, and a concern with setting the agenda by suggesting stories and interpretation for the media and staging events specifically for coverage. A professional approach to campaigning is marked by a number of features:

the subordination of all goals to that of election victory;
the reliance on survey and focus-group research to guide the party's appeal to
    voters;
the pre-eminence of the mass media as the means for reaching voters;
the importance of communications specialists in campaign terms.

Chapters 3 to 6 analyse the ways in which the parties have come to terms with the new methods. Before then chapter 2 provides a contextual background.

2

CONTEXT

It is difficult to generalize about election campaigns because no two elections are ever quite the same, even in one country. Students of elections often regard the verdict as the outcome of (a) long-term forces such as demography and underlying party loyalties, and (b) short-term factors surrounding each election, which reinforce or change those predispositions. The same kind of approach can be applied to election campaigns. Even within a period of three or four years each election is shaped by a different combination of short-term forces like public mood, political personalities and issues, party records, national and international events and more gradual changes in the composition of the electorate, election laws and communications technology. The purpose of this chapter is to discuss the more significant features of the political environment in which British election campaigns are held. It discusses, in particular, the recent developments in electoral behaviour, campaign themes, parties and mass media.

Electoral Change

Since 1945 British society has become more middle class, more 'up-market'. As late as the 1970s market researchers divided society into an approximate 60–40 split between working and middle class. Today, depending on definitions, the manual working class has fallen to between a third and 40 per cent of the workforce. Since 1979 the steady increase in home ownership, now covering two-thirds of households, decline in trade union membership from over 13 million to less than 8 million, greater reliance on private transport and extension of share ownership to 20 per cent of the adult population, are signs of this embourgeoisement. Some four-fifths of voters now belong to 'mixed' social-class categories, e.g. working-class home-owners, or white-collar wives of working-class husbands. The greater ambiguity of class identity has helped to weaken partisanship. Indeed, a person's housing tenure, whether owner-occupation or council tenancy, is now a better predictor of party vote than social class. The social changes have political consequences, for the groups declining in size – council-house tenants, trade unionists, manual workers and inner-city residents – have been disproportionately core Labour voters. A calculation of the net political effects of such social changes in the parties' hypothetical natural vote is that between 1964 and 1987 they cost Labour some four per cent of the vote and boosted the Conservative vote by nearly three per cent (Heath, Jowell and Curtice 1991).

It is sometimes suggested that these social changes are connected with the growth of electoral volatility, although this feature has also been linked with the spread of television, better education and the voters' disappointment with the records in office of both major political parties. Volatility may be measured in different ways. Between a fifth and a quarter of voters claim to decide how to vote during the election campaign and about a third actually change their voting intention over the lifetime of a Parliament, features which have been pretty stable for the past twenty years. A second measure is party loyalty. Surveys conducted between 1964 and 1987 showed a fall in the number of people identifying with the Labour and Conservative political parties, particularly with Labour (see table 2.1). Of those claiming to identify very strongly with the two parties the fall has been sharper,

Table 2.1 Trends in party identification

	Con. %	*Lab. %*	*Lib./SDP %*
1964	39	42	12
1966	36	45	10
1970	40	43	8
Feb. 1974	35	40	13
Oct. 1974	34	40	14
1979	38	36	12
1983	36	31	17
1987	37	30	16
1992	42	31	12

Source: British Election Study cross-section surveys

from about a half in 1964 to a quarter in 1992. In theory, this means that many voters are potentially up for grabs at elections.

A third measure lies in the opinion polls and results in by-elections. Support for the Labour and Conservative parties was fairly steady in opinion polls and by-elections in the first two postwar decades. In these years campaign managers were able to divide the electorate into two pretty fixed camps – the working class, council estates and trade union members were solidly Labour, the middle class, home-owners and the 'aspiring' working class were solidly Conservative. Work, family, neighbourhood and friendships all socialized many people into an allegiance for one or other of the two big parties. 'Other' parties attracted very little support. Since then there have been big shifts among voters. In the course of the 1979–83 Parliament, for example, each of the three main parties (including the new SDP–Liberal Alliance) saw its share of support in the opinion polls fluctuate by as much as 20 per cent. Whereas only one seat changed hands at by-elections in the twenty years after 1945 one in three seats have changed since then, almost invariably at the cost of the government of the day.

More recent research suggests that this fickleness may have been due less to changes in social structure or public mood and more to the initiatives of the politicians. These include Labour's move to the left and split after 1979, the creation and then collapse of the Social Democratic party and the Conservative's move to the right under Mrs Thatcher. In other words, a good part of the change in party support may be a response to the different signals communicated by the parties.

What is undeniable is that the share of the electorate now regularly voting for the Labour and Conservative parties has fallen considerably in recent years. At the general elections between 1945 and 1970 an average of 91 per cent of voters supported the two parties; since then it has fallen to 76 per cent. And the class base of the party system has declined. In 1964 some two-thirds of the working class voted Labour and two-thirds of the middle class voted Conservative. But in elections since 1979 less than half of the working class vote Labour and just over half of the middle class vote Conservative. Indeed the rise of support for a centre party (be it Liberal, Alliance or Liberal Democrat) means that most people now vote for a party not of their 'natural' class. Another way to describe the impact of these changes is to say that the stable, class-based two-party system that prevailed in Britain between 1945 and 1970 has steadily weakened.

Yet for all the talk of volatility, it is still the case that most voters (nearly 80 per cent) have already decided how to vote before the campaign begins. A party has little chance in the short period of a campaign to overturn a voter's long-standing allegiance to another party. Over thirty years ago, Labour's Richard Crossman stated: 'The election is the end of a long process'.

We can adopt the notion of a normal or expected vote to gain some idea of a party's baseline support, the share of the vote a party will *normally* gain, other things being equal. For Richard Rose, 'The normal vote reflects long-term structural influences, and the current deviation reflects short-term cyclical fluctuations' (1992: 452). It can be compiled from recent figures on party identification, local election results, national elections and opinion polls and used to test if parties do better or worse than expected in elections. In the general elections between 1945 and 1970 the two main parties averaged similar levels of support – around 45 per cent each. But because Labour usually enjoyed a lead over the Conservatives in its share of party identifiers it could be judged to have 'under-performed', the Conservatives to have 'over-performed'. The task of Labour campaigners, therefore, was to mobilize the party's 'natural' majority in the largely working-class electorate, while the task of Conservatives was to retain their supporters and attract converts.

Since then, the party balance has shifted dramatically. Table 2.2 shows that in general elections between February 1974 and 1992 the Conservative share of the vote varied between 43.9 per cent (1979) and 35.8 per cent (October 1974) and the Labour vote between a high of 39.2 per cent (October 1974) and a low of 27.6 per cent (1983). The Conservative mid-point in these elections was 39.8 per cent, 6.4 per cent higher than Labour's 33.4 per cent, giving normal votes of some 40 per cent and 34 per cent respectively, for the two parties. In the 1992 election both parties (Conservative 41.9 per cent, Labour 34.4 per cent)

Table 2.2 Normal vote 1945–92

	Con. %	Lab. %	Lib. %	Other %
Mean, 1945–70	45.2	46.1	7.1	1.6
Mean, Feb. 1974–92	40.7	34.4	19.5	5.5
Range, Feb. 1974–92	39.8 +−4.1	33.4 +−5.8	19.6 +−5.8	5.5 +−1.1
General election result 1992	41.9	34.4	17.8	5.0

Source: R. Rose, 'Structural change or cyclical fluctuations?' *Parliamentary Affairs* 1992: 453

just managed to exceed their normal vote. The figures clearly show that over the past two decades the Labour and Conservative parties do not enter an election on equal terms, regarding their natural levels of support. Labour has been second best and 'getting out the vote' has no longer been sufficient for victory.

Politicians and political scientists have concentrated more attention on political issues than on party images. Politicians often think in terms of 'our' agenda, i.e. those issues which their party is perceived as handling better than other parties, and then try to fight the election on them. But studies suggest that this approach is of limited use for understanding electoral behaviour. If people had voted purely on the basis of their policy preferences in 1983 then the outcome would have been a virtual dead heat between Labour and Conservative rather than a decisive Conservative victory. Had voters decided in 1987 on the basis of their preferences on the key issues of unemployment and health then Labour would have just won, rather than suffering another crushing defeat. And on the basis of surveys about voters' main issue concerns (education and unemployment) Labour would have gained a handsome victory in 1992.

Issues, therefore, are only part of the story. Ivor Crewe (1993: 115) reminds us that voting is not like shopping in a supermarket, for dissatisfied voters cannot simply change policies or the government after a few weeks. Parties offer a service, namely governing the country, and have to persuade voters that they can do it competently. Voting for a party may be more like choosing a doctor or solicitor where a client relies on the professional's competence and reputation. Voters are interested in a party's image, particularly such features as its perceived trustworthiness, potential governmental competence, ability to manage the economy and the likelihood that it will keep its promises. A problem for Labour in 1987 and 1992 was that, for all its popularity on a number of issues, many voters simply did not trust it, particularly on the economy. Martin Harrop suggests that, because of their interest in a party's image, marketing experts are more likely to appreciate the distinction than political scientists (Harrop 1990: 278).

Campaign Change

National campaign techniques have gradually changed, largely as a consequence of developments in communications technology. Before the 1959 election television did not cover the election, few public and no private opinion polls were conducted during the campaign and no party employed an advertising agency in a significant way. Campaign managers in headquarters had little sense of a campaign plan or an overall communications strategy and professional communicators played limited roles, such as designing and placing advertisements and posters. Today, by contrast, the national leaders are supported by research and professional help, fight media-oriented, particularly television-oriented, campaigns, 'target' groups of voters, 'pace' the campaign and fight on 'their' agenda. Parties at the centre self-consciously adopt campaign strategies and employ professional communications advisers to help them.

It is worth stressing that the developments of opinion polling, advertising and television are almost entirely employed by campaign managers at the centre and not in the constituencies. The limited opportunities to spend money (see below, pp. 33–4) restrict the local candidate's ability to use the new campaign techniques. Some four-fifths of constituencies are safe for the incumbent party so the overall election result is effectively decided in the remaining hundred or so marginal seats. Some targeting of seats is done as the party headquarters provide limited help in the form of advice, computers, staff and funds to the marginal. Poor attendances have resulted in the wholesale abandonment of public meetings and a decline in the amount of door-to-door canvassing. Perhaps the main change at the local level has been the use of computers. Since 1986 local authorities have supplied local parties with electoral registers on computer tape. Parties with up-to-date records of the names and the voting intentions of the people on the electoral register can use computers for niche marketing and to direct personal letters to target voters, according to their party loyalty, issue concerns and even socio-economic backgrounds. Letters can be directed, for example, to elderly voters outlining a party's policies on pensions. But the success of direct mail depends upon the local party activists collecting reliable data on the voters and keeping it up to date. So far the use of direct mail in British campaigns still lags behind that in the US.

Party managers have become increasingly aware of the need to communicate with voters over the long term, not just during the three weeks of the election campaign. Some influences on the voter stemming, for example, from childhood or schooling are too remote for the parties to influence; a government's record in office or memories of what the opposition did when it was last in office are largely beyond the campaigners' control, although skilled communications may influence public perceptions. A party in government is particularly well placed to use office to dominate news bulletins and shape the agenda before the election is declared. A government's policy proposals, ministers' speeches and initiatives and the Prime Minister's activities satisfy the media's criteria of 'news' and are sure to be reported. Another advantage is that in contrast to the election period the broadcasting media are not obliged by rules of political 'balance' to give equal coverage to the other political parties.

But a British government's efforts in image projection and management pale in comparison with those of the United States, where the use of the White House for campaigning has been developed to a fine art. President Reagan's staff ruthlessly used photo-opportunities, tours, speeches, press conferences and other initiatives to dominate the media and help his chances of re-election in 1984. White House officials seemed to judge the performance of government by the contents of the television news programmes: 'For the Reagan White House every night is election night on television' (Kernell 1986: 138). Reagan spent some two-thirds of his time in the White House on public relations and ceremonial duties, compared to only one-third on policy matters (Foley 1992: 96–7). Less successful in managing the media was President Carter, even though his pollster advised him at the outset, 'Government with public approval requires a continuous political campaign' (Sieb 1987: 184).

In spite of the more professional communications approaches there has been a good deal of continuity in the electoral messages of the Labour and Conservative parties. Because a party is already a known quantity to most voters it is not entirely free in the choice of credible appeals which it can make; many voters already have an image of a party, one that usually changes slowly. A party has either to build on this or try to change it gradually. To some extent, voters' perceptions of Labour and Conservative are mirror images of each other and have been so for many years. A study of the parties' standings on issues in opinion polls shows that for much of the postwar period they have 'owned' different issues (Budge and Fairlie 1983; Harrop and Shaw 1989: 71). Labour dominates the 'caring' issues of pensions, health, education and employment. The Conservatives have long been ahead on the issues of law and order, defence and immigration, as well as taxes and (except for the early 1970s) prices and prosperity. These differing strengths and weaknesses of the political parties remained largely intact in the 1992 election.

The Conservative party has been seen as more united than Labour,apart from short spells in the 1960s, 1974 and post-1992. It has also been regarded as the more likely of the two to provide competent economic management and to defend Britain's interests against other countries. Since the beginning of the century Conservative electioneering has regularly attacked the opposition party of the day for lacking patriotism, threatening private property and enterprise and neglecting the nation's defences. Labour has been widely regarded as the party of 'fairness', in the sense of favouring policies which promote equality, help the less well-off and protect the welfare state and full employment. What recent elections, particularly 1992, show, however, is that the electorally decisive arena is the economy and perceptions of which party is more likely to deliver prosperity.

A party's positioning on the issues depends only partly upon its traditional values; whether it is in or out of office also matters. At election time a government persistently boasts about the strength of the economy it has achieved compared with the mess it inherited from the opposition. For the government to blame the other side for its economic difficulties is now a standard theme of campaign rhetoric. The new Labour government in 1964 made great play with the £800 million balance of payments deficit it inherited from the Conservatives. This struck such a chord that voters were still blaming the Conservatives for the country's economic problems some years later under a Labour government. Mr Heath's government blamed the rising inflation rate it inherited in 1970 on the short-term decisions of the outgoing Labour government. When it regained office in March 1974 Labour in turn exploited the coal strike and industrial disruption which preceded the election.

More positively, a government puts a favourable gloss on its record and warns against the dangers of change. In 1959 the Conservative government exploited the mood of prosperity and warned voters 'Don't let Labour ruin it'. When in government again, the party's slogan in the last week of the 1987 election campaign was virtually identical. In 1970 Harold Wilson boasted 'No Prime Minister in this century has fought an election against such a background of economic strength as we have today', and regularly attacked the 'doom and gloom merchants' and 'the knock Britain brigade'. His successors as Prime Minister have regularly recited statistics in election speeches and interviews to show what economic progress there has been under their stewardships and attacked media critics and political opponents for 'talking Britain down'.

Governments usually excuse their own shortcomings by pointing to the unacceptable alternative. They try to make an election issue of the opposition party. 'Is that really what you want?' ministers ask. In its 1979 manifesto Labour pointedly overlooked its own recent winter of industrial discontent and reminded voters:

> When Labour came to government in March 1974, Britain was facing its most dangerous crisis since the war. The Tory programme of confrontation and social injustice brought the country almost to its knees. Unlit streets, unheated homes, shut-down factories – these were the fruits of the Tory three-day week . . . but . . . Our country has come a long way since.

Conservatives have reaped rich electoral dividends from the winter of discontent under the last Labour government. In 1979 and every subsequent general election the party's manifesto and election broadcasts have referred to it. In 1992 the Conservatives did not have much of an economic case to set before the electorate. Instead their communications hammered at Labour on tax and spending, and leadership – two areas which, surveys told them, were Labour weaknesses. The thrust of such campaign communications is: 'You may not think much of us, but look at the alternative'.

A recurring election theme of the opposition is that it is time for change, to counter the government's claim for a mandate to finish the job, or to carry on with its excellent work. In 1964 the Labour opposition's campaign theme was 'Lets GO with Labour'. In the 1960s and 1970s the opposition exploited public concern over rising prices to berate the government of the day. Conservatives did this effectively in 1970, making use of a shopping basket in election broadcasts to remind voters of how the price of goods had risen under Labour. Labour retaliated in the 1974 general election, by sending its most prominent female politicians, Barbara Castle and Shirley Williams, both armed with shopping baskets, to compare price levels in the shops with those in 1970. In 1979 the Conservative slogan in the final week was 'It's Time For Change'. In 1992 Labour used virtually the same slogan.

Parties frequently accuse their opponents of having a hidden agenda, policies that will be so unpopular that they keep quiet about them. Since 1979 Labour has regularly charged that the Conservatives have plans to cut back or tax some welfare benefits and privatize education and health. Surveys in 1992 showed that most voters believed the health accusations. Conservatives base their charges that a Labour government will increase taxes on their 'costing' of the party's spending promises and translating this sum into extra income tax. They also frequently point to the sinister left-wing politicians and trade union leaders lurking behind the leader. In 1955 the pro-Tory *Daily Express* ran a famous cartoon which showed a smiling Aneurin Bevan lurking behind the party leader Clement Attlee. The implication was that the left was poised to take over from a moderate Labour leadership (see figure 2.1). In February 1974 a controversial election broadcast showed the faces of moderate Labour frontbenchers giving way to prominent left-wingers. The consistent message is that behind the 'moderate' image Labour presents to the voters, 'extreme' left-wingers are waiting to take over.

Party leaders may also try to invent or exploit a sense of crisis, warning voters that they have not yet understood the dangers of electing the other party. Usually the opposition does this but the government may do so if it looks like losing the election. In 1966 Mr Heath trailed by a large margin in the opinion polls and warned voters that the country was facing its greatest threat since 1938 – that of national bankruptcy. In 1970 Heath, again tagged by the media as an inevitable election loser, once more wore the mantle of a prophet of gloom. In the final weekend he appealed: 'I have to say to the British people "For heaven's sake wake up". I want them to recognize what the real issues are, because Labour has pursued a policy of diversion with a bogus story of sham-sunshine'. In 1992 John Major, also facing defeat according to the opinion polls, claimed in the last few days, that 'The United Kingdom is in danger. Wake up, my fellow countrymen! Wake up now before it is too late!'

Party Change

The outcomes of elections decide whether or not parties have the opportunity to realize their policy goals and fulfil their leaders' ambitions for office. Politicians and party activists often invoke military or sporting analogies to distinguish elections from routine activities. When an election is announced a party is said to be put on a 'war footing', as opposed to 'peace time', 'troops' are called to 'battle', a speech is a 'rallying cry' and the opposition is frequently designated the

Figure 2.1   A cartoon carried in the Conservative-supporting *Daily Express* in the 1955 general election. It expresses a familiar Conservative election charge that the left wing (here represented by Aneurin Bevan) will dominate a Labour government.

'enemy'. The party's campaign planning document is usually called a 'War Book', and for planning purposes parties use the 'D-(minus)' system, numbering each day in a countdown to 'D-Day' – polling day. The media also use military or sporting-contest metaphors in reporting the campaign.

But to fight elections political parties require resources, particularly workers, funds and professional staff. How well equipped are British parties? We have already noted a weakening of popular attachment to the main parties. It may be a sign of the voters' low commitment to parties that so few are willing to participate in activities that involve a public proclamation of their loyalties. A MORI poll in January 1993 found that only 4 per cent of voters would canvass in person for the party or speak out at another party's meeting, and a mere 2 per cent would canvass by telephone or discuss the advantages of the party with strangers in the street. Parties are not, relatively speaking, as well resourced in members or even money as they were twenty or thirty years ago. In the 1950s the Labour party claimed about a million individual members, a figure that has fallen to about 300,000 today. Over the same period Conservative membership has declined from a figure of some 2.8 million in the 1950s to less than half a million, and the majority of both parties' members are hardly active.

Disillusion with the policies of the Labour government in 1966–70 led to a large exodus of party activists from local parties (Seyd and Whiteley 1992) and something similar has happened among Conservative associations in the early 1990s (Whiteley, Seyd and Richardson 1994). The decline has had the effect of reducing the number of those eligible to perform political chores, fill offices in the constituency parties and stand in local elections. The parties have also found themselves under severe financial pressure. By the end of 1994 Conservative Central Office reported an accumulated deficit of over £16 million and both Labour and Conservative parties have had to make severe reductions in staff. Compared to the major political parties a number of pressure groups are better financed and have larger and more active memberships.

It is fortunate for the parties that British elections are relatively cheap when compared with the sums spent in other countries, or even with pre-1918 elections. Candidates in the constituencies are strictly limited by law on how much money and on what they can spend. In 1992 successful candidates spent around £5,000 on their constituency campaigns, with the Conservatives spending a bit more than candid-

ates for other political parties. Most is spent on leaflets and clerical
chores. The strict spending limits preclude local parties from using
opinion polls, large-scale telephone canvassing or paid advertising in
the local media and contrast sharply with the position in the US (see
chapter 10). In real terms the local campaign spending has fallen by
about a third compared to 1945.

There is, however, no control on the parties' central expenditure.
Nor is there any requirement on them to publish their spending figures
for advertising, opinion research, election broadcasts and leaders' tours
and rallies. Not until 1964 did a party (Conservative) spend over £1
million in a campaign, a figure that was not breached again until 1979
(once more Conservative). Since then election spending has risen
sharply, with Labour following on the heels of the Conservatives
and by 1992 almost catching up. Labour's 1992 spending doubled
compared to 1987. It is difficult to compare the costs precisely because
of differences in what the parties declare as campaign expenditure and
which periods they cover. The parties' estimates of their spending for
the 1992 election are presented in table 2.3. In real terms total spending
in 1992 fell compared to 1987 and the cost of both elections in real
terms was less than in 1935 and 1964 (Pinto-Duschinsky 1991).

State finance for the parties would be a way of reducing the two big
parties' dependence on interest groups for funds. There is in fact
already a good deal of indirect state subsidy for the parties' campaign
activities. They receive free broadcasting time for their television and
radio election broadcasts, use of halls for election meetings and
distribution of local candidates' election addresses in the campaign.
Pinto-Duschinsky (1991) calculates that the value of these subsidies in
kind during the election actually exceeds the total local and central
campaign spending of the parties. The exclusion of political advertising
from the broadcasting media also acts as a limitation upon the level of

Table 2.3 Parties' central campaign expenditure (1992)

	1987 (£ million)	*1992 (£ million)*
Conservative	9	11.2
Labour	4.3	10.6
Liberal	1.9	1.8

Source: Michael Pinto-Duschinsky, 'Labour's £10 m campaign spending closes the gap
with Tories', *The Times* 30 November 1992

campaign spending and the impact of money in campaigns. Parties may, however, spend freely on press advertising and in 1987 50 per cent of the parties' total election spending went on national press advertising. In 1992 the Conservatives cut this spending back by two-thirds and spent more on posters, election broadcasts and sets for John Major's rallies. Although Conservatives have outspent Labour in postwar general elections and won more often, it is doubtful if money wins elections. The Conservatives heavily outspent Labour on press advertising in elections from 1979 to 1987, but not in 1992. Indeed Labour spent even more if we credit advertisements from public sector trade unions to the party. One always has to remember that people are more likely to be influenced by the news and current affairs coverage of the election on television and in the press.

A political party is not a unitary entity. A party machine consists of many different sections or departments, covering research, publicity, organization, campaigns, women, trade unions, finance and so on. At election time there will also be specialist units which concentrate on marginal or 'special' seats, overseas electors, postal votes, relations with the mass media, the party leader's tour and so on. The efforts of these groups affect the final outcome but observers may sometimes be struck by the extent to which they are wrapped up in their own activities. A major division in a British party's organization is between those career staff employed in its London headquarters and those in the constituency parties. The professional staff in London operate nationally, servicing the party leadership, developing policy, trying to generate favourable publicity and liaising with constituency parties. But local parties are voluntary bodies, employing very few or, more usually, no career staff and much time is spent recruiting members and raising funds. Candidates rely on their local members' goodwill to deliver leaflets, raise funds and canvass support at election time. Norman Tebbit, as Conservative party Chairman, once compared himself to 'a general whose troops may desert at any time and I can't do anything about it' (interview). For the national leaders winning or losing a general election is crucial, affecting their own careers and their ability to implement policies. But some members of the constituency party may be consoled for national defeat by winning the seat or running the local council. For some constituency parties electing a few local councillors is a more realistic political goal than striving to elect an MP.

The Labour and Conservative parties are hardly models of efficient organizations. A Prime Minister understandably ranks the party machine rather low in his list of priorities and party leaders have rarely sought to strengthen the party headquarters, perhaps fearing the emergence of a rival power centre. Central Office chairmen have often been appointed for their political support for the leader of the day, rather than for their proven electoral or organizing skills. No postwar Conservative leader has taken much interest in Central Office and Mrs Thatcher, according to aides, was often scathing about its performance. She became almost apoplectic when the Chairman, Lord Thorneycroft, recommended that Ted Heath should be recalled to share the platform with her at one of the party's final election press conferences in 1979, a suggestion she regarded as defeatist. Her unease about the party Chairman Norman Tebbit and his campaign strategy led her to appoint another minister to Central Office to 'shadow' Tebbit, seek advice elsewhere about polling and strategy and insist on a last-minute change in advertising (see below, p. 64). Her Chancellor of the Exchequer, Nigel Lawson (1992: 698), wrote that as a result of the tensions Central Office was 'divided into two warring factions, who spent far more energy trying to get the better of each other than they did in fighting the enemy'.

Most Labour leaders, from Hugh Gaitskell on, have also complained about the campaign effectiveness of their party's organization. Key appointments, including the General Secretary and Campaigns and Communications Director, are made by the NEC, at times over the leader's opposition. Leaders have often sought to keep the drafting of the manifesto, the results of private opinion polls and key campaign plans under the control of their office. In 1959 Hugh Gaitskell's relations with the party's General Secretary and the head of publicity were poor. Harold Wilson's lack of confidence in Labour's electoral machine was succinctly noted in the 1966 Nuffield election study: 'In all of the Prime Minister's electoral thinking, the National Executive Committee and the party staff at Transport House played very little part' (Butler and King 1966: 30). The tensions continued during the 1970s and 1980s. The party organization was in no sense the source of Labour's strategic thinking about elections. Most party leaders despaired of its efficiency and looked elsewhere for advice on strategy.

Political parties require the services of professionals. At constituency level the key figure is the agent, usually the party's only fulltime official. Election law requires the candidate to have a designated agent who is accountable for expenditures designed to promote the candidacy. But

less than a tenth of local Labour parties and fewer than half of local
Conservative parties now have the resources to employ a fulltime
agent. In 1951 Labour had fulltime agents in about half the seats, and
the Conservatives had one in virtually every seat. Most Conservative
fulltime agents are concentrated in the safe seats which can afford to
employ them. For a time in the 1970s the party had a scheme of
centrally employed (and paid) agents who were directed to the
marginal seats but the scheme lapsed as a result of financial pressure
and constituency jealousies.

A party agent is expected to be interested in politics and support his
or her political party. But excessive political commitment in a
professional can be a disadvantage. A political party may be divided on
key policies or change policy direction quickly, as the Conservative
party did in the transition from Edward Heath to Margaret Thatcher
or Labour did when Foot replaced Callaghan and again under Kinnock
after 1987. Much more of the agent's time is spent in fundraising
activities than in debating politics. As Richard Rose says, 'A good
agent is more like a clergyman than like a bishop or a theologian'
(1974: 176).

Parties also have their own research departments. At general
elections researchers provide the arguments, quotes and statistics to
support the party's speakers. The Conservative Research Department
was created in 1929 out of the Parliamentary Secretariat. It came into
its own after 1945 and again after 1964 when, having lost office, the
party embarked on ambitious policy reviews. Labour's research
department was founded in 1932. It works on home or domestic policy
and a separate international department works on foreign policy. Both
parties recruit staff mainly from recent university graduates, some of
whom regard a post as a stepping-stone to becoming a Member of
Parliament. The work brings the researcher into contact with ministers
and MPs, briefing them, servicing backbench committees and helping
ministers with speeches. Six of Mrs Thatcher's final Cabinet in 1990
had had previous Research Department experience and in the 1992
Parliament 26 Conservative MPs had at one time worked in the
department.

The different centres of power in the Labour party have sometimes
created difficulties and opportunities for researchers. By tradition the
department has been more left wing and more oriented to the party
conference than the Parliamentary party. In the 1960s and 1970s senior
staff often criticized the work of a Labour government and complained

of the influence of the civil service on ministers. In these years its concentration on preparing long-term policies brought it into conflict with the then Labour government. Harold Wilson was furious at the department for producing a draft manifesto, *Agenda for a Generation*, which he felt was a device for putting left-wing pressure on him. Wilson again, before the 1974 election, and James Callaghan, before the 1979 election, voiced similar complaints about the left-wing thrust of the policy work of the department and its neglect of what they regarded as its more important task of providing research to support the government (Minkin 1980).

In the run-up to the 1992 election the Conservatives employed 25 desk officers who combed through opposition speeches, articles and policy documents for damaging material. Such 'bullets' of information, to be used in ministers' speeches or fed to sympathetic journalists, are essential for a negative campaign. The department prepared 65 dossiers in the 12 months before the election was called and produced 21 publications on the theme 'You Can't Trust Labour' during the first two months of 1992.

Attracting well qualified and politically sympathetic publicists has proved to be a problem for both political parties. The task of the publicist is to help the party to gain favourable media coverage. The job includes briefing the media, liaising with the party's polling and advertising agencies and supervising the preparation of a communications campaign for the general election. Conservatives have usually drawn their directors from outside Central Office, from press or public relations, and suffered a high turnover. No director has yet served the party in that post in two successive general elections. The three most recent appointments have come from advertising (Brendan Bruce, 1989–90), television (Shaun Woodward, 1991–2) and the Research Department (Tim Collins, 1992–5). Although the Director is responsible to the Chairman of the party and through him to the party leader, the appointment is in the hands of the party leader. This frustrated Norman Tebbit when, as party Chairman (1985–7), he found that all the names he proposed for the post to Mrs Thatcher were turned down and the party fought the 1987 election without a Director of Publicity.

Publicity, in Labour, was for long a career post and appointments were made from within the party machinery. Until his retirement in 1978 Percy Clarke (who had held the post since 1963) was one of only three people since 1945 to have held the post of Press and Publicity Director. (The title was changed to Campaigns and Communications

Director in 1985). In the sixteen years since Clarke's retirement the post has been held by five different people, including an ex-MP, an ex-trade union public relations officer, two former television producers and a special adviser to the deputy leader. The Director is appointed by and reports to the NEC and is a member of the campaign committee. At times he has often been caught up in the warfare that has existed between left and right and the party leader and the NEC. But under Neil Kinnock the Director's effectiveness depended crucially on his closeness to the party leader.

Media Change

Perhaps the most significant change in the campaign context has been in the role of the mass media, particularly television. Modern elections have become mass-media elections. Parties and candidates can only communicate with millions of voters through the national press and broadcasting networks and much national campaign activity is tailored for television. Campaign managers have developed techniques to feed or counter a partisan press and cope with an increasingly active but statutorily impartial television system (see chapters 8 and 9). In a recent general election a Labour MP, Austen Mitchell, complained that he was treated as an intruder when canvassing because he disturbed people who were following the election on television! A constant refrain of campaign managers about an election activity is: 'If it's not covered by the cameras, then there is not much point in doing it'. In some respects there are two election campaigns, one in which politicians address voters, another in which they address the media journalists, but as a means of communicating with voters.

The British broadcasting media are independent of political parties and have only an indirect relationship with the government. Although the broadcasting media are free from editorial direction by the government, both the British Broadcasting Corporation (BBC) and independent television companies are subject to government regulation: the Boards of Governors of the BBC and Independent Television Corporation (ITC) are appointed by the Home Secretary, the BBC's licence fee is determined by the government and it operates under a charter decided by Parliament. The BBC and ITV are also expected to maintain a balance between the parties in their coverage of politics.

The political impact of television advertising was first seen in the US

Presidential election in 1952 (see above, p. 14). Perceptive British politicians also noted that over 20 million people had watched the Coronation on television in 1953 and wondered how the new medium could be used for politics. Before 1959, however, television and radio refused to cover a general election, ceasing all political coverage from the beginning of the campaign until the close of polling. This was despite the fact that three-quarters of households already had television sets and the election was the main source of news in the national press. The BBC observed its duty to be politically 'balanced' by ignoring the election, apart from providing time for the parties to transmit their own election broadcasts. It feared that coverage would infringe the law restricting spending on the promotion of candidates.

The position is very different today. The broadcasters have steadily increased their campaign coverage, carrying debates between and interviews with leading political figures, allowing voters to question politicians, providing expert analysis and interpretation and using outside cameras to report events live. Voters claim that television is their main source of information about politics and the most trusted as well. As Blumler (1974) notes, in covering elections the British media, notably the broadcasters, are subject to a variety of pressures and expectations. In 1992 87 per cent of the public claimed to view television news at least once a day before the election campaign began and 83 per cent during it; for reading the national press the respective figures were 66 per cent and 63 per cent. The same survey reported that 88 per cent considered that television had covered the election 'very' or 'fairly' well, compared to 62 per cent who gave a similar evaluation to the press. More striking was the finding that 78 per cent thought that the BBC and ITV could be relied on to give unbiased and truthful coverage, compared to only 23 per cent who thought the same of the press (Butler and Kavanagh 1992: 179).

Parties compete not only for votes but also in setting the campaign agenda, i.e. what the election is about. This creates tensions between the parties and news organization teams (Semetko et al. 1990). Behind the public party battle there lurks another, less overt, struggle between politicians and television journalists over election coverage. Most voters expect to be entertained as well as informed, some look mainly for reinforcement of their political loyalties, and some are more open-minded and seek guidance. The politicians want to ensure that 'their' issues, statements and photo-opportunities are adequately covered by the mass media. Parties are now intense in covering all media outlets and opportunities, monitoring broadcasts and trying to dominate the agenda. They are also more willing to employ the services of media advisers, in support of their own communications officials, to help with news management, press conferences, current affairs programmes and interviews. Politicians are therefore both media communicators and media audience; in both roles they are highly partisan.

What, however, should be the role of the broadcast journalists? Is their main role to carry the parties' soundbites and photo-opportunities or make an independent contribution of their own, interpreting and contextualizing what the politicians are doing? At the BBC Blumler found that some were *sacerdotalists*, viewing an election as intrinsically important and regarding it as their duty to provide full and serious coverage of the parties' activities. Others were *pragmatists*, arguing that the amount of election coverage should be based on news values and take account of audience size and interest.

British parties have some control over broadcasting coverage, through their party election broadcasts (PEBs). But these lack credibility and quickly lose viewers. More significant – and what constitutes much of the battleground between politicians and broadcasters – is how the election is covered as part of news and current affairs reporting. Because this audience is, compared to the election broadcasts, more 'inadvertent' and drawn from across the political spectrum, the reporting may have more impact. Campaign managers are more interested in gaining coverage on the relatively non-political early evening programmes and the main news bulletins; in 1992 the BBC and ITN attracted audiences of around a third of the electorate for their main evening bulletins. And even if the amount of coverage of a party's activities is balanced according to a stop-watch, the broadcasters have some discretion in selecting which issues, personalities and events to cover as well as in presenting them.

At first the politicians adapted to the introduction of television by providing activities for the cameras, e.g. Harold Wilson's walkabouts in 1970. By 1974 they had moved from adapting to trying to manipulate the medium, by providing specially staged events for morning, early evening and late evening coverage. Television relies on pictures and the parties strive to control the pictures transmitted by scheduling events, rallies, leaders' visits to hospitals, factories, schools and so on to carry the message. The reasoning is that if the broadcasts are limited to what the party allows them to film then the party managers can effectively determine what the television shows. The rhythm of the campaign day, beginning with the morning press conference, continuing with afternoon 'events' and ending with the leaders' evening rallies, became geared to the deadlines for lunch-time, early evening and peak-time television news programmes. In turn, however, the television reporters are reacting against the parties' more blatant attempts at manipulation, insisting that they will not necessarily cover photo-opportunities or the unveiling of a poster, but judge campaign events more strictly on their 'news values'. The parties' media management has now evolved to the stage where the politicians and the parties' communications directors regularly complain to the broadcasters about coverage in an attempt to influence the media.

Until the arrival of television, politicians communicated with a mass electorate largely through the national and provincial press. The golden age of the press was not, however, an age of politically impartial newspapers. The links between parties and the press were often closer than today, newspapers usually advised their readers how to vote and, before 1914, the parties sometimes subsidized a paper to keep it in business, in return for support (Koss 1984). In recent years the *Morning Star* has been the only national paper owned and financed by a party – the Communist party.

The role of the press in election campaigns remains significant although it has changed in recent years. Table 2.4 reports the readership and circulation figures for national daily newspapers. Some three-

Table 2.4   Partisanship and circulation of national daily newspapers (1992)

Name of paper	Circulation ('000)	Readership ('000)
Daily Mirror	2,903	8,035
Daily Express	1,525	3,643
Sun	3,571	9,853
Daily Mail	1,675	4,303
Daily Star	806	2,628
Today	533	1,408
Daily Telegraph	1,038	2,492
Guardian	429	1,214
The Times	386	1,035
Independent	390	1,083
Financial Times	290	668

Source: Butler and Kavanagh, *The British General Election of 1992*, 181–2

quarters of the adult population read a daily paper, one of the highest figures found anywhere in the world. In 1992 the two best-selling tabloids, the *Mirror* and the *Sun*, had respective daily readerships of some 8 and 10 million, each equal to nearly a quarter of the electorate. Both papers are highly partisan, one for Labour, one for Conservative, and the coverage of both at election time relies heavily on a mix of propaganda, stunts, smears and innuendo.

The broadsheets have an overwhelmingly middle-class readership and provide more campaign coverage than tabloids. Seymour-Ure suggests that the broadsheets appear to have news and editorial values closer to the broadcasters in their interest in balance, while the tabloids resemble television in their emphasis on graphics and personalities (1992: 69). But tabloids and broadsheets devote similar amounts of space to election coverage – about 30 per cent of the total – and the same to opinion polls – about 5 per cent (MacArthur 1989: 98). In the 1992 election, for example, broadsheets led on four out of every five days with a campaign story, the tabloids on half of the days. On virtually every election day the broadsheets had front-page lead stories and all the national papers, except the *Sun*, had more front-page lead stories about the election than they did in 1987. The *Mirror* devoted 100 per cent of its editorials to the election, the *Daily Express* 97 per cent and the *Daily Mail* 79 per cent. The national newspapers clearly still care about elections.

Assessing the quality of the press coverage of election campaigns is a more subjective matter. Martin Harrop (Crewe and Harrop 1986) and Colin Seymour-Ure (1974: 234) have claimed that during the 1960s, probably as a reflection of the lack of marked disagreement between the parties and as a response to the balanced television coverage, the press became less partisan and more willing to discern merits in the party which it did not support. A study of the 1964 general election commented 'The traditional complaint that Labour has a bad press could not be raised in 1964: those who view any trend towards objectivity in the right-wing press as 'disloyalty' had more to complain about' and 'Some sections of the press, and particularly the national press, showed a greater disposition towards objective and fair reporting of the campaign than hitherto' (Beith 1965: 201, 203).

In recent elections, however, there has been a return to full-blooded press partisanship. One cause may have been that since 1979 all the popular papers have become tabloids. In 1959 there were two tabloids and they accounted for a third of the total circulation; by 1992 the respective figures had changed to six and over four-fifths. A second cause may have been the leadership of Mrs Thatcher and the sharper polarization between the parties that resulted. She made a virtue of being a conviction politician and rejecting consensus politics. The tabloids both reflected and contributed to this polarization. Nigel Lawson complained that Mrs Thatcher, her press secretary Bernard Ingham and the partisan *Sun* fed on one another (Lawson 1992). Mr Ingham, according to Lawson, would often feed a line to the *Sun*, the paper would carry it, and then Ingham would highlight it in his digest of the daily press he prepared for Mrs Thatcher. Mrs Thatcher then marvelled at her hot line to the British people! It is interesting that the Conservative tabloids were less partisan when Edward Heath was Prime Minister and have not been happy with John Major since his 1992 election victory. Perhaps there was a Thatcher factor.

Table 2.5 Party supported by daily newspaper readers (1987 in brackets)

Newspaper		*Con. %*	*Lab. %*	*Lib./Dem. %*
		\multicolumn{3}{c}{*Party supported by readers*}	
Daily Telegraph	1992	72	11	16
	(1987)	(80)	(5)	(10)
Daily Express	1992	67	15	14
	(1987)	(70)	(9)	(18)
Daily Mail	1992	65	15	18
	(1987)	(60)	(13)	(19)
Financial Times	1992	65	17	16
	(1987)	(48)	(17)	(29)
The Times	1992	64	16	19
	(1987)	(56)	(12)	(27)
Sun	1992	45	36	14
	(1987)	(41)	(31)	(19)
Today	1992	43	32	23
	(1987)	(43)	(17)	(40)
Daily Star	1992	31	54	12
	(1987)	(28)	(46)	(18)
Independent	1992	25	37	34
	(1987)	(34)	(34)	(27)
Daily Mirror	1992	20	64	14
	(1987)	(20)	(55)	(21)
Guardian	1992	15	55	24
	(1987)	(22)	(54)	(19)

Source: MORI

Paradoxically, this revival of press partisanship has occurred at the same time as popular attachment to the political parties has fallen (see p. 23). Moreover, the partisanship is expressed in more contemptuous Labour 'knocking' copy than was the case earlier (see below). The growth of partisanship may also explain why much of the public regard the press as a less credible source of information than television. For the most part the political leanings of newspapers match the preferences of their readers (table 2.5). In 1992 some two-thirds or more of the readership of *The Times*, *Express*, *Mail* and *Telegraph* supported the Conservatives and some two-thirds of the *Mirror* and 55 per cent of *Guardian* readers supported Labour. Until recent elections the *Sun*, incredibly, was regarded by a large majority of its readership as a pro-Labour paper and even in 1987 and 1992 appreciably less than half of its readers voted Conservative. People do not buy or read the *Sun* for its party politics.

Conclusion

The context alters from one election to another. Some of the change is gradual; the physical replacement of the electorate, due to deaths and the comings of age of voters, amounts to between 1 and 2 per cent of the electorate annually but cumulatively can produce a big change over twenty years. Other changes may be more abrupt, as television started to cover the election in 1959, or as parties introduce new issues, policies or arguments. Labour's policies and leader, for example, were very different in 1983 from 1979 and they had shifted again radically in 1987. Some of the changes have been mutually reinforcing, providing both challenges and opportunities for more professional approaches to campaigning. The electorate appears to be less constant to the parties and politicians are convinced that voters are more easily moved by campaigning. Campaign managers have come to terms with television as the main source of voters' information and impression about politics; the growth in the number of media outlets in radio, television and press requires them to devote more effort to news management. Increasingly, they have turned to professionals to fine-tune campaign strategies and make the best use of publicity and public relations techniques.

The next two chapters explore the ways in which the Conservative and Labour parties have adapted to the pressures for professionalization.

3

POLITICAL COMMUNICATIONS: CONSERVATIVES

The Conservative party has been a pioneer among British parties in using the latest publicity techniques in election campaigning. It was an innovator after the 1914–18 war, in 1950, in 1959 and again in 1979. The party was stimulated to experiment with new methods by the creation of a mass electorate in 1918. Party officials were impressed with the government's propaganda techniques in the 1914–18 war and sought to emulate them. Election defeats, notably in 1945, 1966 and 1974, were a further spur to internal party reform and the adoption of more professional methods of communications. In several respects communicators have found the party a more attractive client than Labour. It has more money, a more commercial ethos, a more sympathetic tabloid press and is usually more focused on winning elections. There is a clearer locus of authority in the party leader, and the Chairman and Central Office are constitutionally subordinate to the leader. As a rule there is no doubt about who is the client – the party Chairman and, through him, the leader. The structure has made for speedier decisions than in Labour's case.

Origins

In Central Office responsibility for communications lies with a specialist department led by a Director of Communications (until 1979 the post was titled Chief Publicity Officer). The post has usually been occupied by a person recruited from outside the party organization, one with a background in the press, advertising or public relations. After 1918 the Conservative party managed to recruit some ex-intelligence officers who had worked on 'political warfare' during the war. The first fulltime publicity chief was Major Joseph Ball, who left MI5 to take up the post in 1927 and then became Director of the newly established Conservative Research Department in 1929 (Rhodes-James 1969; Pinto-Duschinsky 1982: 93–101). For the 1929 election the party launched a massive 'Safety First' poster campaign, designed by the advertising agency S H Bensons, urging voters to support the Prime Minister, Stanley Baldwin. The agency continued to prepare posters and leaflets for the 1931 and 1935 elections and more than half of the party's election expenditure was consumed by posters and publicity in the press. The party was also an innovator in the use of cinema and advertising. It used Baldwin in newsreels and his staff prepared brief speeches for him, to reduce the danger of his being cut short by editors. This was, perhaps, the first conscious development of the 'soundbite' (Cockett 1994: 559). It also created a news service which supplied pro-Conservative stories to sympathetic provincial papers.

Between 1934 and 1945 Conservative publicity was handled by the National Publicity Bureau, a front organization created to avoid the alleged 'dead hand' of Central Office. Critics claimed that the party headquarters were too dominated by party agents and unaware of the possibilities of new forms of communication (Pinto-Duschinsky 1982). The bureau was also a means of overcoming the inhibitions of some businesses about contributing to a political party.*

After the party's resounding defeat in the 1945 election the Chairman, Lord Woolton, made sweeping reforms of the party organization and Central Office. With his background in retailing Woolton appreciated the importance of public relations and in 1946 recruited E. D. 'Toby' O'Brien, a journalist, to be Director of Information Services. This was the first occasion that a party had employed a professional publicist to improve its propaganda and communications. When O'Brien arrived at Central Office he found that there was no press cuttings service and that press releases were

---

* There are analogies between the bureau and the development of political action committees in the United States and the Shadow Communications Agency for Labour (see below, p. 93).

sent only to *The Times*, *Daily Telegraph*, *Financial Times* and Press Association (Pearson and Turner 1965: 228). The party appointed Colman, Prentis and Varley (CPV), a London advertising agency, to place advertisements in the national press. Within Central Office Mark Chapman-Walker provided the link with CPV and eventually replaced O'Brien as Chief Publicity Officer in 1949. Churchill and Eden showed little interest in publicity and left the publicists and party Chairman a free hand.

1959 Breakthrough

In 1957 the party reappointed CPV, this time to handle all the advertisements for the next election. In an interview with Richard Rose in 1959 Chapman-Walker explained the decision to appoint an advertising agency:

> CPV have many creative people who are accustomed to selling a product in a very perceptive way. They understand the importance of telling a person what he wants to hear. It is better to work through an agency than to build a staff internally, because an agency can afford more creative people. (Butler file)

Within the agency the account was the responsibility of Geoffrey Tucker, whose thinking had been coloured by a talk about working-class Conservatives in 1958 from Mark Abrams, who was conducting surveys for the Labour party (see p. 80). Tucker wrote a two-page memo, based on the talk, which stressed the importance of using ordinary language in advertisements and noted the interest of the new working class in consumer goods and home ownership. He was sure that these ambitious working-class voters no longer regarded Labour as 'their' party. Oliver Poole, formerly Central Office Chairman (1955–7) but then Deputy Chairman of the party, and an influential supporter of the new methods, circulated the paper to Cabinet ministers.

Between January 1957 and 1959 the party launched a press and poster campaign at a cost of £468,000, easily the most expensive advertising campaign until then. The advertisements presented familiar party themes – the Conservatives as the party of opportunity, prosperity, home ownership and all the people. The aim of the campaign was to improve the party's image by associating it with positive themes such as affluence and the family, rather than to promote particular policies. One series of ads contained the slogan 'You're Looking at a Conservative', which accompanied photos of ordinary people as well as sports stars like the cricketer Colin Cowdrey and the show jumper Pat Smythe. Sir Tim Bell, who was then beginning his advertising career with CPV, recalled in 1993 that the series of adverts was a breakthrough:

> Those adverts broke down the apartheid in the social and political system. The idea was deeply rooted that if you were working class you were Labour and if you were middle class you were Conservative. The ad was saying that it was now permissible to vote Conservative. (Interview)

The most famous advertisement, mixing the positive with the negative, was: 'Life's better with the Conservatives: Don't let Labour ruin it' (figure 3.1). Ronald Simms, the publicity chief, claimed that he invented the basic slogan but Lord Hailsham, the party Chairman, substituted 'better' for the original 'good' and CPV suggested 'ruin' for the original 'spoil' (Pearson and Turner 1965). Another version is that Hailsham invented the phrase, 'Things are better under the

Figure 3.1 Perhaps the most famous postwar election poster. It combines a positive message about prosperity with a warning against voting Labour.

Conservatives' to which Tucker made the changes and added 'Don't let Labour ruin it' (Tucker interview). The advertising was directed at target voters, particularly housewives, skilled workers and young voters. The *Life's Better* slogan was carried on posters which portrayed a handsome young family standing proudly beside its new house or new car. The persuasiveness of the message was helped by economic prosperity. These were years of full employment; average take-home pay had increased in real terms by some 20 per cent since 1951; easier hire-purchase facilities had boosted consumer spending on cars, fridges and foreign holidays, and there was a general mood of economic optimism. The introduction of commercial television familiarized voters with advertising and, by extension, political advertising. When the election was announced the posters were taken down for fear of infringing the law on election expenses.

The essential principles of effective political communications were observable in the Conservative advertisements prior to the 1959 election. They were expressed in simple language, continued over the long term, complemented party policy, and relied on professional help (Hennessy 1961).

In spite of the party achieving a handsome victory in 1959 not all Conservatives were comfortable about political advertising or the party's use of an agency. The doubters included the new head of publicity George Hutchinson (1961–4), a former journalist. Some in the party hierarchy appeared to regard the use of public relations and opinion polling in politics as somehow unethical and some may have feared that it represented a reflection on their own skills. 'They [CPV] will take over policy', was the fear of one official. Poole's answer was to ensure that the Research Department vetted all CPV adverts for compatibility with party policy. The role of the agency was confined to making suggestions for posters and press ads and senior staff were never invited to meet Conservative ministers face to face to discuss their work. 'We were rather looked down on', recalled Geoffrey Tucker (interview).

In 1959 the political and economic conditions were in place for election victory. In 1964, however, good presentation could not overcome difficulties with the political product. Throughout 1963 the Conservative government was dogged by the Profumo scandal, France's rejection of Britain's application to join the European Community, doubts about Macmillan's leadership, his retirement, and then the bitter divisions surrounding his replacement as Prime

Minister by Lord (Alec) Home. Sir Alec, as he became, was not at ease with campaigning or with television. In a recent interview he confessed, 'Well, I was bored by the whole business of presentation as far as television was concerned because I think television is bound to be superficial. I was wrong' (Hennessy 1986: 65). As a fourteenth earl he was hardly a suitable personification of the Conservative message that it wanted to modernize Britain. The party trailed in the opinion polls and Labour, under its new leader Harold Wilson, had seized the initiative. As Richard Rose notes, the work of the publicists was handicapped by 'the behaviour of the party they were seeking to boost' (1965: 372). If the Conservatives had been an innovator in 1959, Labour appeared to have overtaken them by 1964 in integrating survey research and advertising in their communications campaign (see below, pp. 80–1).

Projecting Heath

Between 1963 and 1966 the party suffered two general election defeats and the retirement of two weakened leaders. In defeat Conservatives often blame 'poor communications'. After the 1964 election reverse some Central Office officials increasingly recognized the importance of adopting a more professional approach to publicity and opinion polling and were conscious that Labour had stolen a march on the party. George Hutchinson left to become Managing Director of the *Spectator* and after some short-term appointments the party managed to appoint Geoffrey Tucker in 1968, on secondment from the American advertising agency, Young and Rubicam. It was under him that the Conservatives made a breakthrough in their campaigning communications.

Tucker was convinced that the next election would be won or lost on television and the campaign dominated by the party leaders. His problem was that Edward Heath, who had been elected leader in 1965, was not good on television, hated the medium and resented people making suggestions about how he could do better. Heath came across as stiff, aloof, lacking the popular touch. Tucker wanted him to be seen as warmer and more relaxed and to speak in a more colloquial style, above all to combine informality with authority. It was a tough battle and not a completely successful one, for Heath was determined to resist what he dismissed as 'gimmicks' and 'packaging', which to him were too redolent of Harold Wilson.

Tucker was influenced by his contacts in America and the writings of the media guru, Marshall McLuhan. The latter claimed that because television was a 'cool' medium the success of the performer depended on the 'low-pressure style of presentation'. The politician should not make speeches or lecture to people in their living-rooms but engage in intimate conversation, and create a good 'impression' – through voice tone, facial expression and body language – on the voters, who would not pay much attention to what he was saying. Advisers were fond of drawing a distinction between Heath's private voice, which could be warm and relaxed, and his public voice which they feared alienated voters. In a lengthy letter, on 4 August 1969, Tucker wrote to Heath:

> I put only one problem to you. How does one make certain that the private voice, which comes over on television in a direct interview, also comes over when you are addressing a rally and is then picked up for television? This will be a major factor for us at the next general election and is a difficult one to crack.

Tucker returned to the theme in another letter, dated 17 December 1969. He warned the leader against trying on television to orate like Winston Churchill:

> A politician has to conform to his own speech rhythms and to use his language and not those of other people. That is what I mean by the private voice and the importance of the private voice is that it is the voice for television – a voice that you use in talking to people in their own homes.

A video machine was installed in Heath's private residence so that he could rehearse his speeches and be his own critic when they were played back. But the leader proved a reluctant student and more than once told Tucker that he had better things to do with his time than provide film footage for television; at times he said that he would not go on television at all.

In the 1970 election the Conservatives made a breakthrough in the use of advertising and public relations. William Whitelaw, the Chief Whip, provided political approval for all initiatives, Sir Michael Fraser, formerly Director of the Research Department between 1951 and 1964, now Deputy Chairman of Central Office, spoke for the organization, the agency Davidson Pearce placed the ads, ORC (Opinion Research Centre) supplied the research and Tucker recruited a team of volunteers in communications. Crucially, Conservative publicity was being left to professionals recruited from outside Central Office. Groups specialized in speechwriting, copywriting, broadcasts and advertising. The team brought from the advertising industry an emphasis upon strategy and communicating concisely and in everyday language. By the middle of 1969 Tucker was able to state the objectives and methods of the campaign in a one-page document (see Appendix, pp. 75–6). The objective was 'To convince all C2 women and men under 35 and women of all classes under 35, that the personal prosperity they have lost under Labour will be restored to them by a Conservative Government'. The method was:

> Advertising [which] will both reinforce the current level of dissatisfaction felt by many of the electorate and show how a Conservative adminis-tration will put matters right. It will highlight the incompetence of the present Labour administration and contrast this with the competence of the Conservatives.

The advertising should emphasize Labour's record of increased direct and indirect taxation and highlight the Conservative promise to reduce the rate of direct taxation. Above all, the advertising would have to make people '*believe that a Conservative Government will make a difference to them as individuals*' (original emphasis). Working-class housewives become a particular target of the advertising and election broadcasts. The team decided that the best way to appeal to the housewives was to concentrate upon the increased prices of the goods which they were buying. Husbands might get bigger wage packets but would house-wives see any of the extra cash?

The party also made innovations in its party election broadcasts. Tucker brought in James Garratt, of James Garratt and Partners, the largest maker of television advertisements in Britain. He in turn recruited the television director Dick Clements and Barry Day, the creative director of the McCann Erickson advertising agency, to write the television scripts. The team were known as the Communications Group and borrowed from the techniques of British television and American political advertising. Barry Day's view was that by 1970 people expected to get most of their information from television: 'Therefore, we should make our election broadcasts like ordinary programmes. That way we could blend with the media background' (interview).

The team replaced the 'talking heads' of politicians (which, their research showed, bored voters) with snappy newsreel film, modelled on the 'News at Ten' programme, introduced by two well-known broadcasters who also happened to be Tory MPs. Viewers had become used to advertising on television, so the broadcasts made a simple point about rising prices by providing striking visuals of a 'vanishing pound' and a 'frozen wage packet'. The former advertisement showed a £1 note being attacked by a pair of scissors. As each segment was cut away a voice-over announced the date and reduced value of the pound, concluding with the claim that a continuation of Labour policies would lead to the 'Ten Bob Pound'. The second advertisement showed a woman's hand removing a block of ice from a domestic fridge with a frozen wage packet embedded in the ice. The message was 'Vote Labour and You'll Get it Again – in the Family Economy Size'.

The broadcasts focused single-mindedly on rising prices and their sophistication was acknowledged by Martin Harrison, who commented on 'a professional polish never previously achieved in party election broadcasts' (Butler and Pinto-Duschinsky 1971: 224). But, in spite of the praise from professional communicators and party managers, Conservative private polling and BBC Audience Research surveys suggested that the broadcasts were no more appreciated than straight talks to camera and did not make a net gain in votes.

As Prime Minister, Heath periodically invited Tucker, Day and Garratt to suggest ideas for election broadcasts and major interviews. They were disappointed to discover how little film of the work of Conservative ministers had been preserved, proof positive to them of how ministers had ceased to think politically. 'We were always aware that Ted was now surrounded by the civil service machine and he was thinking like it. The party communicated to get into office, but did not do this as an ongoing process' (Day, interview). Barry Day later recalled that if an advertiser '*stopped* advertising when he had a brand leader on the market, his competition would think he was mad' (Worcester and Harrop 1982: 9).

Mr Heath showed a similar detachment about election timing. The industrial action taken by miners in pursuit of a wage claim in excess of the government's guidelines not only damaged industry, but increasingly led to pressure for the government to call an election. In December 1973 and January 1974 he listened to the views of ministers, Central Office and regional officials and backbenchers. Most of the advice pointed to the advantages of 7 February. In early January the party's private opinion pollster suggested that a late January or early

February election would offer a good chance of victory but that a later one would be more risky, as the issue of the miners' challenge to the government might be overtaken by other issues. The Prime Minister's political secretary, Douglas Hurd, concurred. Mr Heath listened to the advice, ignored it, dissolved later, and lost. His subsequent judgement was that he had got the timing wrong – he should not have called an election at all!

The production of the party's broadcasts for the crisis election in February 1974 was again left to Garratt, Day and Tucker, and organized around the theme of 'Firm but Fair'. The team's second election programme was perhaps the most controversial broadcast made until then. The programme set out to show that Labour was moving to the left and was unwilling to stand up to the unions or check Communist influence in the unions. One sequence showed the faces of Harold Wilson and James Callaghan dissolving into those of Tony Benn and Michael Foot and then back to the originals. A nationaliz-ation sequence suggested that Labour would take over insurance policies, mortgages, pay packets and bank accounts, and concluded by showing a young couple losing their house. None of these accusations could be based on the Labour manifesto, but they could be said to be implied or contained in various party documents. The broadcast made some people inside Central Office unhappy and subsequent broadcasts were less hard-hitting. The judgement of Martin Harrison was:

> This was a sorry broadcast in its ethical blindness, its clumsy cascade of visual gimmicks, and its abysmal view of the electorate's intelligence. It confirmed the fears of what can happen when ad men are given their head without adequate political control. (Harrison 1974: 160).

One young Research Department official who was present at the making of the programme to check the accuracy of statements on Conservative policy, felt, in retrospect, that he had been 'conned' (interview). Opponents of the use of outsiders complained that the communicators were operating with too little political direction and demanded that the leaders should pay more attention to the party's grass-roots and less to experts in public relations and polling. According to one observer, 'The election had been lost, it was said, because the "old politics" had been too easily abandoned in favour of the "new politics"' (Pinto-Duschinsky 1974: 87).

After the party's defeat in the February election the communications team was influential in pushing the idea of a national unity appeal for the next election. This jelled with the thinking of a number of other leading Conservatives and was backed by private and public polling about the public dislike of adversarial politics and support for the idea of an all-party coalition government (Sherbourne interview). In June Mr Heath appointed a small team of young sympathizers (Douglas Hurd, Nigel Lawson, John MacGregor and Tony Newton) to consider the survey findings and make recommendations. The group approved the national unity approach and suggested a much lower profile for Mr Heath in the second 1974 election. Survey research as well as doorstep opinion suggested that he was not an electoral asset to the party and more emphasis was placed on 'the team' of shadow ministers, notably Margaret Thatcher. But the party suffered another defeat in the October 1974 election.

Those associated with the two losing campaigns blamed bad election timing and failures in presentation. Others drew more radical lessons. Mrs Thatcher succeeded Heath as leader in February 1975 and she and her supporters thought that the party in government had been wrong to abandon the free-market approach and that the U-turns over economic policy had confused the electorate. She was determined to change the philosophy and the policies of the party. Her views were accurately represented by the political editor of the *Spectator*. In an article, 'Mistakes of the image makers' (27 April 1974), Patrick Cosgrave wrote:

> The view that a political philosophy, a political party, a set of measures and a group of men who are to govern, are in any way equivalent to a commercial product, to be sold with aggression in the electoral market place, whether it is spelt out openly by such as Mr Day, or implicit in an election campaign, is demeaning and diminishing to any civilized view of public life and service, let alone to traditional British ideas about the conduct of the public business.

Cosgrave accused Day of downgrading the importance of party organization and policy and criticized his publicly stated analogy between selling a party's programme or philosophy and selling a commercial product. What mattered was the adoption of policies based on a coherent set of beliefs. Mrs Thatcher supplied a set of beliefs but used the latest public relations techniques to a greater degree than any of her predecessors.

Arrival of Saatchi

In late 1977, Margaret Thatcher installed a new Director of Publicity, Gordon Reece. He had earlier worked on broadcasts for the party (the first in 1967 on the case for selling council houses to tenants) and advised Mrs Thatcher on her campaign for the party leadership in 1975. Reece did not disparage research but placed more reliance on his intuition and hunch about what moved voters. He took the existing level of Conservative support for granted; four or five years' personal experience of living under Labour should be enough to guarantee their loyalty. He also believed in political 'pacing', claiming that an election was probably decided long before the dissolution of Parliament and the campaign was but 'the final sprint or the last fence in a race'. His target voters were 'soft' Labour or Liberal voters and working-class women. Women, he believed, were the opinion formers in a household and the way to reach them was to present Mrs Thatcher on relatively non-political or light entertainment programmes. These voters were more likely to read the *Sun* and the *Mirror* than *The Times* and *Guardian*, and were moved more by impressions than argument ('You have to create impressions. That's what people vote on, not issues'). Advertising would be placed in the tabloids ('the only audience that matters'). He knew that some MPs and officials (not least Chris Patten, the party Director of Research) disapproved of his 'down-market' approach, but he countered that *The Times* or *Newsnight*, which they read or watched, were ignored by the voters he was seeking to reach. Political advertising might not convert Labour supporters but he would be content if it 'made them think Conservatives are good for you' (Reece, interview).

It was Reece's decision that the party's entire communications programme should be handled by a single agency. He wanted to appoint an agency that had enough resources to handle all the party's communications needs – press and poster advertising, television and research – but was also small enough to want to impress, 'to make its name'. After approval from Mrs Thatcher and the party Chairman, Lord Thorneycroft, the contract was awarded early in 1978 to the Saatchi & Saatchi agency. This agency had been formed in 1970, was the sixth largest in Britain and was British-owned. Successive party leaders had stipulated that Central Office could only use a British agency – a difficulty in an industry that was dominated by US firms. For the first time in British general elections a party's election broadcasts would be made by an advertising agency. Reece was given a free hand by the leader and Chairman and was effectively the agency's client. Like Tucker in 1970, Reece thought that the success of his job would depend on the impact made by Mrs Thatcher on television.

The agency worked to a brief about the party's policies and objectives written by the Research Department. Saatchi's qualitative research with target voters was crucial to the development of the strategy. This showed that few people were aware of how poor the Labour government's performance on unemployment and prices was, compared with that of the 1970–4 Conservative government. The advertising and broadcasts, therefore, were designed to promote public awareness of the government's poor record on productivity, unemployment and prosperity. 'We wanted to make them dissatisfied with the government, to promote dissonance. In opposition the only message is "Time for Change"', said Tim Bell, Saatchi's director of the Conservative account (interview).

A large poster campaign was launched in summer 1978, aimed mainly at semi-skilled workers, first-time voters and women in Labour households (the usual Conservative target voters) and emphasized jobs, prices and law and order. Bell also took the view that the Conservative supporters had nowhere else to go, 'So we had to spend our time winning new supporters' (interview). The press advertising was concentrated in the popular papers, particularly the *Daily Mirror* and the *Sun*. The poster and broadcasting campaign had been designed to contain the anticipated recovery of government support during the summer and some Conservatives later claimed that it had succeeded so well in this that it had probably dissuaded Mr Callaghan from calling a dissolution in the autumn. The most famous poster was 'Labour isn't working', with a slogan placed above a long dole queue, emphasizing Labour's poor record on unemployment. It was a sign of how the tone of ads had changed from 1959 that the posters invariably used strong knocking messages:

'Labour still isn't working'
'1984 – What 5 more years?'
'Cheer up. They can't last forever'
'Educashun isn't working'

Mr Reece acknowledged the problem in presenting Mrs Thatcher. In part this was because she was the first woman leader of a major British party and in part because she was widely regarded as 'bossy', 'uncaring' and unfamiliar with the problems of ordinary people. She made adjustments to her hair, teeth and wardrobe, lowered her voice and spoke in shorter sentences. She was more receptive than Heath to advice (from Reece, Bell and the playwright Ronald Millar) about how she could improve her presentational skills. Each time she appeared on television Reece commissioned a private opinion poll to assess audience reactions and then discussed the findings with her. He wanted her to relax and therefore tried to avoid forceful television interviewers. Such interviewers tended to provoke Mrs Thatcher and her abrasiveness in turn alienated target voters. Mr Reece also encouraged her to appear on less explicitly political programmes such as the Jimmy Young Show on radio and early evening regional and national news programmes; these attracted larger audiences than current affairs programmes and included the C2 or skilled working-class voters, the party's target audience. He ensured that her activities were timed for the film to be processed and broadcast at peak times; these were geared more to providing photo-opportunities for the cameras than interviews and comments for the journalists. The attention to the leader's television and public appearances and the control exercised over access to her was so meticulous that some commentators dubbed the campaign 'The Selling of Maggie'. But Mrs Thatcher made a point of inspecting all posters and advertisements and on occasion vetoed suggestions.

During the election campaign Conservative advertisements and broadcasts reiterated the case for change and the themes of 'freedom, choice, opportunity, small government and prosperity' (Bell 1982: 17). Above all, they attacked the Labour government's record, the obvious approach for an opposition: 'it's the classic slogan for capturing a national mood when people are in fact tired of a government' (Bell 1982: 28). The poster and press advertisements highlighted the government's record on inflation, unemployment, taxation and hospital queues – unflatteringly. The advertising and communications of the last week of the campaign were built around the slogan 'It's Time for a Change'.

It is easy to write that a winning campaign did so many things correctly – because it won. But the contrast in 1979 between the cohesion and sense of purpose in the Conservative communications and Labour's was marked. For example, all but one of the Conservative election broadcasts were made before the election began. Labour's were made at the last minute and, as one of those responsible admitted, it showed (Delaney 1982). The Conservative election success prompted much discussion about 'The Marketing of Margaret', of Labour having been 'out-Saatchied at every turn' and of how slick advertising and professional communications had transformed elections. Yet Labour's election defeat in the wake of the winter's industrial disruption was a virtual certainty.

Saatchi & Saatchi were retained for the 1983 election. The agency was aware that there were party critics who thought that some of its communications in the 1979 election had been too facetious and that a more serious tone was required now that the party was in government. The agency's qualitative research showed widespread public cynicism about politicians and scepticism about their ability to tackle the major problems facing the country. People were looking to government for a sense of direction and discipline more than a display of caring and compassion. They did not hold the government primarily responsible for the country's economic and other difficulties and were prepared to acknowledge the shortcomings of individuals and the decline of family and neighbourhood as major causes of social problems.

At the party's first election strategy meeting at Chequers in January 1983 the agency's presentation to Mrs Thatcher argued that the election campaign should:

1 Emphasize continuity.
2 Highlight the Conservatives' qualities of leadership.
3 Take account of voters' lowered expectations of what governments could do: 'This is to encourage the electorate to take a realistic view of politics, with low expectations of what politicians can achieve'.
4 Take advantage of the fundamental changes in public attitudes: 'The Conservative party can be positive and aggressive in its communication. There is no need to be defensive, even on unemployment'.
5 Wrong-foot the opposition appeal of 'It's Time for a Change'. The Conservatives should present themselves as the party of radical reform and urge people to 'Stay the Course'.
6 Be true to what the party is doing: 'The Conservatives' main weakness is an image of being inflexible and uncaring, but their perceived strengths outweigh their weaknesses'.

The advertising campaign was geared more to attacking the alternatives than defending the government's record. One advertisement claimed that voting Labour was the same as agreeing to 15 unpopular itemized statements. Another listed 11 similar policy promises of Labour and Communist manifestos under the heading, 'Like Your Manifesto, Comrade?' Such negative and controversial ads, like those of 1979, had a deliberate tactical objective. According to Barry Day, 'By forcing an issue – which might or might not surface naturally during the campaign – the party forcing the issue dictates to a considerable degree what the campaign will be about for one or more valuable days in that limited campaign period' (interview).

An advertisement planned for the final Sunday was to have been an unprecedented three-page spread listing Labour, Conservative and Alliance policies. It was entitled 'IF' (the title of Mrs Thatcher's favourite poem by Kipling) and had already been approved in principle by Cecil Parkinson, the Chairman. One page warned of the unpopular policies a Labour government would implement, another of the desirable developments that would follow the election of the Conservatives, and the third warned that a vote for the Alliance would produce a Labour government. But Cecil Parkinson, partly because he was convinced that victory was assured and partly because he was worried over the costs, vetoed the ad. After the election he claimed that his action had saved the Conservative party nearly £3 million and a frustrated Bell mourned the waste of what he regarded as his best ever advertisement. There was also some post-election wrangling between Central Office and Saatchi over who should bear the greater part of the cancellation costs to the newspapers.

The party developed its public relations in other respects. Harvey Thomas, who had previously staged rallies for the American evangelist Billy Graham, was employed as Director of Presentations for the 1979 and later elections. Mrs Thatcher's rallies and party conferences became spectacular showpieces, employing the latest gadgets to increase their effectiveness on television. Christopher Lawson, a former marketing manager with Mars in the US, was employed as the party's Marketing Director between 1981 and 1983. He introduced direct mail, telephone canvassing and designed a logo for the party.

After another election victory there was no question that Saatchi & Saatchi would not handle the advertising for the (next) 1987 election. But relations between the agency and Mrs Thatcher before and during the election were much more fraught this time. Some of Mrs Thatcher's closest advisers, including the Cabinet minister Lord Young and party Treasurer, Lord McAlpine, maintained close links with Tim Bell, who had left the agency somewhat acrimoniously in 1984. Mrs Thatcher was an admirer of Bell's political flair and presentational skills and wanted him to be involved in the campaign; she now regarded him as personifying Saatchi & Saatchi. He had become more than a communications helper; he was a personal friend, courtier and trusted political adviser. But Norman Tebbit, the party Chairman, and the agency were not prepared to have him involved in the Conservative campaign in any capacity whatever. Michael Dobbs had been a personal assistant to Bell at Saatchi (1979–81) and became a deputy chairman at the agency. Dobbs took paid leave to act as chief assistant to Mr Tebbit in Central Office; his misfortune was that he became *persona non grata* to Mrs Thatcher and for a time she would not accept his appointment at Central Office. Lord Young was appointed to Central Office as a deputy chairman, with a remit to keep an eye on Mr Tebbit (some of her friends whispered that he had designs on her job) and provide a link with Bell, who continued to advise Mrs Thatcher. Mr Tebbit made two attempts to recruit a Director of Publicity after Sir Gordon Reece left in late 1985 but Mrs Thatcher vetoed each candidate. These were the ingredients of what turned out to be an explosive relationship.

A strategy presentation by Dobbs to the Prime Minister and her advisers at Chequers in April 1986 was badly received. The research on which it was based had been conducted during a low period in Mrs Thatcher's political fortunes. The government, Mr Dobbs reported, was seen as harsh, uncaring, extreme and lacking a sense of direction. Conservative supporters were particularly critical of the government's record on health and education. And Mrs Thatcher's image raised particular difficulties. She was told that she was seen as 'bossy' and 'fussy' and although voters acknowledged her strengths, many did not link them to any sense of purpose. The agency recommended that the government could protect itself against the opposition cry of 'It's Time for a Change' by showing that it was still forward looking and more positively presenting its policies on health and education. The presentation did nothing to improve relations between Mrs Thatcher and her party Chairman Norman Tebbit or to boost her self-confidence at a difficult period.

Mrs Thatcher received more reassuring advice from another advertising agency, Young and Rubicam (Y & R). Its approach to studying the values and lifestyles of the electorate divided the voters into value groups, which cut across conventional market research social classes (see Gold 1986: 109–16). It assumed that for each voter there was one dominant value which affected his or her behaviour and attitudes, why a person liked or disliked a product, supported some policies but opposed others. The largest group was the *middle majority* which amounted to nearly two-thirds or 63 per cent of the population. The most pro-Conservative category among them were the so-called 'succeeders' or 'achievers', who were high-income earners, ambitious, optimistic, pro-establishment and pro-authority. The largest single category were the 'mainstreamers', who were conservative, patriotic, home centred, traditional and had voted for the party in 1979 and 1983. Mrs Thatcher identified these as 'Thatcherites'. But in 1985 and 1986 they were turning to other parties, particularly the Alliance. This research suggested that too much of the Conservative message was oriented to the 'succeeders' and that the 'mainstreamers' felt neglected and were particularly disappointed over education, law and order and the NHS. Defectors from the Conservative party still accepted many Thatcherite values and wanted to see the Prime Minister exercising strong leadership and taking action to meet their concerns over education and health.

A key figure in bringing the research to Mrs Thatcher's attention was Geoffrey Tucker, now a consultant for Y & R. He had close links to Lord Whitelaw, the deputy Prime Minister, John Wakeham, Chief Whip, and Sir Ronald Millar, a speechwriter for Mrs Thatcher. The agency was commissioned to carry on with the research, using funds raised by the party Treasurer, Lord McAlpine, without Tebbit's knowledge. The research was regularly distributed to a select group of senior ministers and Number 10 staff, but not to Mr Tebbit, who chose not to receive it, nor Saatchi who were not impressed by the work. Mrs Thatcher, however, found the work useful in 1986; it confirmed her own electoral intuition and it was important in restoring her self-confidence.

Saatchi played the key role in presenting the 1986 Conservative conference, which proved to be the launching pad for the party's recovery. The agency devised the conference theme, *The Next Move Forward*, suggested some of the contents and themes of ministers' speeches and co-ordinated the publicity. In particular ministers were urged to concentrate on future plans in their departments and to give voters a clear perception of what the party stood for.

Mrs Thatcher was not a passive recipient of advice about advertising for the election. She insisted that the campaign should be positive about her government's record and her radical policies for the future. When the Saatchi team presented over 80 election advertisements to her in Downing Street on 24 April she expressed disappointment that there was not more material on the government's achievements. 'The trouble is that when politicians ask for a positive campaign, they really

want to blow their own trumpets' said one member of the agency. Mrs
Thatcher particularly wanted the communications to highlight the
government's achievements on health. Tebbit's view was that

> It was too big a task to overcome public disbelief, including that of our
> supporters, that the government handled the health service spending
> issue well . . . Indeed, success would have been surprising in view of the
> government's earlier rhetoric on cuts. Therefore the strategy was repair
> and containment on that issue. (Tebbit, letter to author)

A week later the Prime Minister approved the more positive advertising
copy.

During the election the polls suggested that the government was
coasting to another decisive victory. But Mrs Thatcher's concern over
the advertising and panic at apparent slippage in an opinion poll
combined to create the famous 'Wobbly Thursday' in the Tory high
command one week before polling day (see Young 1990: ch. 15; Tebbit
1988: 335; Butler and Kavanagh 1987: 107–10). On the Wednesday
night it was learnt that the Gallup poll to be published in the next day's
Daily Telegraph showed the Conservative lead over Labour down from
double figures to 4 per cent. A Gallup pollster was telling Mrs
Thatcher's advisers that the party was losing the election. On the
Thursday morning further gloomy tidings came in the form of the latest
Y & R research – *mainstream* voters, it reported, were becoming
disillusioned and Labour was gaining on many of the key image
questions. It urged the party to be more positive in its communications,
concentrate more on Mrs Thatcher and show voters what they stood to
lose under Labour.

The information spurred an already uneasy Mrs Thatcher to
demand changes in the party's advertising. At Lord Young's behest
Tim Bell produced some advertising copy which stressed the government's accomplishments on taxes, schools and health, and a slogan,
'Britain is a success again, don't let Labour ruin it'. Saatchi's also
worked on new posters but Mrs Thatcher had already decided that she
wanted Bell's, 'which I believed would be better' (1993: 584–5). After
harsh words between Lord Young and Norman Tebbit, in which the
former, on the leader's behalf, virtually instructed the latter, Saatchi's
adapted the idea under protest and modified the slogan to 'Britain is
Great again, don't let Labour wreck it'. The advertisements were
spread over the pages of national newspapers on each of the last four

days of the campaign, always accompanied by the slogan 'Britain is Great again'.

After the election various people claimed sole authorship of the slogan, proof that victory has many fathers. But it is clear that all three advertisers were working on almost identical slogans and that the message was essentially no different than the party's 1959 slogan 'Life's better with the Conservatives. Don't let Labour ruin it'. The rows over the advertising were given full publicity after the election and it was no surprise when Saatchi's decided that they would no longer handle advertising for the Conservative party. The tension and disagreement between Downing Street and Central Office, conflicting sources of advice, and the clashes between the party's appointed agency and other consultants, are a model of how not to run a campaign. Tebbit afterwards complained of 'a cacophony of discordant and ill-co-ordinated advice . . . too many cooks spoil the broth, especially when the appointed Chef does not know who is putting what in the pot behind his back' (letter to author).

Projecting John Major

During 1989 and 1990 the party considered presentations from a number of advertising agencies, but made no move to appoint one. In late 1990, with Mrs Thatcher still in office, it was planned by the Central Office Director of Communications, Brendan Bruce, that the party would put Sir Tim Bell in overall control of communications. He in turn would commission different groups to deal with broadcasts, advertising and other aspects of communications, much as the Tuesday Team had operated for President Reagan in the 1984 Presidential election. It was virtually certain that Mrs Thatcher and the Chairman, Kenneth Baker, would agree. But before action could be taken on this in late 1990 both Thatcher and Baker had been ousted, and a new Prime Minister and a new party Chairman were installed. The new Chairman, Mr Patten, turned down the key recommendations and in January 1991 he replaced Brendan Bruce with Shaun Woodward, a television editor and before that a producer of current affairs programmes.

Woodward and Patten regarded the appointment of an advertising agency as urgent. The search was organized by a public relations firm, Shandwick, which invited agencies to submit a communications strategy suitable for a large, but unnamed, corporate client which was about to launch a new product. One agency BBH (Bartle, Bogle and Hegarty) was very much the front-runner but it decided late in the day that it did not want to handle what it learnt would be the Conservative account (see below). It was a surprise when Saatchi were reappointed. The agency would be involved in all aspects of the communications strategy – broadcasts, press conferences, posters and advertisements. The change of party leadership to John Major was both a challenge and an opportunity for Saatchi. For the first time it would be working for a Conservative leader other than Mrs Thatcher.

The agency's research confirmed the party's long-standing weakness on the 'caring' social issues, although Mr Major certainly softened the image of the party. But the change of leader now appeared to give more credence to Labour's criticisms about the limits of markets and the importance of policies being based on fairness and social justice.

In a memorandum in early July 1991 Saatchi warned that fighting on 'caring capitalism' or the 'social market' approach (at this time Chris Patten was making speeches advocating these themes) was Labour's ground. The approach contained an implied admission that the free market alone would not improve the social services. Yet the government had just introduced market forces into education and health. There was therefore a contradiction between post-Thatcher Conservative rhetoric and the policies actually being applied. A second danger was that the party could not compete with the Labour party when it came to projecting a caring image. The party therefore faced what the agency called a 'double danger' – a confused public perception of its message, and fighting on Labour ground.

The Conservative problem was that many dragons from the 1970s had been slain. The power of the unions had been reduced; the breakup of the USSR removed a military threat and thereby reduced the importance of defence; the privatization programme was nearly complete; and the state of the economy ruled out further tax cuts. The last frontier appeared to be the public services. The agency argued that the party should return to its traditional strengths in economic management and remind voters that good public services had to be paid for. This would enable the party to fight on its own territory of economic management. But what did John Major want?

'What an agency wants from a client, be it a party or Procter & Gamble, is a clear answer to the question of what it stands for, why people should support the party or buy the product', said Jeremy

Sinclair, of Saatchi (interview). The agency had no difficulty in knowing what Mrs Thatcher stood for, but Woodward took some weeks to provide clear answers to the agency's two key questions:

Do the Conservatives favour lower taxes?
Do the Conservatives favour more public spending?

'The delay in answering was because the client (John Major) was probably still not clear in his own mind', said a Saatchi executive.

A good example of the American influence on British campaigns was seen in the visit to the United States in late September 1991 of Shaun Woodward, Bill Muirhead, a Saatchi executive, and Sir Tom Arnold, a Central Office vice-chairman. They were interested in learning from the successful 1984 Reagan campaign which had been fought in an economic recession. They met Richard Wirthlin, pollster to former President Reagan, and Roger Ailes, Bush's campaign manager in 1988. One lesson was that Reagan had used the last few months before the campaign to dictate the agenda through co-ordinating his speeches and press conferences, tours and legislative initiatives. This was the inspiration for the launching of a pre-election campaign for the first three months of 1992.

Shortly after the annual party conference in October 1991 party leaders decided to launch a lengthy pre-election campaign by linking the daily communications output from Central Office with the ongoing work of the government. They sought to dominate the news media via Parliamentary Question Time, Prime Minister's Question Time, control of the Parliamentary timetable, legislation and of course the Budget. In these months election preparations were never far from ministers' minds and the Cabinet regularly devoted a session to the current political situation (Butler and Kavanagh 1992). In a paper for the Cabinet on 19 December the party Chairman Chris Patten appealed for co-operation from other ministers and warned that the campaign was a half-way house between normal activity and election conditions: 'It requires us to place political priorities above rigid Departmental considerations and for Departmental heads to be prepared to insist upon adherence to the timetable where Departmental officials may regard this as extraneous to the announcement itself'.

This campaign was co-ordinated by the No. 12 Committee of senior Cabinet ministers, so called because it usually met at the Downing Street residence of the Chief Whip, Richard Ryder. This group handled the day-to-day tactics. Ministers were urged to accept – and solicit –

invitations to media interviews, provide Central Office with an effective rebuttal of Labour policies and consider updating their 'television presentational skills'. There was also a political session at the end of each weekly Cabinet to agree themes. Labour mounted its own campaign at this time (see p. 102).

In the last weeks of 1991, a small group, consisting of Chris Patten, Maurice Saatchi and Shaun Woodward, visited each Cabinet minister to agree the minister's contribution to the near-term campaign. They drew on polling by Gallup about the salience of issues and voters' perceptions of the competence of the parties on the issues. According to Gallup in October, on the two most salient issues, unemployment and health, the party trailed Labour by large margins, but had good leads on cost of living and law and order (see figure 3.2). The position resembled that in September 1986, seven months before the 1987 election, when unemployment and health had also been the main issues and the Conservatives trailed badly on both. But by the time of the election the party had considerably improved its standing on both. Conservative issues were: the economy (taxes and inflation), law and order and defence. Labour issues were unemployment, health and welfare. Saatchi's reflected in a memo: 'Most of our *strong* issues have *low* salience' (e.g. defence); 'Most of our *weak* issues have *high* salience' (e.g. health). Any Conservative strategy must seek to raise the salience of issues on which the party had a lead, and promote a positive message about the government's record on those on which it trailed Labour.

The agency advocated linking the costing of Labour's spending to the tax implications. The party's researchers calculated that the total cost of Labour's spending plans would be £35 billion. Now that the Labour party had ruled out higher borrowing to finance its spending plans, the agency looked at the £35 billion in terms of what it would mean for extra income tax. The tax attack was first raised in July 1991, via a poster, general election broadcast and press conference all on the same day. It was raised again in the controversial tax bombshell poster in early January 1992 which claimed that Labour would cost '£1,000 more tax a year for the average tax payer' – a forerunner of the April election campaign message. Each time the attack was co-ordinated with press conferences, an election broadcast and ministerial speeches.

The party managers prepared a so-called pre-election campaign to set the agenda for a forthcoming election and open up a clear lead over Labour by the time of the Budget in March 1992. For each issue week of this campaign the government and Central Office tried to integrate press conferences, photo-opportunities, ministerial statements and activities, Research Department documents, media interviews, regional visits and other activities to seize the agenda and place the opposition on the defensive. Ministers were issued with media soundbites which were to be used in all interviews and speeches. On the economy, they should reiterate:

'You can't trust Labour.'
'You can't trust Labour to run the economy.'
'You'll pay £1,000 more tax under Labour.'

On law and order, they should say:

'Labour are soft on crime. They make excuses for criminals, and ignore victims.'
'We believe in tougher sentences, and more bobbies on the beat.'

Because the Conservatives would be fighting an election in a recession Saatchi could not invoke the time-honoured claim that 'Britain's better off with the Conservatives. Don't let Labour ruin it'. It anticipated that Labour's position would be:

The Tories have failed.
They deserve punishment.
It's time for a change.

The agency decided that the answer to the expected line of attack should be:

You can't trust Labour.
It could be worse.
Labour would start a new recession.

Inevitably this approach meant that the campaign would be predominantly negative: 'We had to demolish Labour and say that they would make things worse', said Maurice Saatchi (interview).

The 1992 election, however, is hardly the story of carefully planned timing. John Major succeeded Mrs Thatcher in December 1990 and, according to the opinion polls, greatly improved Conservative election prospects. But throughout 1991 the recession, rising unemployment and continuing news of bankruptcies depressed the voters' mood. John Major, it was often said, was impatient to gain his own mandate from the voters. But each time there was a window of opportunity for an election, it was closed because of bad news – disappointing local election results in May, a by-election reverse at Monmouth in June and then disappointing opinion polls in the autumn. The Treasury insistence that there would be stronger signs of economic recovery in

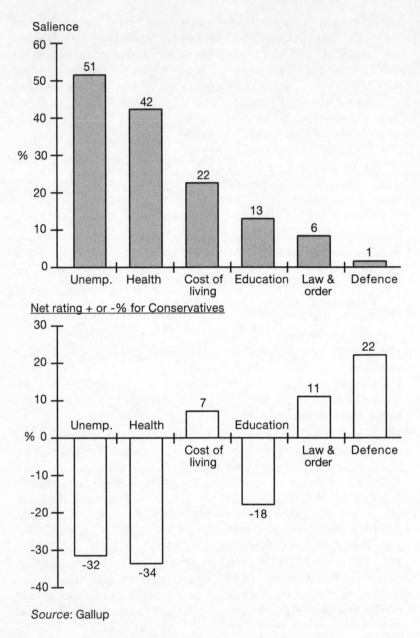

Figure 3.2 (a) Issue salience/rating October 1986.

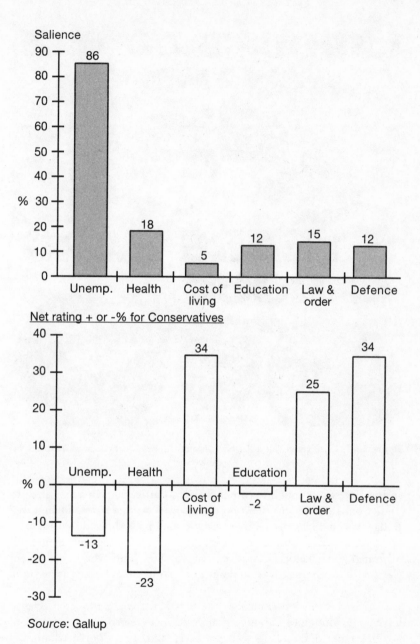

Salience

Net rating + or -% for Conservatives

Source: Gallup

Figure 3.2 (b) Issue salience/rating October 1991.

Figure 3.3 Conservative 'attack' advertisements in 1992 on Labour as the party of
high taxes.

spring 1992 was enough to convince Chris Patten that the party should
soldier on. In fact signs of economic recovery were not convincing, the
Budget was not warmly received and opinion polls showed that Labour
and Conservative were on level pegging. As in 1979, a government had
mistimed the electoral and economic cycles. John Major called an
election because there was no point in hanging on and being seen to do
so.

During the election campaign the tax theme was hammered relentlessly. The launch of Labour's manifesto was greeted by a poster, 'Oh
no, it's a tax demand'. Another poster, 'Labour's double whammy'
(figure 3.3), referred to more taxes and higher prices. 'Five years' hard

Labour' added higher mortgages to higher taxes and higher prices. These themes were restated in election broadcasts, press conferences and leaders' speeches. Indeed, this was so much the case that at the party's daily press conference journalists groaned when it was announced that yet again the topic would be Labour's spending and/or tax plans. Even sympathetic journalists complained to campaign managers about the negativism of the Conservative campaign. During the election Maurice Saatchi in his meetings with John Major and Chris Patten and the agency strongly reinforced the tax message: 'If we made a difference in 1992, it was in pushing tax', said one Saatchi executive.

In the general election there was continuing tension over strategy between some members of John Major's staff in Downing Street and some of the Central Office staff. After the first week of the campaign John Major decided to revamp the schedule of press conferences and abandon the 'Meet John Major' question and answer sessions, on the grounds that they were too bland, bored the journalists and made poor television. His decision to take a soap box on his campaign tour and address voters directly reflected his own unhappiness at how he was being 'packaged' by Central Office. Some of the Number 10 staff took a dim view of Central Office. One senior staff member explained its campaign ineffectiveness: 'Its trouble is that it is like a Rolls-Royce that comes out of the garage once every four years' (interview). As the campaign proceeded the political differences between some associates of the ousted leader, Mrs Thatcher, and the new regime were exposed. There was steady criticism from some of her supporters about the need for a more vigorous campaign, as well as the promotion of more Thatcherite policies. There were also disagreements between Saatchi, which argued for a substantial press-ads campaign, and Chris Patten, who was sceptical about its value. In the end the agency appealed directly to the Prime Minister, private funds were raised and a modest press-ads campaign was launched.

Campaign strategies have to make assumptions about key groups of voters – about their hopes and their fears. Some of this thinking is guided by research, some is derived from party ideology and some is based on hunch. A number of Labour leaders had been impressed by opinion poll findings that the public was concerned about the standard of public services and that most voters were willing to pay more taxes so that spending on health, education and the social services could be increased. It would not be fair to claim that they simply followed the polls in this, for the research fitted in with their political values and they would probably have argued the case without the polls. The Conservative calculation was that the Thatcher years had convinced enough people that benefits had to be paid for and that most were not willing to pay more taxes. Most of the survey evidence on narrow questions about taxes and spending, and commentators' interpretations of it (see p. 184), suggested that Labour's reading of the electoral mood was correct. Before and during the election the Tory tax campaign appeared to be a damp squib. The election result and post-election surveys suggested the opposite (see below, pp. 231–2).

Conclusion

The Conservative party has been a pacemaker in using advertising and modern publicity techniques in British politics. Labour effectively copied the techniques from 1986 onwards. The electoral record suggests that the Conservatives have been more successful than Labour in campaign communications. The party's structure has provided speedier decisions and allowed the communications team to work to a clearer brief. But much depends on whether the client – the party Chairman or the Director of Communications – has the ear of the party leader. Conservative leaders, certainly when in Downing Street, and their staffs have often regarded Central Office with a mixture of indifference and irritation, notably in 1986 and 1987, and some distancing between the two was apparent again in 1992. Conservative general election communications since 1978 have been remorselessly attacking. It was predictable that in 1979 the Conservative opposition would attack the Labour government's record, the failure of the incomes policy and the winter of industrial disruption. A government's record is often the battleground, hence the judgement, 'governments lose elections, oppositions do not win them'. It was less predictable, however, that in government, Conservative campaign communications would also focus so negatively and so successfully on the Labour alternative.

It is important to keep the electoral impact of communications in perspective. The product matters more than the presentation. Prosperity could be presented effectively by the Macmillan government in 1959, for the evidence was easily seen. Strong leadership could be credibly presented in 1983, as could economic prosperity in 1987. In 1992 economic success could not be a credible theme but the weaknesses of Labour gave ample scope for negative campaigning.

The British party system still offers voters a choice between rival teams of politicians bidding to form a government. The Conservative party and its communicators in general elections since 1974 have been benefited from the voters' perceptions of the competence and trustworthiness of the rival parties. The underlying political factors have mattered more than all the skilful communications. According to Woodward, 'No matter how skilled the presentation and publicity, we would not have won in 1992 without the political fundamentals changing from 1990. The most important of these was the replacement of Mrs Thatcher by John Major as leader' (interview).

Appendix: Conservative communications strategy for next general election

To convince all C2 women and men under 35, and women of all classes under 35, that the personal prosperity they have lost under Labour will be restored to them by a Conservative Government.

Advertising will both reinforce the current level of dissatisfaction felt by many of the electorate and show how a Conservative administration will put matters right. It will highlight the incompetence of the present Labour administration and contrast this with the competence of the Conservatives.

This will be done by specifically drawing attention to:

1   The substantial increase in taxation imposed on individuals by the present Labour Government in *both* direct and indirect taxation. And to highlight that the Conservatives are pledged to reducing the rate of direct taxation.
2   The very big increase in the cost of living which has occurred since Labour came to power, using wherever possible specific examples, e.g. housing, fuel, food, etc.

Advertising will underline the importance of people thinking twice before believing what Labour politicians may promise in order to get back into power next time.

We recognize that the most important consideration in the success of this advertising will not be simply to communicate how Labour have failed, and to present what the Conservatives will do to rectify matters; but the degree to which the advertising makes people *believe that a Conservative Government will make a difference to them as individuals.*

Tone:

The tone of the advertising will be simple and human. It will show a concern with the readers' individual problems. It will show a determination to do things that will benefit individual voters personally.

April 1969

4

POLITICAL COMMUNICATIONS: LABOUR

Political communicators have experienced particular difficulties working for Labour. Some problems have arisen from the party's ethos, particularly the notion that it has been the party of the working class and trade unions and has an ideology. For many Labour politicians this self-image has defined the party's message and its electoral market; they claimed to know what ordinary people wanted without the help of market research. Another difficulty derived from the party's structure and forms of decision-making; theoretically, these were designed to facilitate the accountability of the parliamentary leaders to the membership, but in practice were hardly geared for making quick decisions or granting the leaders much discretion. By contrast, advertising people in the private sector emphasize speed, individual initiative and results. They tend to concentrate single-mindedly on results, in this case winning the election, whereas employees of the party headquarters have other organizational concerns.

Much of Labour's communications with the electorate has traditionally been divided between the Research and the Press and Publicity Departments, both responsible to the National Executive Committee (NEC) not the party leader. The former department has been primarily interested in developing party policy, the latter in communicating with the public via posters and press releases. Neither department until recently contained anyone with professional experience in advertising or public relations but relied on periodic help from MPs with a journalistic background and sympathizers in the media. Only in 1962 was somebody with professional skills recruited in the Publicity Department. Not surprisingly, professional communicators from the private sector have often been struck by how introverted, non-voter oriented and complex Labour's political communications are. This chapter traces the uneven way in which the party has accepted modern communications.

Politics without Marketing

Labour's communications advisers have usually derived their authority and sense of security from the support of the party leader. Hugh Gaitskell, the leader between 1955 and 1963, faced resistance in the NEC over commissioning opinion polling (not least from his deputy leader, Aneurin Bevan, and from the party's General Secretary) and over advertising, usually from the political left. Denigration of opinion pollsters and public relations experts has found a ready audience from sections of the party. After the 1979 election an advertising consultant to the party complained of its 'hypocrisy' about advertising, which 'did not help the morale of the people working for the Labour party' (Delaney 1982: 27). A similar story could be written about the 1983 and 1992 elections. In trying to draw on the skills of the professional volunteers party leaders have often been tempted to by-pass the party machine. With the possible exception of February 1974 Harold Wilson's five election campaigns as party leader were largely planned by himself and his 'kitchen cabinet' (in the two 1974 elections this consisted of Marcia Williams, Joe Haines, Bernard Donoughue and communication advisers like Denis Lyons and Peter Lovell-Davis). He and his entourage had little time for the party headquarters (see Donoughue 1987: 46). This was true of all his successors except for Michael Foot in 1983.

An offer by communications specialists to help Labour's campaign make use of modern methods in 1959 was rebuffed by the NEC, which preferred to rely on traditional organizational efforts and policy publications. As Rose observes, campaigning strategy was regarded as the prerogative of fulltime politicians and MP-journalists (1967: 63). Labour was the party of the working class, which constituted by far the majority of the electorate: it only had to 'get out the vote', which it would do by good organization and by enthusing the party workers with policy leaflets and documents. In 1959 the party published one and a half million copies of a glossy policy statement, *The Future Labour Offers You*, addressed primarily to party members but probably read by very few. The Nuffield study of the general election that year questioned the party's approach:

> The Labour party's unconcern with building a more favourable party image during the long period between election campaigns is striking [because studies showed that] Labour voters responded much more readily to the appeal of the party's image than to individual items in the party's policy or to organizational efforts. (Butler and Rose 1960: 25)

Richard Crossman expressed the traditional thinking when, on reading a draft version of the Nuffield study, he rejected the above passage:

> A Left party, moreover, is inevitably more concerned with policy than with image, just as a Right-wing party is inevitably more concerned with personality and image than with policy. A Left party is inevitably democratic in a way that a Right party is not. (Butler file, 11 January 1960)

Communicating with Voters: 1964

After Labour's third successive election defeat in 1959, however, enough politicians were convinced of the case for employing the skills of advertisers, copywriters, account executives and pollsters. Hugh Gaitskell in particular had been dismayed by the party's publicity in the 1959 campaign: 'You only realize what's wrong when you are in the campaign. You can do all the preparations but you only find out if they work when the thing is happening', recalled John Harris (now Lord Harris of Greenwich), who was Gaitskell's personal assistant at the time (interview). In January 1962 Harris was appointed the party's first Director of Publicity, following the abrupt retirement of the previous press officer, and he was a supporter of new methods.

At a private meeting in the House of Commons in early 1962 Labour supporters in the media and public relations discussed ways in which they might help the party. As a result of the meeting a volunteer team from advertising and research agencies was formed. The main figures were David Kingsley, Mark Abrams, Ros Allen, Brian Murphy, Peter

Davis (later Lord Lovell-Davis) and Denis Lyons (later Lord Lyons). Kingsley, Murphy and Allen were in advertising, Davis in the press and Lyons in public relations.* The survey research and polling expertise of Abrams was an integral part of the communications planning (see pp. 128–9). His surveys debunked claims that Labour supporters were a majority of the electorate and influenced the party to target its communications at floating voters and voters in marginal seats.

Davis was responsible to John Harris and recently recalled that his main problem at the time was to avoid offending the Labour party machine at Transport House: 'We had constantly to make clear that we would not challenge the party's policies or command structure or in any way undermine the party's officers' (interview). The group had no official standing, members were unpaid and Harris in turn reported to the party's campaign committee, drawn from politicians, NEC and party officers. Gaitskell and his successor, Harold Wilson, were prepared to contract the party's communications to outsiders. Some Labour officials and politicians, just like their Conservative counterparts, disliked the use of public relations and outsiders (see p. 50). Communicators were surprised at the reaction to the following statement they had drafted about the objective of party propaganda:

> To persuade our targets that they should vote for the election of a Labour Government at the coming general election. (Rose 1967: 75)

This gave rise to a heated discussion on the morality of such an aim and the dangers of pandering to voters! The similarities with the development of the party's Shadow Communications Agency 25 years later are remarkable (see below, p. 93).

Prior to the election a small planning group commissioned and co-ordinated the work of other specialist groups on posters, adverts and broadcasts, and copy was submitted to senior politicians for approval. Labour's first ever national press advertising campaign in 1962 sought to project the party as efficient, energetic, modern and classless. It also exploited the popularity of Harold Wilson, who had become party leader in 1963 after the death of Gaitskell; his youthfulness and

---

* But there were tensions, particularly concerning the role of David Kingsley. The late Percy Clark, then Labour's Press and Publicity Director, warned Harold Wilson in 1970 that he would resign if Kingsley continued. Apparently Clark found him too forceful in his views. Kingsley was retained but assumed a low profile.

Figure 4.1 Labour's slogan in the 1964 general election. The message conveys Labour's freshness and energy in contrast to a Conservative party exhausted after 13 years in office.

meritocratic background made a sharp contrast to the new Conservative Prime Minister Sir Alec Douglas-Home. Before the campaign Wilson made a series of speeches, which portrayed the Conservatives as an old-fashioned, amateurish and incompetent party. More positively, he presented himself as a competent national leader, thoroughly versed in economics and the machinery of government. He appeared to personify the party slogan 'Let's GO with Labour and we'll get things done' (figure 4.1). Labour propaganda concentrated on the party's strong issues of housing, pensions, education and the state of the economy. Spending on advertising and public relations for the 1964 election increased three-fold compared with 1959. If 1959 had been a communications breakthrough for the Conservatives, 1964 was a turning point for Labour.

In retrospect, Labour's successful 1964 election campaign has acquired an undeserved reputation for professionalism and dynamism. To overturn a Conservative majority of over a hundred seats was a remarkable achievement. But much of the most effective communications had

been done long before the election began. The pre-election publicity
and the series of speeches by Wilson showed a greater sense of purpose
than was evident in the general election. A problem was that there was:

> no Labour campaign, no central directive or plan. One man decided
> tactics from day to day, essentially on his own, playing by ear and not
> according to some premeditated source. . . . He had no inner circle of
> advisers, no elaboration of strategic-position papers and day-to-day
> polling. He went out of his way to avoid being seen taking professional
> advice. (Butler and King 1965: 150)

At least two committees were involved in the making of television
broadcasts and it was not clear which one had final authority. The
broadcasts were not co-ordinated with the larger strategy and,
according to Martin Harrison, 'Interminable committee meetings
parodied Parkinson; the senior politician on a programme tended to
view it as "his" broadcast' (1965: 175).

In view of the narrowness of Labour's victory in the 1964 election (a
majority of four seats), a fresh election was sure to follow soon and the
publicity team was kept on standby. It developed the slogan 'You *know*
Labour Government works' for the 1966 election. The group's main
problem was liaison with the politicians; over some 18 months it
worked to four different MPs deputed to act as a link with the
government. According to Butler and King, 'The members of the group
felt that they did not know who they were dealing with, and that it was
impossible to get anyone to take decisions' (1966: 32).

The 1966 Labour government was dogged from the outset by
economic problems. The government and the party, represented in
conference, were at loggerheads over many policies. Although the
communications team remained largely intact, planning for an election
took place only fitfully from 1968 onwards. During 1969 the 'three wise
men', as Kingsley, Lovell-Davis and Lyons were now dubbed, met
every second Tuesday in Number 10 with Harold Wilson and Marcia
Williams and Gerald Kaufman, from Wilson's political office. Relations
between Wilson and the party machine in Transport House were poor
– 'Harold used us as a sort of liaison committee asking us to deliver
messages to Transport House' (Kingsley, interview). The publicists
were strong advocates of private polling and the NEC agreed to fund a
study of party activists (see p. 130), 'We wanted the research to educate
the party, to change its culture, but the findings aroused little interest',

recalled Kingsley (interview). In April 1970 the team developed the controversial 'Yesterday's men' theme, to run as a poster and an advertisement in the press. This portrayed glum-looking Conservative leaders in lurid colours, and ridiculed the attempts of former ministers to make a comeback (figure 4.2). Although there was some party criticism that the poster was negative and vulgar, the volunteers defended it as part of a phased communications campaign which would be sustained over the summer and culminate positively in the presentation of 'Labour's winning team'. They argued that the Conservative advertising was overwhelmingly negative copy and that Labour had to expose the incompetence of the opposition before making a positive case (Butler and Pinto-Duschinsky 1971: 133).

The team assumed that an election would be held in October 1970 and, like most of those involved in election planning, were taken aback when Harold Wilson summoned them to Downing Street in May and informed them that he had just visited the Queen to request a summer election. The imminence of the election meant that 'Yesterday's Men' was never properly launched. Wilson also vetoed the 'Labour's winning team' idea and asked for something different. Davis recalled, 'The trouble is that politicians think that you can pluck slogans out of the air' (interview). Kingsley strongly objected to the way in which the publicity plans had been thrown overboard by Wilson and after the election decided not to become involved again. In some desperation the two men came up with 'Now Britain's strong let's make it Great to live in', and this was used in all leaflets and posters.

Until the declaration of the results on polling day in 1970 Harold Wilson enjoyed a reputation as a formidable campaigner. His approach to campaigning – stronger on tactics than on strategy – was not dissimilar to his approach to government. He kept his ideas to himself and a few trusted advisers and was confident that his nimble mind would deal with all eventualities. He dispensed with elaborate pre-press conference preparations, and daily strategy sessions, which are usual today, were introduced only informally in 1970. Encouraged by the opinion polls which showed that Labour had a big lead and that he was more popular than Ted Heath, Wilson thought that victory was assured. But the approach was discredited when Labour lost the election. Wilson was no longer regarded by colleagues as an electoral asset to the party.

In the 1974 election the party demonstrated that it had learnt some lessons from the Conservative campaign in 1970. Wilson's authority in

Figure 4.2   Classic Labour and Conservative 'knocking' posters.

the party had fallen sharply and there was more emphasis on Labour's 'team'. The same stage backdrop was employed for all Wilson's public speeches and greater care was taken over placing television film crews in the audience. However, very little advertising was done for the two 1974 elections and the slogan for the February 1974 election, 'Back to work with Labour', was suggested by Tony Benn. Lovell-Davis and Lyons continued to advise Harold Wilson on communications and election broadcasts. He was comfortable with them and they were members of a small group that he convened every morning to discuss tactics, prior to meeting the party's campaign committee. After Wilson resigned in 1976 his successor as Prime Minister, Jim Callaghan, looked elsewhere for help.

Attempting the Impossible

In 1977 a minority Labour government had to face the possibility of being forced into an election at short notice. In May Edward Booth-Clibborn, who ran an art design agency and was a Labour supporter, was asked to organize the publicity. He recruited other Labour sympathizers from the communications industry, notably Tim Delaney and Trevor Eke in advertising. Their understanding was that they would control advertising and broadcasts and not be encumbered with Labour party committees. But the volunteers chafed at the constraints they worked under. When the Conservative party appointed Saatchi & Saatchi as its advertising agency, Booth-Clibborn wrote to the Prime Minister on 4 April 1978:

> Significantly, in appointing Saatchi & Saatchi, the Conservative Party have moved away from the more traditional staid advertising agencies they have used in the past, and chosen an agency which has a reputation for being aggressive, publicity conscious, energetic and creative. Their work may even be considered controversial.

The implication of the memo was that Labour should take advertising more seriously and appoint an agency. If so, it failed; using volunteer outsiders was just tolerable for the party but employing an advertising agency was not.

In late 1977 Mr Callaghan began to hold a series of 'White Drawing Room' meetings of senior colleagues, political advisers, party officers and the communicators, to plan for the election. These were fairly secret and consisted of people with whom Mr Callaghan felt comfortable. Labour's official campaign committee represented different sections of the party and was too large (up to 40 on some occasions) to be an effective decision-making body. Mr Callaghan participated fully in the discussions but resisted many of the communicators' suggestions, particularly advice that he attack Mrs Thatcher and exploit his greater experience and popularity. He was determined to present himself as a senior figure on the international stage, in the company of Helmut Schmidt and President Carter. When he was told by advisers that the voters were more interested in events nearer home he turned on his heels.

The communications team soon encountered a major difficulty, one that every group working for the party has had to face. Was its client the party leader Mr Callaghan, or the NEC? If the two had been in broad agreement on policies and electoral strategy this would not have presented a problem. But they were publicly at odds on many issues. The Labour government lacked a majority in the Commons, was deeply unpopular and the constant parading of internal divisions only added to its problems. The NEC contained many of the government's most bitter left-wing critics, who complained that the government was betraying socialism with its pay policy and public spending cuts. Most members of the NEC and the research department were determined to have at least an equal say to Mr Callaghan in deciding the contents of the manifesto and the election strategy and to fight the next general election on a left-wing programme. Mr Callaghan had come to dread his meetings with the NEC. At campaign committee meetings Tony Benn and Eric Heffer, on the left of the party, attacked opinion polling and most suggestions for advertising. Indeed, in 1978 the NEC refused Mr Callaghan's request for funds for polling, although friendly trade unions eventually provided some help. Booth-Clibborn recalls the attacks of the left: 'They saw advertising and polling as symbols of selling out socialism: they did not need polling because Labour was the party of the workers' (interview).

Other volunteers found themselves drawn into lengthy meetings with party officials who often appeared to be suspicious of public relations. One complained of a 'deprofessionalization of the organization, a total disinterest in what the electorate wanted'. According to Tim Delaney, 'Too many wanted Labour to be whiter than white. They weren't really interested in modern communications. It's a legacy of sanctimonious socialism' (interview). And,

You had officers who were terrified you would reduce their power. They were more interested in following procedures than winning the election. Coming from the outside I was struck by their obsessive interest in getting power and keeping it and the love of being able to say 'yes' or 'no' to us. (Interview)

Mr Callaghan passed up the option of holding an election in autumn 1978, because he was not sure he would win it (see p. 135). The decision came, however, as a great surprise to most of the Cabinet and his campaign team. A forced election was now possible and it came when the government lost a vote of confidence in the Commons in March 1979. The Callaghan government was the first in 55 years to have no control over the decision to dissolve. The campaign strategy for a hypothetical October 1978 election relied heavily on the Labour government's partnership with the unions and its success in reducing inflation. The campaign slogan would be 'Keep Britain Labour and it will keep on getting better'.

Over the winter months, however, union activists challenged the government's pay policy and strikes plunged parts of the country into chaos. The winter of industrial troubles fatally undermined public support for the government. Tables 4.1 and 4.2 show how the support for Labour in crucial areas of voter concern had collapsed compared to the previous August: then Mr Callaghan had been more highly regarded as a leader than Mrs Thatcher and Labour was thought to have the best policies and best leaders. By March the position had been reversed on all three (although there was some recovery during the election). Moreover, the original strategy of appealing for a mandate to consolidate an anti-inflation policy in co-operation with the trade unions was in tatters. 'By spring all our positive messages, planned for the previous October, had been destroyed', said Roger Carroll, who had taken leave as political editor of the *Sun* to be a Callaghan

Table 4.1 Approval of government's handling of main issues (1979) (% approving minus % disapproving)

Common Market	−19	Cost of living	−51
Immigration	−28	Economy	−48
Law and Order	−21	Strikes and labour relations	−62
Education	−9	National Health	−23
Employment	−48	Old age pensions	9

Source: Gallup, March 1979

Table 4.2 Changes in which party has best policies (1979)

	August 1978	February 1979	Change Aug.–Apr.
Prices/Inflation			
Con.	31	39	+8
Lab.	40	27	−13
Industrial relations/strikes			
Con.	32	39	+7
Lab.	41	26	−15
Unemployment			
Con.	36	39	+3
Lab.	29	24	−5

Source: MORI, in Butler and Kavanagh 1980: 130–1

speechwriter. The speechwriters drafted a series of hard-hitting speeches exploiting fear – 'fear of the unknown Mrs Thatcher, fear of a return to a three-day week and fear of a doubling of VAT and unemployment' (Carroll, interview). But Mr Callaghan was uneasy and refused to deliver the speeches. 'I think his wife said to him, "Jim, you've built up a reputation as a statesman over 30 years, don't let these young men destroy it in a few weeks"' (Carroll interview).

The choice facing Labour's campaign team was whether to try to correct the party's main electoral weaknesses – on handling the economy – or to concentrate on its strengths on the social agenda and employment. They decided on the latter. In looking for issues to regain the support of traditional Labour voters who had strayed in the previous few months, the publicity advisers suggested concentrating on issues which appealed to the economic interests of working-class voters and on which Labour still had some credibility. The team identified these as:

Welfare – pensions, family allowances, health services.
Jobs – creating and saving jobs, decent unemployment benefits.
Interests of public sector – public expenditure, staffing levels, comparative wage levels.
Economic planning and control – incomes policy, price and rent controls.

It recommended that Labour speeches and publicity should emphasize pensions, family allowances and the comparability of wages in the public and private sectors. These three issues would be combined into a programme of *Fairness to all*. Surveys showed that the most common unprompted reason offered for voting Labour was that 'Labour looks after the workers' or 'the less well off'. And Mr Callaghan, to exploit his greater electoral appeal over Mrs Thatcher, accepted an invitation to take part in a television debate between the party leaders. The plan was aborted when Mrs Thatcher refused the invitation (see below, p. 213).

A classic illustration of the political divisions and organizational conflict within the party was seen in the fate of the candle poster, shown on page 98. This poster was originally approved by the White Drawing Room group and was then shown to the NEC and the party's campaign committee for their formal approval. The majority of the 30-member committee, angry at what they regarded as a *fait accompli*, vetoed the poster. Another poster appeared in January 1979, using the slogan 'Keep Britain Labour and it will keep on getting better'. This had originally been prepared for an October 1978 election but was now hopelessly timed, as it coincided with a lorry drivers' strike. Decisions about the party's election broadcasts gave rise to further conflicts between Booth-Clibborn's group and the party's long-established broadcasting committee, which included two Labour MPs, Austin Mitchell and Philip Whitehead, both of whom had extensive broadcasting experience. Each side claimed that it should have control. On one occasion Mr Callaghan was woken by a phone call from Booth-Clibborn at 2 a.m., and asked to decide between the rival teams; he authorized the volunteers to do the broadcast, but faced complaints that he was undermining the party's machine (Butler and Kavanagh 1980: 136).

The campaign was not a rewarding experience for the government nor for its volunteers. By the final days Mr Callaghan had grown weary of the bickering, sensed electoral defeat and had lost confidence in Booth-Clibborn. He ruled that the party's publicists rather than the volunteers would do the final election broadcast. The Conservatives spent much more money than Labour, made more innovative election broadcasts and party campaign managers enjoyed a closer relationship with the advertising agency. On the admission of the campaign's creative director Labour was outgunned by Saatchi's (Delaney 1982). Labour's advertising people were regarded with suspicion by party officials and different sections of Transport House gave competing advice about press advertisements and broadcasts. Senior Labour politicians and advisers acknowledged the impact of Saatchi and concluded that at the next election the party should break with tradition and employ an advertising agency. But all the problems with communications paled in comparison with the unfavourable under-lying political realities.

The 1979 Parliament was a harrowing one for Labour. The party suffered a split, the rise of the Social Democratic party, a bitter internal battle over reform of its constitution, Tony Benn's protracted challenge to Denis Healey for the deputy leadership and the replacement of Jim Callaghan as leader by Michael Foot. The insurgent left wing produced something of a cultural revolution in the party, removing from Labour MPs the exclusive right to elect the party leader and making them submit themselves to reselection by constituency parties within the lifetime of a Parliament. The NEC and conference gained greatly in authority at the cost of the Parliamentary party. The party, it seemed, was so preoccupied with its internal squabbles that it forgot about the electorate. It entered the election in 1983 having made hardly any preparations. No opinion polling had been done since the 1979 election and arrangements for private polling and advertising were finalized only on the eve of the campaign. Michael Foot was unsympathetic to modern media techniques and showed little interest in the campaign preparations. Decisions were often left to an unwieldy 30-strong campaign committee.

In February 1983 a small advertising agency, Wright and Partners, was contracted to handle Labour's publicity for the local elections in May. Because the general election followed a month later, the party decided to retain the agency, giving it only days to prepare broadcasts and adverts. Wright argued that the party must think positively and contrast the government cuts in welfare and the high level of unemployment with what could be achieved in the future. Hence the slogan: 'Think positive, act positive'.

Labour's 1983 campaign is now widely regarded as a shambles, as politicians and officials did their own thing. Throughout the campaign the agency had difficulties in getting the attention or co-operation of senior politicians and officials. Party managers failed to provide the agency with an adequate brief; there was no meeting during the campaign between the agency and the party's pollster; party leaders were often filmed in depressing settings; little central control was exercised over the television appearances of leaders and many were often scheduled in locations distant from television studios; and there was no evidence of coordination in what they were saying. After the election politicians and advertisers agreed that there had not been a proper client–agent relationship, largely because the party did not provide a clear brief and the agency was too small to cope with the heavy demands of an election campaign. The contrast with the Conservative campaign was marked.

Although party leaders were critical of the agency's efforts the best communicators in the world could not have delivered an election victory in 1983. Labour entered the election with too many 'negatives' – about its leadership and policies on defence, nationalization, industrial relations and taxation. The party's left-wing manifesto was an albatross, some of its proposals clearly embarrassed shadow cabinet ministers and few voters had confidence in Labour. An already weak position was further eroded by open policy divisions between party leaders during the election and a poorly conducted campaign. Labour just managed to beat the new Alliance for second place in popular votes, but the election result was the party's worst for over fifty years. Tim Delaney had warned after the 1979 defeat that, 'Without a more professional approach . . . to problems of political communication, one party will be talking through Saatchi & Saatchi to the people, while the other will basically be talking to itself' (Delaney 1982: 31). The warning was prophetic. But the problems went deeper than poor campaigning. It was a confirmation of a long-standing trend. The party's share of the vote had declined at almost every general election since 1951. Its 27.6 per cent share of the total vote was a fall of 11.4 per cent from its last victory in October 1974: its vote share was two points ahead of the Alliance and 15 behind the Conservatives. The survey evidence of the lack of popular confidence in Labour or support for many of its key policies was devastating (see above, pp. 87–8).

Marketing Kinnock

Neil Kinnock, Labour's new leader, was determined to profit from the 'never again' feeling and despair after the crushing election defeat and poor campaign in 1983. The 1987 election was to be a breakthrough in Labour's adoption of modern communication methods. The key person in this transition was Peter Mandelson who was appointed as the party's Director of Campaigns and Communications in October 1985. He was the first holder of the post to have had an established career in television, having been a current affairs producer with London Weekend Television, in addition to a strong political and family history in the party. It is therefore no surprise that he was more presentation-

minded and more aware of the world outside party headquarters and
Westminster than his predecessors; he believed that the party should
spend more time communicating with the electorate rather than with
its own (declining) party membership. He was not impressed with his
legacy:

> There was a deprofessionalization – that's the only word I can think of –
> in the party organization. Professional communications encountered a
> series of political, organizational and managerial obstructions in
> headquarters. It started under Harold Wilson and Jim Callaghan, who
> let the headquarters go. You had to bring in outsiders to help sort it out.
> (Interview)

He was also helped by the skills of Patricia Hewitt, Neil Kinnock's
press officer. She appreciated that the development of ENG (electronic
news-gathering) meant that there would be continuous television
coverage of elections, and that news editors would be seeking virtually
instant responses to every key speech and statement. The party must
meet this development by staging events, creating photo-opportunities
and persuading speakers to include succinct passages that television
producers would use. Both Mandelson and Hewitt were backed by
Kinnock, who was determined to bring in people with communications
skills from outside the party.

As well as looking outside the party machine for a more professional
approach to communications, Kinnock was determined to gain greater
control over campaign strategy. Formally, this was the responsibility of
the NEC, not only a diverse body but one which the leader could not
rely on to support his initiatives. The first step was to create in 1983 a
Campaign Strategy Committee which would 'advise' the NEC on
campaign strategy and co-ordinate campaigning. It contained representatives from the NEC, Parliamentary Labour Party (PLP) and
Shadow Cabinet and decided on broadcasts, opinion polling and
campaigns. The more centralized form of decision-making would
certainly help those in the party who wished to change radically Labour's
approach to election campaigning. It was also part of Kinnock's
attempt to modernize the party, as well as to by-pass the NEC, until he
had an assured majority for his initiatives.

Soon after his appointment Peter Mandelson invited Philip Gould,
an advertising consultant, to review the party's communications and
make recommendations for the future. His 64-page report was

delivered in December 1985. It complained that Labour's communications lacked coordination, had little impact on voters and failed to employ clear direct language. It also criticized the proliferation of communications groups, whose lines of responsibility were often unclear. Its key publicity recommendations included:

Greater concentration on securing publicity through the mass media rather than relying on campaigning by local constituency parties.

A Shadow Communications Agency (SCA) would be set up and a fulltime co-ordinator would recruit volunteer members from the communications industry. 'Its role will be to draft strategy, conduct and interpret research, produce advertising and campaign themes, and provide other communications support as necessary.'

The Director of Campaigns and Communications would be in complete charge of communications.

The party's messages should be simplified, repeated and orchestrated around its selected themes.

Opinion polling and separate qualitative research should be more integrated into the planning of the campaign.

Concentration on winning votes: 'All campaigns should have the influencing of the electorate as their first priority'.

Labour's decision to rely on volunteers from the communications industry rather than employ an agency was dictated in part by finance and in part by the reluctance of any established advertising agency to work for the party. It was rumoured that an agency that took the party's account risked losing some of its private sector work. More positively, unless an advertising agency was very large it would be able to address only a part of Labour's communications requirements; drawing upon volunteers would enable the party to recruit a wider range of talents. The BMP (Boase, Massimi, Pollitt) advertising agency, which had handled the 'Save the GLC' campaign and worked for the TUC in the past, seemed ideal. BMP's Managing Director, Chris Powell, had advised the party on communications since 1971 and supported the idea, but other board members were opposed. In the event many of the Agency volunteers were drawn from BMP, floor space was rented from the agency and Powell became its Chairman. If BMP had agreed to be recognized formally as the party's advertising agency then the Agency would not have been created. Its involvement was so strong, however, that it was *de facto* the party's agency. The reliance on volunteers was a reversion to the Wilson approach for the 1964, 1966 and 1970 elections, and was inspired by the Reagan use of media volunteers in the Tuesday Team in the 1984 Presidential election.

The establishment of a new Shadow Communications Agency was ratified by the NEC in March 1986, Philip Gould was appointed as co-ordinator of its work and he worked directly to Mandelson. The latter's task was to gain support for the Agency's suggestions from the leader, frontbenchers and the party machine. A re-organization of the Campaign Strategy Committee resulted in Mr Kinnock's office and Mandelson gaining more control over communications and giving more initiative to the Agency. The volunteers dealt with all aspects of communications – design, speechwriting, research, copywriting and art direction, advertising and broadcasts. For the first time in the party's history all campaigning communications – publicity, press briefing, broadcasting and polling – would be co-ordinated by one body. These were the first steps in Kinnock's modernization of the party – centralizing more control in his office, by-passing opponents on the NEC and upgrading the influence of professional communicators.

The Agency launched a number of campaigns in 1986, including *Freedom and Fairness*, and *Investing in People*. Party conferences were staged more professionally and speeches and addresses by party leaders took place against carefully designed backdrops. Locations were sought for television film and press photograph backgrounds which would associate the party with youth, vigour, progress and build up a more positive image. Patricia Hewitt did not want the leader filmed amid derelict housing sites, closed factories or run-down hospitals but with 'people – bright, attractive people presenting an image of the broader base Labour has to capture, *not* people who present an image of old-fashioned Labour die-hards' (Butler and Kavanagh 1988: 61–2). The party adopted a red rose as its symbol and Labour leaders wore sober suits and white shirts. The party won endorsements from pop and sports stars, leaders appeared on TV chat shows and Mr Kinnock took part in a pop video. The Agency made several presentations of its work to candidates, party workers and joint NEC/Shadow Cabinet meetings. It suggested words, phrases and themes which were to be repeated and orchestrated in attacking the Conservatives and defending Labour. The qualitative research suggested that Labour's target voters were unhappy about the future of the country, public services and the 'real' economy, although many reported that they were better off financially. Labour leaders were urged to exploit this dissatisfaction, emphasizing the government's responsibility for the decline of industry, rising unemployment and deterioration of social services, and to present Labour as the party of hope, one that would defend the social services. The impact of the communicators must have promoted some awareness among party campaigners of the principles of political marketing – the need to take account of the views of the electorate, have a clear, distinctive message and create an efficient party organization which could deliver the message. But the party's major weaknesses, which the team was never able to overcome, were the widespread doubts about its economic competence, its defence policy and Neil Kinnock, as well as fears that a Labour government would increase taxes on ordinary people.

Once again Labour's build-up to a general election was unfortunate. At the time of the party conference in October 1986 it led in the opinion polls, but thereafter support steadily fell away. The Conservatives had a successful conference, defence became a major issue, Neil Kinnock paid a trip to President Reagan in Washington which attracted little favourable publicity, and the poll ratings of the leader and the party slumped. Then, in February 1987, a left-wing candidate was adopted to fight the safe Labour seat of Greenwich at a by-election. The candidate was a gift to the Tory tabloid press which attacked Labour's 'loony left' and the seat was lost to the Alliance. Entering the election Labour was struggling to hold off the Alliance for second place. Indeed one Gallup poll actually placed the Alliance just ahead of Labour. The party's qualitative research showed a marked decline in the party's standing on many questions.

Yet Labour's election campaign gained much praise. Labour's appeal to voters was on the social, caring issues – not the economy, defence or law and order. Hard-hitting advertisements attacked the Tory record on jobs, health, education and pensions, above the slogan, 'The country's crying out for change – vote Labour' (figure 4.3). In the words of the Agency leaders, the advertising was designed to set the agenda and attacked the government on the social issues: 'Advertising is best at attacking the enemy rather than putting forward a consistent viewpoint. Our theme was "we care"; our advertising said the Conservatives did not' (Gould, Herd and Powell, 1989: 73). The broadcasts, particularly Hugh Hudson's film portrait of Kinnock, received appreciative reviews, the activities of the leaders were linked to the party's chosen theme of the day and television was used effectively (figure 4.4). The campaign, press conferences, advertising, media events and speeches concentrated on its 'social agenda', and the

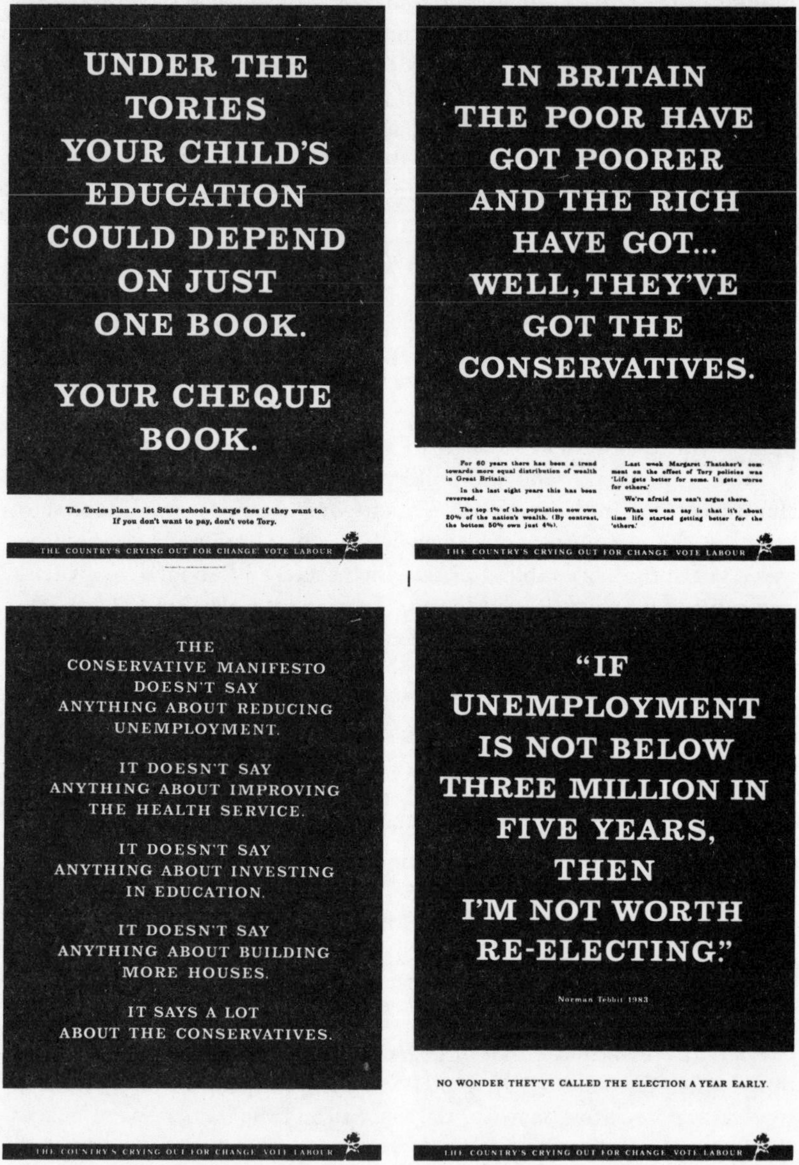

Figure 4.3 Labour's 'attack' advertisements in 1987.

Conservatives were rattled (Thatcher 1993: 580; Young 1990: ch. 15). A Gallup election-day poll for the BBC found that 47 per cent of voters thought that Labour had run the best television campaign, compared to 21 per cent who thought the Conservatives had. But Labour still lost the election by a wide margin. The party's 'brilliant' campaign had increased its share of the vote by less than 4 per cent; the 30.8 per cent of the vote was its second worst result in the past fifty years. Gallup found that 36 per cent of voters identified themselves as Labour; they thought of themselves as Labour supporters even if they did not necessarily vote for it in the election. The figure was close to the 35–38 per cent share of support the party gained in the local elections and the opinion polls throughout 1986. Labour therefore was still 'under-performing' by some 4 per cent. For its defenders the campaign had other compensations: 'It was important that we demonstrated that Labour showed that it could campaign competitively – that things were done as planned, that people did not contradict each other. We succeeded in that' (Mandelson interview).

Clearly, it was not the presentation but the nature of the product that was at fault – the manifesto, leadership, policies and memories of the last Labour government. The party's general election report accepted that good communication was not sufficient to overcome weaknesses on core policies: 'The policies themselves . . . of the party ultimately determine success or failure'. Again, Labour's defence policy was a liability; unilateralism was not only unpopular with voters, it was not accepted by many party spokesmen. In addition, many skilled working-class voters – the party's target audience – did not trust Labour to run the economy competently. Philip Gould reflected, 'Voting for a government comes from too deep a place in people to be shifted fundamentally in such a short period of time. We could change their minds, but not their votes' (interview). The campaign was therefore a failure in marketing terms, for 'A party committed to a process of modernisation must address its core values and associated traditions in such a way as to shift the perceptions of voters towards its position' (Sackman 1994: 475). The next stage in the modernization of the party would have to deal with the product and the conclusive election defeat was a spur to the process.

The party's post-election qualitative research showed that many target voters regarded Labour as a party of the past not the future, a party that placed protecting the poor ahead of encouraging the go-getters. It was not a party for those who aspired to better things – who

Keep Britain Labour.

Published by the Labour Party, Transport House,
Smith Square, London SW1P 3JA.

The poster was the work of John O'Driscoll, Caroline Bard, and Tim Delaney

Figure 4.4 Labour's failed attempt in the 1979 election to remind voters of the Conservatives' 'Winter of Discontent'. The poster was vetoed by party campaign leaders (see page 89).

were found across the social spectrum. Many workers wanted to 'get ahead' – own their own homes, buy shares, earn more money – and saw the Conservatives as the party which could help them. Labour had fought on its social agenda – but it was the economy which bothered these key voters. The findings had strong echoes of Mark Abrams's survey for *Must Labour Lose?* after the 1959 election defeat (see p. 129). Changing minds and votes was not a task that could be accomplished in four weeks; it needed five years. Labour would have to modernize drastically and quickly and cover policies as well as presentation. To become a more *responsive* party Labour would have to respond to voters' aspirations and fears, convince people that the party had changed and integrate communications specialists into the party organization (Sackman 1994: 467). The pre-1987 party reforms would have to be carried further.

The effort to modernize the party further began early in the 1987 Parliament with hard-hitting presentations from the Agency to the Shadow Cabinet and the NEC about the scale of the decline in the party's electoral fortunes and deterioration in its image between 1964 and 1987. It reported that the party was tied to a diminishing working class and many supporters voted for it out of tradition. Labour's image contained many negatives, notably its perceived ties to unpopular trade unions, weaknesses on defence and the perception that it was extreme, divided and backward looking. The party would have to restore the electorate's trust in its leadership and economic competence; it must *reposition* itself as a changed and modernized party and this would have to embrace changes in policy. There was little dissent when these presentations were made to the Shadow Cabinet or NEC; three election defeats meant that the reformers were pushing at an open door. The presentations helped to make the case for a far-reaching review of party policy, one which would culminate in Labour dropping unilateralism, virtually abandoning nationalization and economic planning, adopting constitutional reform and becoming a West European Social Democratic party. The research was an encouragement and a lever for the modernizers (Hughes and Wintour 1990).

It was not until the middle of 1989, two years into the Parliament, that Labour managed to regain a lead in the opinion polls. Although it did well in that year's European elections, in which the Conservatives lost 13 seats and Labour gained 13, the surveys showed that the party, in spite of a substantial opinion poll lead, still had much ground to make up. An Agency paper, presented to the NEC and Shadow

Cabinet in October 1989, predicted that Conservative attacks on Labour would include

'Kinnock's fitness to be PM'.
'Labour links to the Unions'.
'Labour will put taxes up'.

Another presentation in December 1989 anticipated that:

The coming election will be based around (in order of importance):
financial well being: spending power, taxation, interest rates;
self-determination: opportunity;
defence;
social support;
national pride.

Here was the essence of Labour's problem with the voters. In spite of the economic recession, voters still saw it as more likely to accentuate their personal financial difficulties, the Conservatives more likely to alleviate them. The party had to appeal to what the Agency called 'the aspirational classes' (essentially working-class achievers and middle-class voters who felt under pressure from the recession and high interest rates); so far, such voters believed that Labour identified with their fears, but not with their successes. In July 1990 the Agency made another presentation to the Shadow Cabinet, at a time when the party had a lead of 12 per cent in the opinion polls. This reported how the party's image had improved in many respects. But even when Labour enjoyed a commanding lead on voting in the polls many voters feared that it would do worse than the Conservatives in controlling prices, improving the standard of living, managing the economy and avoiding tax increases for the great majority. Voters also worried how Labour would pay for its spending proposals. In March 1991 when NOP and MORI reported a six-point lead on voting intention for Labour, the party still trailed 41 per cent to 18 per cent on the question 'Which party would you trust to run the economy?' and Mr Kinnock trailed John Major by 73 per cent to 32 per cent on who would make the best Prime Minister.

The Agency identified two crucial groups of target voters. One was termed the *money centre* and consisted largely of 'soft' Labour and floating voters, was predominantly working class and based in the north and midlands. There was also the *concerned centre*, largely middle class, based in the south and worried about education and the environment. But, crucially, both groups were worried about Labour's tax policies and economic competence. How could Labour pay for its proposals to improve the quality of life, without raising taxes significantly, or 'resolve the paradox of the electorate's desire for higher public expenditure with their aversion to higher taxation'? The report bluntly stated that as things stood the Conservatives were on course for an election victory: 'At the death, in the polling booth, people may be more likely to vote for the devil they know, and dislike, rather than the devil they don't fully trust'. These concerns were still being restated at the end of the Parliament. Labour campaigners could point to progress on many fronts, but not on the crucial areas of economic competence, taxation, leadership or trust.

There were also weaknesses in campaign organization. Peter Mandelson resigned as Director of Campaigns and Communications in June 1990. Mandelson had been an effective client for the Agency and was close to Kinnock. His successor, John Underwood, lacked his skill in feeding the media or 'squaring' the senior politicians, and resigned after twelve months in the post. He in turn was replaced by David Hill, until then Roy Hattersley's special adviser. The changes led to a vacuum in campaign planning and Agency members took more initiatives. In addition, many members of the campaign team felt that senior politicians and Neil Kinnock himself failed to show a continuing interest in the planning of the campaign. In the two years prior to the election Mr Kinnock did not attend any meeting of his entire campaign team and took no effective part in campaign planning. Some dissatisfied strategists decided to take action. Two years before the election a Campaign Advisory Team (CAT) began to meet each Thursday at 9 a.m. This consisted of key figures – from the Agency, Kinnock's office and party headquarters. Its members were John Cunningham the campaign co-ordinator, communications director and general secretary from party headquarters and Lord Hollick. The meeting was held in secret and notable absentees were other senior figures from party headquarters. The purpose of the meetings was to have a central planning group integrating all aspects of the campaign. But there was a serious breakdown of communications between key figures; John Underwood did not have good relations with the leader's staff, and some of the latter were hardly on speaking terms with each other. The existence of this 'secret' group was to be attacked after the election. As the Agency came to take more initiatives between late 1991 and the general election, so there was resentment from some NEC members and senior staff at headquarters. In a post-election critique one party official, Jim Parish, complained of the Agency's 'wholesale takeover of the campaign' and that it 'denied headquarters staff any real role in campaign decisions'.

In its near-term campaign in the first three months of 1992 Labour held three or four press conferences a week to launch a steady stream of policy and campaign documents. In January it launched a *Made in Britain* campaign, which highlighted the party's plans for industrial regeneration. But this had little effect in face of the Conservative onslaught on the tax implications of the party's plans (see p. 68). It then moved on to a social campaign in February. Like the Conservative campaign (see pp. 68–9) this promoted a policy area or linked policy areas each week, but Labour concentrated on the modernization of the health and education services. The election battleground was marked out in advance – health for Labour versus tax for the Conservatives. One verdict on the strategy was that although 'Labour's spokesman proved quite adroit at exploiting political openings . . . in the circumstances of a generally hostile press communicating its message remained an uphill task and the results were often disappointing' (Shaw 1992: 12).

Policy Failures

Politicians and communications advisers insist on the separation of policy and presentation. For much of the time this is accurate and both sides have an interest in declaring it to be so. At times, however, effective communications cannot be divorced from the nature of the product being promoted. Over time the constant survey evidence about unpopular policies and leaders or dislike of a party's image has effects on most voter-conscious politicians.

In this context it is worth considering two policy questions that exercised Labour's campaign planners and proved controversial in the months following the 1992 election. Some members of the Agency felt strongly from late 1991 onwards that the party should revise its tax plans and, therefore, its spending commitments; both of these had been drawn up before the recession took hold. The package of public spending proposals and priorities had been agreed by the Shadow Cabinet in 1990. The only firm spending pledges were increases in old age pensions and child benefit and extra funding for the NHS, which would be financed by higher taxes on the better off. Spending in other areas would be allowed only as and when resources were available. But some advisers were conscious of Labour's electoral weakness on tax and were sure that the Conservatives would exploit it. One adviser argued that Labour should promise not to increase taxes because it would only delay economic recovery and others warned that unless the spending commitments were reined back (thereby avoiding the need for tax rises) the Conservatives would 'cost' Labour's policies and repeat the charge, 'Labour equals higher taxes', as in 1987. They feared that unless Labour could protect itself against this charge the election was as good as lost.

On the other side, some Shadow ministers, particularly those whose programmes were promised more money, pointed to survey evidence that a large majority of voters were prepared to pay more tax for better services. Influential figures like Roy Hattersley, the Deputy Leader, and John Smith, the Shadow Chancellor, favoured a clear choice between the parties – Labour's programme of 'fair' taxes and more spending on welfare versus the Conservative stance of tax cutting and restraint on spending – one that they calculated would work to Labour's benefit. Politics, namely the reputations and feelings of politicians who had made the promises of further spending in their areas of responsibility, and political convictions (particularly, the belief in redistribution and greater equality), suggested a different tax and spending programme to that favoured by most SCA advisers and was decisive.

Mr Kinnock shared the fears of the advisers. Early in 1991 he had privately suggested to John Smith that a part (12p) of the standard rate of income tax should be hypothecated for the NHS – as a health tax. This would enable Labour to reduce the standard rate of tax and force health to the top of the agenda (Kinnock interview). But John Smith showed little interest in the idea or in revising the party's spending plans. In September 1991 the Agency made a private presentation of the public perceptions of Labour's economic policies to Neil Kinnock, Smith, Gordon Brown and Tony Blair. The message was gloomy. The party would have to do something to counter the charge that it would put up taxes. Mr Kinnock was already convinced and challenged the Agency to persuade John Smith. He, however, resented the suggestions from the publicity advisers. He was aware of the problem but was determined not to show his hand on taxes in a Shadow Budget until the

Chancellor had delivered his Budget in March. He was not going to risk his reputation for fiscal prudence until he had a fuller picture of the nation's finances, did not want to appear to be vacillating on tax and hoped to surprise the Conservatives with his response. Members of the Agency were warned to keep off the subject. Smith had a contingency plan; if the Conservatives cut 1p off income tax, then Labour would repeal it and cut one per cent from national insurance rates. But this was kept secret from Kinnock, for fear that he would reveal what was to be a Labour surprise in the Shadow Budget.

Mr Kinnock and members of his private office grew increasingly frustrated that the party was not answering the Tory tax attack; more specifically, they were frustrated with John Smith. The leader eventually and unfortunately showed his hand at a dinner for journalists at Luigi's Restaurant in the West End on 14 January. Although recent Labour party documents on economic policy had dropped the idea of phasing in higher national income contributions over the lifetime of the Parliament, Mr Kinnock now drew journalists' attention to an earlier policy document which stated that the party retained the option of phasing in the contributions. The media seized on the incident to publicize the tensions between Kinnock and Smith (Butler and Kavanagh 1992: 90–1). The incident was a symptom of the difficulties at the top of the party about taxing and spending, and specifically of Mr Kinnock's impatience with Mr Smith and the latter's distrust of the leader. Nothing came of the initiative, except to irritate Mr Smith, who felt that the leader was reacting to adverse opinion polls and trying to 'bounce' him into making a pledge not to increase taxes. On the day of the restaurant encounter a *Guardian* editorial called on Labour to modify its tax policy and an opinion poll showed Labour trailing the Conservatives. The two men were concerned to defend Labour against charges that it was a high tax party but had different solutions. One person who was very close to these events has commented:

> This is when we started to lose the election. We were never ready for the Tory tax campaign, were thrown into disarray by it and never fully recovered our stride. It's a terrible thing to say, given the predictability of the Tories' tactics and the need for us to be ready for anything at that stage. But, for a variety of reasons which are probably best not gone into, Labour was not able to deal with the situation. (Interview)

Another troublesome political issue was proportional representation (PR), a move supported by a minority of Labour MPs. Some of the communications team also felt that a willingness by the party to examine the case for electoral reform might provide reassurance that a Labour government would seek consensus and not give in to the unions or the left wing. They wanted the topic to be broached well in advance of the election. Mr Kinnock agreed to set up a working party under a Labour-supporting academic, Professor Raymond Plant, to examine the topic and at the October 1991 party conference the group's remit was extended to cover elections for the House of Commons. Mr Kinnock felt inhibited from declaring his own view partly because he thought that it would pre-empt the work of the group and partly because of the well-known opposition of his Deputy Leader, Roy Hattersley, and some other senior figures. The issue was developed in the last week of the general election campaign when Mr Kinnock stated at a press conference that the Plant group's membership would be broadened to include other parties. The Conservative party and its tabloid supporters seized on the statement as a Labour bid for Liberal support, and warned that a Liberal vote would 'let Labour in by the back door'. The advisers wanted Mr Kinnock to grasp the issue well in advance of the election. One said: 'The last thing we wanted was for him to do it in the campaign. It then would look like a "fix". I took the view that if Neil lost the election then he was out. Electoral reform might have improved our vote. He had nothing to lose' (Hollick interview).

After the election, some of the initiatives of the communications team attracted much criticism. The 'Jennifer's ear' election broadcast (see below, pp. 158, 209) and the triumphalist rally at Sheffield, for example, were criticized in the General Secretary's post-election report to the party. Many on the left and the right disliked the new methods, and the left in particular resented the Kinnock project of modernizing the party and many of the policy changes. As far as the latter were concerned the party had, at the behest of pollsters and publicists, abandoned its principles in the search for 'designer socialism'. The party should have relied on the voices of so-called 'real people'. Kim Howells a Labour MP claimed: 'There is no substitute for slogging around the streets, talking to people, and getting the message across' (Jones 1992: 152). But more important than any of these problems was the electorate's lack of trust in Labour and confidence in its economic competence. Reading and listening to the criticisms of the communications from Labour MPs and activists, one senses that they were a form of scapegoating from those who resented Kinnock's changes to the party's structure and policies, or from those who had been downgraded or by-passed in the process. The product was still more decisive for the electorate than the presentation.

Conclusion

Labour has had a fluctuating relationship with professional communicators. In 1964 the party was probably ahead of the Conservatives in its use of survey research and communications expertise. Thereafter, disputes over who does what within the party organization, disagreements on policy, complex committee arrangements and downright suspicion of the whole business of public relations and professional communications have made the volunteers' task difficult. Fifteen years after working for the last Labour government, Tim Delaney was not convinced that the party had made much progress. Before 1979 he was part of the team that advised Callaghan, found it necessary to participate in secret meetings 'to get things done' and met hostility from the party headquarters and NEC. In 1992 Philip Gould and the Shadow Communications Agency faced similar difficulties. Delaney complained:

> The trouble is that Labour goes through the motions. Of course, it wants slogans, ads and professionally made broadcasts. But these are add-ons, a cosmetic. . . . Marketing can only work if it is taken on board fully and that's never happened in Labour. There are still people there who say 'We are the party of the working class, we do not need manipulators'. (Interview)

He added: 'Modern communications techniques are an essential part of modern politics. Why be amateur about it? You can lose on your own amateur terms or win on their [Tory] professional terms' (interview). Lord Hollick, a successful businessman and a member of the Shadow Communications Agency, reflected: 'Labour people love to have meetings, so that they can be informed about things, but they do not like to have meetings to decide things. That is a crucial difference between Labour and business and, probably, the Conservative party' (interview).

Labour's Agency was wound up after the 1992 election. But this did not mean that the party had turned its back on professional communications. In November 1993 it appointed Butterfield, Day,

Devito, Hockney (BB&H) to be its advertising agency. The agency's director, Les Butterfield, had been a volunteer member of the Shadow Communications Agency.

Political communications are more likely to be effective when the product is sound and the communicators are backed by a leader of authority. Wilson in 1964 and Kinnock in 1992 provided the latter. But the product was sounder in 1964. Before the election Labour had already made significant policy changes in *Signposts for the Sixties*, Harold Wilson was widely regarded as a more convincing leader than the Conservative premiers Macmillan and Home, and the Conservative government was dogged by failure, division and scandal. In 1983 Labour's political position – on policies, leadership and image – was so poor that no campaign could have succeeded. In 1987 and 1992, in spite of some recovery, many of the barriers to voting Labour remained.

What emerges from surveys into the voters' mood over the past thirty years, from the post-1959 research (*Must Labour Lose?*) to the post-1992 election surveys, is the deep and recurring fears about the party, fears which the communications have not overcome. Labour was continually seen as a party of tradition, of the working class and the have-nots, not of those who wanted to 'get on' and be better off economically. In both 1959 and 1992 Labour trailed in the crucial areas of leadership and economic competence. The earlier research drew attention to changes in society and in working-class aspirations, and concluded that many skilled workers no longer saw Labour as the party for them. Thirty years later the message was similar. But Labour's relative position had worsened. In 1959, when Labour had lost its third successive election, it trailed the Conservatives by 5 per cent of the vote: in 1992 it trailed by 7.6 per cent. The party was more widely mistrusted, society was even more bourgeois and up-market – more share ownership, home ownership and white-collar jobs – and fewer people thought of it as a party that could realize their aspirations. Changes in society and values appeared to be making Labour a party of the past. A pessimistic Philip Gould wrote immediately after the 1992 election:

> Last time, in 1987, I said that you can't win an election campaign in four weeks – but in four years. After four years' continual campaigning that excuse is no longer available. Campaigning of itself clearly cannot win elections and the causes of Labour's defeat are more complicated, more deeply rooted than I suspect either of us anticipated five years ago. (Letter to author)

In December 1992 an internal evaluation of the recent election campaign stated: 'Perhaps Labour's largest weakness was the lack of a central compelling message articulated by the leadership and agreed by the party'.

A party's persistent failure in the market-place of elections will eventually force politicians and communicators to re-examine its policies and structure. Survey findings and comprehensive electoral defeats made the case for radical change irresistible. The acceptance of modern communications methods was a force for change in the structure of the party and in policy. Like other modernizing European parties Labour was becoming an 'electoral-professional' organization (Panebianco 1988). Under Mr Kinnock the measures to 'modernize' the party included:

Reducing the authority of conference and its policy-making role by the creation of a Policy Commission.

Centralizing power in the leader's office and the Shadow Communications Agency over campaign strategy.

Strengthening the NEC *vis-à-vis* constituencies, particularly in drawing up shortlists of candidates for by-elections.

Distancing the party from the trade unions.

Weakening the power of party activists by the introduction of one member one vote and membership ballots for the selection and reselection of Parliamentary candidates.

Shifting the emphasis from grass-roots campaigning to reliance on the mass media and public relations in elections.

Organizing a policy review which dumped unpopular policies on public ownership, industrial relations and defence.

Granting delegated authority from the NEC to the Shadow Communications Agency in preparing for the election.

The modernization measures, particularly the centralization of decision-making in the hands of the leader and those around him, and the adoption of public relations, are interconnected. Speedy decision-making and short lines of communication (by-passing committees) are important to communicators. The policy changes also do seem to have been part of a larger agenda to marginalize the party's left wing and reassure middle-of-the-road voters and financial markets that Labour is a competent party of government, not a class-specific party. The term 'socialism' and the policy of public ownership were downgraded as 'baggage' and an electoral liability. Labour, in its search for votes, became more like a commercial firm in a competitive market, 'a responsive political organization qualitatively different from the class-based parties of the post-war period' (Sackman 1994: 468). Not surprisingly, many of the new methods and the policy thrust have been seen as interconnected and opposed by the left wing (see Heffernan and Marquesee 1992).

The project had some success. *Labour's Last Chance*, a study of voting in 1992, calculates that the policy changes designed to improve the party's image, were worth an extra 3 per cent of the vote to Labour. Voters acknowledged that Labour had moved to the centre, but they also believed that John Major had moved the Conservative party to the centre, thus limiting the benefits to Labour of its policy changes (Heath, Jowell and Curtice 1994).

5

PUBLIC OPINION POLLS

Campaigners require accurate information about the views of voters if they are to prepare and monitor an effective election strategy. The media also require information about the public mood, to assist their reporting and analysis of the election. In the past politicians and commentators had their own guides to public opinion. Their sources were often quite crude, intuitive and impressionistic, drawing variously on letters to the press, the size and enthusiasm of public meetings or personal contacts with other politicians, political journalists or taxi drivers. Stanley Baldwin allegedly consulted his local railway station manager and Winston Churchill in 1945 relied on the confident forecasts of friendly press proprietors. But even in 1992 Glenys Kinnock was reported as believing that Labour had lost the election when she found a number of voters avoiding eye contact with her in the last few days. What is striking about most of these sources is the lack of concern there is with how representative they are of the broader public. As one political scientist has recently commented, 'All politicians are pollsters of a sort' (Berrington 1992: 73).

Development

Political opinion polls, based on the questioning of a representative, systematically drawn sample of voters, started in the United States in the 1930s. In 1936 a Gallup poll achieved fame by accurately predicting the result of the Presidential election that year. The same election, however, also gave rise to a disastrous 'poll'. *The Literary Digest* magazine sought the voting intentions of its readers and 10 million replied. By a large majority they supported the Republican candidate Alf Landon over the Democratic President Franklin Roosevelt. In fact, FDR won by a landslide. The *Digest* was read predominantly by people with access to a car and a phone, i.e. they were largely middle class and Republican supporters and therefore unrepresentative of the electorate. This was an early warning that it is not the size but the representative-ness of a sample that is important. In Britain a Gallup survey had correctly predicted the result of the West Fulham by-election in 1938, but a more notable *coup* was its prediction of a Labour victory in the 1945 general election. At the time people showed little interest in the poll and few believed it. Twenty years later, when the polls had compiled a good record of prediction, some commentators went to the other extreme and regarded them as almost infallible.

Opinion polls are now commissioned by a wide variety of clients, including companies, pressure groups, local authorities, the mass media and even wealthy individuals. They can be used for private purposes, for example, to help a company or political party plan its communications with the public or to assist pressure groups to influence decision-makers or public opinion. Most political opinion polls are now commissioned by the media and made public. For a newspaper it is a good way of promoting itself. During elections the poll will probably be reported by the main television news bulletins and this may boost the paper's circulation. The poll findings are usually carried on the paper's front page under arresting (and sometimes misleading) headlines (see below). There are also bogus polls – for example, the anti-nationalization surveys in marginal seats in 1959 were financed largely by privately owned steel companies who were threatened by Labour's public ownership plans, and designed less to reflect than to influence public opinion, by showing how unpopular public ownership was. There have also been cases of the Liberals using little-known pollsters in target constituencies and selectively releasing figures in an effort to give the party some 'momentum'.

Political polling has grown steadily in Britain in the postwar period (Worcester 1991). In 1945 Gallup had the field to itself but by 1992 there were five major companies and several smaller ones. The number of national polls at election time has also steadily grown, from one in 1945 to 57 in 1992. If we were to count other regional, marginal and 'special' polls, the 1992 total would easily double. The big increase occurred in 1983, since when there has been a plateau. The growing number of current affairs TV programmes and national newspapers has contributed to the increase. There is now an opinion poll on most days of the election campaign, a deluge on the final weekend and on polling day virtually all newspapers lead with opinion polls' forecasts. Most of the media interest is in the recorded levels of support for the political parties, based on the response to the question 'How would you vote if there was an election today?' This is often presented as a prediction, for weeks or days ahead of the actual election, rather than as a snapshot of opinion about a hypothetical event taken at one point in time. If voters are particularly fickle or undecided the finding may be out of date even by the time it is reported.

Methods

Pollsters draw their samples by either random probability or quota methods. A random sample is drawn by selecting every nth (for example, fifteenth) name from, say, the electoral register for a number of areas or sampling points. In principle, every person in the sampled area has an equal chance of being drawn. A quota sample is drawn by allowing the interviewer to find respondents who together match the social characteristics of the population, say for social class, age, gender and so on. For anyone who refuses or who is unavailable, another person with the same characteristics is to be substituted. Conducting a random probability sample may require the interviewer to visit a residence several times to contact a selected respondent. In the interests of saving time and expense pollsters have increasingly used quota samples. Purists, however, have expressed worry over the growing number of refusals (around 40 per cent) by those first approached or who give other reasons for non-cooperation. How representative, they wonder, are those who are willing to be interviewed? Interestingly, virtually all academic and government-sponsored polls use random probability methods.

Most opinion polling in the United States is done by telephone rather than by face to face interview, and the method has supporters in Britain. In 1992 90 per cent of British voters had phones, although nearly a third were ex-directory. A problem is that the non-telephone owners tend to be disproportionately poor and non-Conservative. They are, however, an ever-dwindling minority and the samples can be adjusted to take account of these shortcomings. Supporters of the method also point to the potential gains from the interviews being supervized and the reduced geographical clustering in interviews. Clustering leads to a 'neighbourhood effect' in face to face quota surveys (for example, interviewers will often go to council estates for unskilled, working-class respondents).

Pollsters also employ panel surveys, a useful technique for measuring and explaining changes in voting intention or opinions during the three or four weeks of an election campaign or over an even longer period. Panels are not without problems, however. One is attrition, stemming from respondents refusing to continue or, in the longer term, moving house or dying; the result is that the panel may gradually cease to be representative of the original population. The panel may also lose in representativeness if respondents strive for greater consistency in the answers given at each interview, or if their political interest is increased as a consequence of being interviewed regularly.

All sample surveys are subject to a margin of error, for no sample can be guaranteed to be an exact representation of the population from which it is drawn. It is often claimed that, statistically, there is a 95 per cent likelihood that, say, the Conservative and Labour vote reported in a sample of 1,000 voters is accurate to within + or − 3 per cent. If a poll shows that Conservative and Labour each have 40 per cent of the vote, the actual figures might vary between 37 per cent and 43 per cent for each. The outcome for a party could be a clear defeat or a landslide victory and the polls could still be 'technically' correct – i.e. within the margin of error. These margins might not matter to a commercial company or even an opinion survey. But they make election predictions under the British first-past-the-post electoral system very risky. In fact the claim about error margin is bogus because it only applies when the random sample is fully achieved – which is rare. Moreover, mistakes may also arise from other factors than the sample size, for example, from incorrect quota controls.

Any sample or any poll is only as good as the questions it asks. Although pollsters try to avoid questions which are 'leading' or worded vaguely, some respondents make distinctions between terms which are not apparent to others. There are marked differences in the perceived competence of the parties on handling, say, 'health' compared to the 'NHS' or on 'jobs' compared to 'employment'. In 1983 Labour private polls found the Conservative lead over Labour as the best party for handling 'defence' was 25 per cent higher than for 'nuclear disarmament' and on 'inflation and prices' was 14 per cent higher than for 'cost of living'. Labour's lead over the Conservatives on the 'National Health Service' was 14 per cent higher than on 'hospitals'.

Poll Reporting

In May 1970 the main polling companies agreed a code of practice for reporting the polls. It urged that every substantial published report of the poll should also carry the size and type of the sample and the date of the interviews. Some of the media reporting of opinion polling, however, still leaves something to be desired. Pressures of time and space mean that qualifications about the margin of error or the size of the 'don't knows' are not always carried. Although the polls are sometimes misreported or distorted, pollsters cannot control how the media headline and cover their data, particularly in the non-sponsoring press. In 1979 the *Sun's* interpretation on election day of the final polls, three of which had a Conservative lead of between 5 per cent and 7 per cent, was 'It's Maggie by a whisker' – an attempt to stiffen wavering Conservatives (Crewe 1982: 121). In 1983 the *Mail on Sunday* carried a headline, 'Jobless say we back Tories', over a survey report that 56 per cent of a sample of unemployed intended to vote Labour and only 26 per cent would vote Conservative! Partisan calculation often encourages this distortion. What is regrettable is that much other interesting material, apart from voting intentions or the rating of party leaders, is often neglected in the secondary coverage.

Yet the polls have on balance led to more informed reporting and analyses of political campaigns, issues and personalities. One can now use evidence where once one had to rely on hearsay or supposition. Sustained exposure to surveys has also improved the capacity of many politicians and campaigners to read the evidence with a discerning eye, even if this is not always reflected in their public statements. One Tory official's assessment of the early private polls conducted for the party was: 'When the old-timers talked nonsense before, all you could do was say "Rubbish", and they'd just say "Rubbish" back. Now you can produce some evidence' (Butler and King 1966: 68).

A negative consequence has been the excessive attention which the media pay to the election 'horse race' which, some critics complain, leads to the neglect of issues and distorts the electoral process. In the 1992 campaign a Loughborough University team found that opinion poll stories accounted for one-fifth of the total election coverage by the six daily tabloids and for 12 per cent of coverage on the main broadcasting news bulletins. In the second and fourth weeks the polls made more front-page stories than any other topic, much of it on the horse race element. During the campaign only eight days passed without the publication of a national poll, on the final Sunday six were published and on polling day eight out of eleven national dailies led their front pages with a poll story (Crewe 1992). Although the media have always been interested in the horse race aspect of elections, polls have added a new dimension. Polls also shape the judgements of commentators because they are widely regarded as the best indicator of how the electorate is responding to the campaign. The use of numbers to describe public opinion, sometimes down to a decimal point, lends the exercise a spurious kind of accuracy.

The reporting of the polls has also become a factor in the campaign. On the night of 31 March 1992 Conservative managers were deeply unhappy at the media attention devoted to the large Labour lead in three polls. That day they had launched a press conference on defence and the 'hidden' CND connections of Labour MPs, and expected that defence would lead the early evening television news. Instead the main story was about Labour 'winning' the election, on the basis of the most recent opinion polls. One frustrated senior Conservative official commented: 'Polls may be ruining the democratic process if they mean that politicians can't be reported on the issues' (Lansley interview).

Another case of influence is the 1970 election which the polls suggested Labour would win by a large margin. The media therefore sought to explain why Harold Wilson was coasting to victory, and the hapless Ted Heath was heading for defeat (see p. 184). According to a recent biography of Heath, 'The leading commentators attached themselves too closely to the travelling entourages of the party leaders – who were themselves mesmerised by the polls', and selectively reported incidents and anecdotes to reinforce the polls (Campbell 1993: 280). In 1992 the polls were again often cited by commentators as proof that the Conservatives were fighting a poor campaign – a highly subjective assessment (see below, pp. 184–5). In the *Independent on Sunday*, on 5 April, Peter Kellner's report on an NOP voting panel was headlined 'Victory is slipping from the grasp of the Tories'. Kellner wrote:

> The Conservatives would have to overcome the lessons of history and the weight of evidence from our panel if they are to retain power with an

overall majority. They would need a swing of at least 3 per cent in the last few days, and 'No governing party in modern times has achieved a late swing of that magnitude'. Looking at the likely defections and gains any late swing is likely to be to the Liberals and away from the Conservatives. And on the questions asking voters to choose between more public spending and tax or less spending and tax, it seems that Labour's public spending promises are having a greater impact than the Tories' charge that 'Labour government means higher taxes'.

Election Forecasts

Until 1970 British opinion polls had a good forecasting record. In 1959, 1964 and 1966 they were virtually spot-on and the error on the winning party's forecast lead was 2 per cent or less. But since then, as table 5.1 shows, in four of the seven elections the error of the average forecast has been larger (1970, October 1974, 1983 and 1992) and they pointed to the wrong winner in February 1974. In 1970, by ceasing to poll several days before the election day, the polls may have missed a late swing to the Conservatives – or they may have been wrong all along. The ORC claimed to detect a last-minute swing to Conservatives among voters in interview towards the end of its final polling, adjusted its figures to give a Tory lead and achieved fame as the only pollster to get the outcome right. In 1992 the final forecasts of the five major pollsters – Gallup, NOP, MORI, ICM and Harris, averaged a 1.3 per cent Labour lead compared with a 7.6 per cent lead in votes for the Conservatives on election day. All the polls were wrong by a margin greater than the accepted range of error, all erred in the same direction, underestimating the Conservative share of the vote and overstating Labour's share. Even the exit polls overstated Labour's vote and misled the television

Table 5.1 The error on the winning party's lead in polls (1970–92)

Election	Average error on lead (%)	No. of polls
1970	6.6	5
1974 Feb.	2.4	5
1974 Oct.	5.6	5
1979	1.7	4
1983	4.3	6
1987	3.2	5
1992	8.9	5

companies in forecasting the outcome. A number of analysts now think that in 1992 the opinion polls were wrong throughout the election, notably in under-reporting Conservative support (Crewe 1992; Jowell et al. 1993).

An election result is the most objective test of whether the opinion polls are accurate. It is doubtful, however, that Dr Gallup would have been pleased that the main interest of the media in polls is for prediction. He regarded the polls as a means of increasing popular feedback to the politicians and improving the quality of democracy.

Immediately after the 1992 election the Market Research Society commissioned a report into the reasons for the error. The report reviewed a number of possible shortcomings, including inadequacies in the electoral register and sampling methods, late swing, differential turnout and tactical voting. Although late swing was the favoured immediate explanation of some pollsters the size of the swing on election day or even in the last few days would have had to be enormous and unprecedented, and was rejected as the major cause of the error. The reported Conservative share in the final polls increased by only 1 per cent on those of the previous week and the gap between the two parties closed by a mere 0.5 per cent (Jowell et al. 1993). Post-election analyses found that Conservatives had disproportionately refused to declare their voting intention before polling day and one polling organization, ICM, found that late deciders, 'won't says' and 'don't knows' voted disproportionately Conservative.* The MRS report also acknowledged that the samples, because of inadequacies in weighting and quota controls, did not fully represent Conservatives.

Voters may also use information from opinion polls to vote tactically. In every general election since 1964, except for 1987, the party ahead in the final survey did worse than predicted on polling day. This has led some observers to wonder if there is an 'underdog' effect, in which some voters deliberately abstain or vote for the second party because they do not want the leading party to win by a large majority. In the last few days of the 1992 campaign forecasts of a hung Parliament were used by Conservatives to warn that a vote for the Liberal Democrats would 'let Labour in', a claim that may have frightened off some wavering

* After the election ICM sought to cope with the greater reluctance of Conservatives (or others) to reveal their voting intention, by using a secret ballot. It found that this increased the number who declared a Conservative allegiance. Other pollsters adjust their results according to how people voted in past elections to check that their samples are representative.

Liberals and Labour supporters. Two days before polling day NOP reported a 2 per cent Labour lead and on election day Gallup reported that 81 per cent expected a close result. 'Good polls actually hurt us. The closer we got to a Labour government the more some people got scared. In the end we could not overcome the mistrust', said Labour's Philip Gould (interview).

There is, however, no good evidence bearing on how the polls influence voters. For what it is worth, only 2 to 3 per cent of voters admit that they are influenced by the polls. To demonstrate that polls do have an influence one would have to show that voters (1) are aware of other voters' first and second preferences, (2) know how most other voters will react on election day in the light of poll findings and (3) assume that the overall effect of the various tactical calculations will not be largely self-cancelling. Moreover, any hypothetical effects of the polls on voting need to be set against the impact on voters of events and political activities reported by the media in the closing stages of the campaign; shifts in the polls or in actual voting may simply be reflecting these other influences (Crewe 1992; Waller 1992).

Campaign Effects

Polls certainly affect the morale of campaign participants. Many campaigners have acknowledged the feverish way in which their mood alters depending upon the latest opinion poll. Even Mrs Thatcher, the so-called 'Iron Lady', was not immune from them. Rumours of a gloomy poll and a reported reduction in the Conservative lead by Gallup a week before polling day in 1987 induced a crisis in No. 10 and a decision to change the advertising strategy (Young 1990: ch. 15). Within hours, however, another poll showed a large Conservative lead and calm was restored. The original poll gave Mrs Thatcher an excuse to change the advertisements – which she wanted to do anyway (see p. 64).

It is par for the course for party leaders to deny the accuracy of unfavourable polls by invoking the enthusiastic reports from 'our people on the ground' in the constituencies. They do this to boost the morale of supporters. In 1983 the Labour leader Michael Foot dismissed the polls' reports of his party's low support, by claiming, 'I have been attending a different election from the one described in the polls', and Neil Kinnock spoke in similar vein in 1987. The comments were treated with appropriate scepticism by much of the media. In 1992 questions were often addressed at the morning press conferences and in media interviews to Conservative spokesmen about why they were 'losing' (in the polls) the election and what would happen after the defeat. In the 1970 and 1992 elections reports based on returns from Conservative canvassers and organizers to Central Office were more encouraging than the opinion polls – and it was the latter that were confounded on election day. The party's publicists and media specialists are expected to comment on the polls – good or bad – because the media cover them so intensively. The effectiveness of the parties' campaign strategies are assessed by commentators in the light of the published poll findings, and like their American counterparts, British politicians explain poor poll findings by claiming that (1) their private polls are more encouraging, (2) the findings differ between polls – 'the polls are all over the place' – or (3) the only poll that counts is the one on election day (Bauman and Herbst 1994).

Polls also affect the behaviour of financial institutions and private investors, usually already nervous because of the political uncertainty induced by an election. Rumours of Labour's gains or leads in opinion polls in 1983, 1987 and 1992 prompted heavy selling of the pound on foreign exchanges and large falls in the value of the stock market.

The public, as well as private, polls are an additional source of information which Prime Ministers can consider when choosing an election date. But Harold Wilson's experience in 1970 is a warning. He was misled by the recovery of Labour party support in the polls and local elections in spring and called a general election in June. Labour lost. Mr Heath ignored reported Tory leads in the public and private polls and the advice of most party officials to go for a dissolution in early January 1974; the delay of a few weeks may have cost him the election. A Prime Minister is more likely to be persuaded when most of the polls point clearly in one direction and are consistent with other cues.

One can point to several cases where polls have influenced the conduct of British campaigns. The favourable reaction in the polls to Labour's election broadcast featuring Neil Kinnock in 1987 persuaded the party to repeat the film. Survey evidence in 1992 also encouraged Labour to give a high profile to the Shadow Chancellor John Smith and Conservatives to try to give a lower one to the Chancellor of the

Exchequer, Norman Lamont. The virtual unanimity of the polls about a 'hung' Parliament highlighted the interest in Mr Kinnock's late campaign invitation to the Liberal Democrats to join Labour's working party on electoral systems, and seemed to confirm John Major's warnings that a vote for the Liberals could let Labour in. And the forecasts by three polls of Labour leads of 4, 6 and 7 per cent on 31 March endowed the party's rally in Sheffield that night with a triumphalist atmosphere which was never envisaged when the event was planned, and was quickly regretted. The financial markets, particularly the long interest rate market, reacted negatively, and gave force to Conservative warnings about the economic risks of a Labour government.

Unfavourable polls may also embolden critics of a party leader or campaign. The failure of the Conservatives to establish any lead, let alone a clear one, in the opinion polls in the 1992 election encouraged commentators and disgruntled Conservatives to attack the party's campaign as directionless and lifeless. Two successive election defeats would probably have made Neil Kinnock's position as leader impossible. But the considerable body of survey evidence suggesting that he was an electoral liability strengthened the case of those who called for his removal.

Opinion polls have therefore become more than a reflection of public opinion, they are a major influence on the conduct and interpretation of the campaign. In 1992 they certainly contributed to the impression that Labour was winning the campaign and may have reinforced among party strategists and the media commentators a false view of the strength of Labour's vote. It is worth quoting at length the post-election view of Philip Gould, a central figure in Labour's campaign:

> Labour's campaign, the pollsters, the broadcast media and the press all submerged the Tory vote. Submerged it because people were guilty and because a kind of social dynamic had been established that made Labour more acceptable than the Conservatives. This led people to be publicly embarrassed and uncertain about expressing support for the Conservatives. But it was also submerged in the sense that many people hid from themselves their real intentions, feelings and view of where their self-interest lay. The strength of Labour's campaign was reflected into a majority shifting from thinking the Conservatives would win into a majority thinking that Labour would win. (Interview)

Polls and the Agenda

Polls may also influence the political agenda. By asking voters to indicate which issues *are* important and which *should be* important, polls may spotlight issues that are neglected by elites but concern voters. Opinion polls were crucial in the 1960s in showing the popular concern over race and immigration, something which the leaderships in the major political parties hardly discussed. In the early stages of the 1987 election the media paid much attention to defence, although surveys showed that voters did not think this important and wanted more on social issues and unemployment (Miller et al. 1990).

By the same token polls may also mislead politicians about the agenda. For several years now opinion polls have reported that large majorities of voters would prefer more public spending on services instead of tax cuts and be willing to pay more taxes to finance such spending. Labour built its election strategy in 1987 and to some extent in 1992 on such a reading of the public mood. Yet in both elections the electorate voted comprehensively and persistently against the party of greater public spending and tax increases. One wonders if some people were giving what they assumed was a 'politically correct' response, in this case agreeing to pay more taxes to finance more spending. A denial might have been perceived as tantamount to being selfish and uncaring.

There was other survey evidence which qualified the altruistic response. Before the 1987 election Labour's private polls reported that by 70 per cent to 24 per cent voters preferred more spending on social services – even if taxes were raised – over tax reductions. But when Nigel Lawson in his pre-election Budget cut 2p off the standard rate of income tax, Labour's proposal to cancel the reduction was supported by only 32 per cent, with 46 per cent opposed. At the time Labour's campaign planners were puzzled. NOP private polls for the party in 1992 regularly found that some 75 per cent of voters said that they were willing to pay more in taxes to fund better public services. But when asked whether they preferred Labour's proposed tax increases or Conservative proposals for tax cuts, the split was almost 50–50. Exit polls found that the number complaining that they would be worse off under Labour's tax and spending proposals was greater than those who calculated that they would be better off. Moreover, when Labour's

Table 5.2 Differences in 'important issues' according to polling methods

(a) 'The most important issue in deciding how to vote' (prompted)

	%
NHS	62
Education	41
Recession	38
Tax	18

(b) 'The most important issue' (unprompted)

	%
Taxation/economy	20
Health	13
Always vote that way	10

private polls asked voters what was most likely to put them off voting for the party, higher taxation was usually the biggest objection.

Table 5.2 reports the different responses of voters, according to whether the 'important' issues are left for the voter to suggest or are prompted by the pollster. There is a marked reduction in the proportion mentioning the 'caring' issues of health and education when they are left to suggest their own views. Questions about which party is regarded as more competent to manage the economy or will improve living standards proved more reliable guides to voting intentions. The lesson of recent elections is that responses to 'iffy' or leading questions on issues, particularly on taxes and spending, need to be handled with care.

Political Effects

Some politicians criticize the 'playback' role of opinion polls as an interference between themselves and the voters and would like to ban them during the election campaign. Many resent the amount of media attention paid to the polls and, perhaps, the pollsters' ability to second guess their own claims about public opinion. In 1967 the Speaker's Conference recommended a ban on polls during the campaign and in 1987 a ten-minute rule to ban them was passed on first reading in the Commons. Public hostility to the polls usually increases after they have wrongly predicted an election. After the 1992 election, Gallup found that over 40 per cent favoured the banning of opinion polls during elections and the media expressed reservations. This reaction is a testament to the narrow role which the public attributes to the polls.

Surveys have other uses than prediction. They are also important for evaluating a winning party's claim to have a mandate for a particular policy or for its programme. During and after the 1987 election they showed that in spite of electoral victory, Conservative proposals for introducing water and electricity privatization, a poll tax and changes in the health service were still opposed by a majority of voters. Similarly, analysis of Labour's last two general election victories in 1974 shows that they were gained in spite of the electorate's growing hostility to key party policies (Crewe, Alt and Sarlvik 1977).

Between elections, opinion polls provide a continuous source of public assessment of how a government is doing, how the party leaders are rated and what the major issues are. Michael Foley (1993) has argued at length that continuous polling about the standing of the leaders and the media interest in the polls have contributed to the rise of presidentialism in British politics. When Margaret Thatcher was challenged for the party leadership by Michael Heseltine in 1990 opinion polls reported that on hypothetical questions about levels of Conservative support under different leaders, the Conservative party led by Michael Heseltine would win a general election, whereas it would lose badly under Mrs Thatcher. This spelt trouble for Mrs Thatcher among the scores of Tory MPs who feared for their seats. Indeed Michael Heseltine used the opinion polls to claim that he could recapture many of the former Conservative voters who had defected since 1987. When Mrs Thatcher withdrew from the leadership race opinion polls removed Heseltine's ploy by reporting that John Major would be at least as great a vote winner.

The continuous polling of the popularity of leaders may also have the effect of undermining the leader's authority. There is some irony in this. The superiority, according to polls, of Thatcher and Major over the Labour leader in 1983, 1987 and 1992 has been advanced as a cause of the Conservative victories in those elections, and added to their authority in the party. But when their poll ratings tumbled – Mrs Thatcher had scored a record low in 1990 until John Major plummeted further in 1993 – their leadership came under intense pressure as many Conservative MPs saw them as an electoral liability. The polls provide a continuous popularity – or more often, unpopularity – contest for the Prime Minister.

Foley (1993: 226–31) is also impressed at how the consistently poor opinion poll ratings for Mr Kinnock undermined his leadership. Critics could use the polls to argue that he was an electoral liability to his party; he ran far behind John Major on leadership qualities and responses to hypothetical questions suggested that the party would do much better under John Smith. In turn, as such polls give rise to media discussion of the leader's 'failure' and analyses of his or her weakness and unpopularity, so they may become self-fulfilling. The tendency is reinforced when the polls ask even more hypothetical questions, such as how people would vote if the leader were replaced by somebody else, usually an unknown quantity. Sir Alec Douglas Home's authority in the Tory party was weakened after the election defeat in 1964. But low poll ratings further undermined him, particularly an NOP poll a week before his resignation in July 1965, which showed that people found him less sincere than Harold Wilson. Since John Major's 1992 election victory a run of bad poll ratings has been a factor in weakening his position. Constant opinion polling may also limit a government's willingness to pursue policies which incur unpopularity. The intense publicity given to polls' reports of voters' short-term hostility to a proposal may dissuade a minister from doing something which he believes is beneficial in the long term.

Conclusion

The 1992 election result was a humbling experience for opinion polls in Britain. But the media clients as well as the pollsters bear some responsibility for the débâcle. The media highlighted the polls and commentators allowed the findings to dominate their assessments. A greater modesty in future about the predictive role of opinion polls in elections would be a positive development. One judicious verdict is that publicity about polls should be limited 'to a point more in keeping with their real significance and usefulness, and in a form more cognizant with their numerous shortcomings' (Sabato 1981: 321).* And in making forecasts, pollsters should take care to consider a broader range of questions (including issue preferences and previous vote) rather than simply relying on the reported voting intention (Waller 1992).

   Banning the publication of polls, as is sometimes suggested, would give more scope to the predictably outrageous and self-interested

---

* One pollster who read the above, commented 'Yes, but persuading the headline-obsessed media to do so will be very difficult' (Waller interview).

claims of the partisan press and politicians, as well as rumours of the findings of private polls. The methods of opinion polls have the merits of being open to public scrutiny, and faults in sample design and question wording can be checked and corrected. Opinion polls still remain the best available guides to public attitudes on political and other issues.

6

PRIVATE OPINION POLLS

The use of private opinion polling by political parties is but one indicator of how political parties have become more self-conscious in their attempts to manage their election campaigns. Just as a commercial company researches its 'market' of potential purchasers so a party needs to understand its 'market' of voters. Parties now commission private polls to test their images, target voters, present policy more persuasively, track issues and themes, and generally improve their political communications with voters. This chapter discusses the role of private pollsters and assesses their influence on parties' election strategies.

Technically, a private opinion poll is no different from any other poll. Both draw samples systematically and ask the same questions of each respondent. But the public, academic and private surveys are commissioned by different clients, serve different purposes and are subject to different pressures and constraints. A newspaper commissions a public poll because it wants a good story or an arresting headline, usually about election prediction, public opinion or political personalities. An academic survey is usually financed by a government or academic agency and is concerned to inform public policymakers or contribute to scholarship by the rigorous testing of hypotheses. The research may not even be published until two or three years after the event. But the political parties who commission private surveys are more interested in findings which will answer their specific questions to help develop campaign strategy and, ultimately, influence electoral behaviour. Much useful information is available to party managers in the public polls; they cannot, however, be guaranteed to ask exactly the questions which the parties want or to provide the answers quickly. In an election speed is usually more important than scholarship. The pressure of time means that private polls do cut corners, asking a few precoded questions and analysing by a few variables.

The two main parties in Britain have commissioned private polls for three broad types of operations. They have used panels of voters to collect what they call baseline data and formulate *long-term* strategy, with particular groups of voters being re-interviewed between and during elections. During 1964–5 the Conservatives commissioned the British Market Research Bureau (BMRB) to conduct a large panel survey of voters, which was sampled in later years when the party needed information on particular subjects. The survey was consciously based on the first nationwide study of British electoral behaviour, eventually published as *Political Change in Britain* in 1969 by David Butler and Donald Stokes. Labour also used a panel study by its private polling agency MORI for the 1974 elections and again in 1986.

During general elections the parties have also conducted *short-term* surveys on reactions to particular issues, themes, personalities and broadcasts. Part of a small panel (usually between 500 and 700) is interviewed regularly, even daily, during the campaign so that movement of opinion can be 'tracked'. A system of 'moving averages' is a way of coping with the small size of the daily sample. In 1992 Labour combined three successive daily surveys, with each new daily sample replacing that of the first day. The data are analysed and presented to the party within 24 hours of the completion of fieldwork. Speed is essential; in a developing campaign information can soon be out of date. There are also *medium-term* surveys, which deal with reactions to by-elections, slogans, policies, broadcasts and generally assess the impact of a party's political communications. If the first type of operation is used to help formulate electoral strategy, the last two are to help in monitoring its operation. Pollsters or market research firms also conduct focus-group studies in which a small group of people (ten or less) discuss a series of issues. Readers of such material claim that it often provides more insights and connections between politics and other topics than the more quantitative polling.

Origins

Labour

British parties have now used private polls for over thirty years. In the 1950s the majority of influential politicians and officials in both parties were uninformed about polls or hostile to them, and were slower to use them than their counterparts in the United States and West Germany. The wartime government had authorized surveys of national morale and these were continued under the 1945 Labour government. But ministers showed remarkable indifference to the reports that arrived on their desks. According to the market researcher Mark Abrams of Research Services Ltd: 'Labour leaders, in their role as Cabinet ministers, energetically abandoned any research and communication activities that might be construed by their enemies as being of use to the Labour party' (1963: 10).

Labour was the first British party to commission polling when it employed Mark Abrams to do a small survey in 1956. Although he enjoyed the support and friendship of Hugh Gaitskell, the party leader, the work was not developed. The results of a second poll, on education, were vigorously debated by the National Executive Committee's (NEC) publicity committee and at one point Abrams was likened to Goebbels! The party's deputy leader, Aneurin Bevan, disapproved of polling – he took the view that it was the job of the politicians to know what voters were thinking and, as Treasurer of the party, influenced the NEC to block funds for research. Gaitskell did not want a row on the NEC and did not pursue the matter.

Some of the obstacles to opinion polling (and modern communications) were pungently analysed by Abrams. They included:

Anecdotalism, or the politicians' preference for face to face contacts and letters as indicators of public mood.

Ignorance, because few Labour politicians had experience of industry or business which, in the 1950s, were already turning to commercial market research.

Puritanism, or the fear that surveys might lead the party to betray its values and traditional policies.

The journalistic perspective, because MPs with a journalistic background dominated the party's publicity committee. Richard Crossman, Barbara

Castle, Tony Benn, Christopher Mayhew and Tom Driberg inclined to the view that writing pamphlets and newspaper articles, particularly by themselves, was the best form of political communication.

Moreover, the party possessed neither the organization nor the political will to make use of such research. Abrams wrote that 'the exercise could have led nowhere. The party simply had no machinery that could have taken survey findings and used them to help shape effective political propaganda' (1963: 17).

The famous post-1959 election survey *Must Labour Lose?* by Mark Abrams and Richard Rose was financed in part by private funds and in part by *Socialist Commentary* (a magazine sympathetic to the revisionist policies of Gaitskell), because the NEC refused to provide the money for a study of the reasons for the party's third successive election defeat. The survey emphasized the limits of the party's traditional working-class appeal and the unpopularity of its links with the trade unions and commitment to nationalization. These findings upset the left but did not surprise the generally right of centre supporters of polling who wanted to modernize the party. The study, particularly the material on the aspirations of the working class, was also closely studied by Conservatives and the party's advertising agency bought 15 copies. Approval or disapproval of polling in the Labour party split largely on right versus left lines and was affected by the message of the polls. Here was another reason why polling had to be handled carefully; findings might exacerbate divisions in the party as well as providing ammunition for the party's opponents. The survey played an influential part in Labour's change of direction in the early 1960s.

By 1962 many of the problems in the party structure remained but the party turned to Abrams again. A change of important personalities facilitated acceptance of polling. The party now had a new General Secretary, Director of Publicity, Deputy Leader, and a volunteer group of professional communicators (see p. 79) who insisted on survey research. The survey findings surprised many by showing that Labour supporters were not a majority among the electorate, that the number of 'floating' or uncommitted voters was larger than expected, and that such voters were not drawn from any particular section of society and were not greatly interested in politics. These became the 'target' voters for the publicity which was concentrated on the floaters in marginal seats, what Abrams called 'the uncommitted voters in the uncommitted constituencies' (interview, Butler file). The research was used to select issues and themes for posters and press advertisements, pre-test advertisements and slogans, and to assess reactions to party broadcasts and leaders (Butler and King 1965: 70). Some Labour MPs and officials claimed that the survey told them nothing new, although a few granted it some influence over advertising and targeting of voters. But the Nuffield authors were not impressed by the dismissals:

> the party's behaviour in 1959 . . . and the vocabulary and thought of several National Executive members seemed permeated with the survey's conclusion . . . . Whatever its influence in 1964, the use of survey research by politicians seems almost certain to remain a permanent feature of British political life. (Butler and King 1965: 71).

The party did little polling for 1966 because: 'the main reason (for not doing surveys) was probably that the party felt that it had learned all it needed to before 1964' (Butler and King 1966: 33). Not until 1968 was the NEC persuaded to provide funds for polling when it appointed an American, Conrad Jamieson, to study the values and mood of Labour party members. Party leaders shrugged off the survey's findings that members were disillusioned with the government and were inward-looking and not interested in communicating with ordinary voters; members were, in the report's title, *Resolutionaries not Revolutionaries*. One communications adviser, David Kingsley, was an advocate of the polling, and hoped that the findings would 'wake people up to the need for a culture change in the party. We failed' (interview). Jamieson was dismissed when he talked to the media about the results of his research into party activists. The party eventually turned in March 1970, to another American, Robert Worcester of MORI (Market & Opinion Research International) as its pollster. MORI's programme of work was based on the expectation of an October election and the 'snap' election in June meant that it did little work for that campaign. The party once again seemed to have problems in taking opinion polls on board or giving effect to their findings and there was 'no evidence that these surveys had any impact among the politicians' (Butler and Pinto-Duschinsky 1971: 190).

MORI enjoyed a close relationship with the Labour leadership in the 1974 elections and continued to poll for the party until the 1987 general election. The MORI private polls tracked a decline in the importance to voters in February 1974 of the 'who governs?' and industrial relations issues, raised by the coal strike, and a rise in importance of prices; this shift in the agenda presaged the late movement in votes to the party. But from 1979 the findings of the private polls were often depressing for the leadership. In the 1983 election MORI spelt out the party's problems:

Labour

Party image poor, divided, out of touch, disorganized, left wing.

Inconsistent, old-fashioned, T.U. linked, but . . . caring for the working classes (?), welfare.

Leadership shabby, not outstanding, not projected, uninspiring, inconsistent, old, sincere but weak.

Policies – low awareness, low confidence, not better than alternative, for welfare, looking after poor/unemployed.

Conservative

Before 1959 the Conservatives had made occasional use of National Opinion Polls and Gallup for *ad hoc* surveys into, for example, by-election reverses. But most leading politicians and Central Office staff were not interested in polling and had no machinery for considering the results. The party's advertising agency, Colman, Prentis and Varley, routinely conducted research into reactions to its advertisements and presented the reports to Central Office. The reports did not, however, spark much interest. One Central Office official claimed that Lord Hailsham, the party Chairman (1957–9), 'simply did not think that this is what politics is about' (Douglas interview). The agency was particularly struck by the material ambitions of many young prosperous manual workers and their unwillingness to identify with the working class (and Labour). This awareness inspired the slogan 'Life's better with the Conservatives' for the 1959 election (see above, pp. 48–9).

The *Must Labour Lose?* survey and Labour's use of polling before the 1964 election impressed one Research Department officer, James Douglas, and he in turn persuaded the department's Director Sir Michael Fraser, to press for polling. In 1965 Central Office encouraged Humphrey Taylor, who had done some polling for the party, to set up a polling company, with the promise that the party would be a major client. The company, at first called Opinion Research Centre (ORC) and now Harris, has provided a continuous flow of research for the Conservative Party ever since. The work was conducted on a large scale for the 1970 election. Just as some Labour supporters of polling hoped that the findings would make the party more voter-oriented, so Conservative advocates correctly anticipated that surveys of attitudes towards personalities and issues would show that the party was appealing to too narrow a social group (i.e. the middle class and the elderly) and that local party leaders needed to be more outward-looking. The private surveys between 1968 and 1970 showed that even when the Tories had a commanding lead on voting intentions many of the people who defected from Labour still identified with the party. The surveys conducted after the surprise election defeat in February 1974 reported the voters' dislike of adversarial politics and widespread desire for a 'national unity' government, particularly among Conservative and Liberal supporters. The findings were encouraging for advocates of the 'national unity' message for the second general election that year (see p. 56).

For some years now the Conservative party has also made use of Gallup omnibus surveys. Aggregating monthly Gallup surveys produces a sample of 9,000 voters, large enough to be broken down for detailed analysis by regional, socio-economic and other categories. In addition, in 1989 and 1990 the party employed the American consultant Richard Wirthlin to oversee an ambitious survey of the values of voters (see below).

Pollsters as Advisers

Like any professional who advises politicians the pollster has to tread carefully. Their advice can be rejected. Labour's pollster (for six elections MORI) has often faced three particular problems. The first has been the lack of a clearly defined single client, a consequence of the party's organizational complexity. Labour's polling agency is formally employed by the NEC (which pays the bill), although the main support for the polling has usually been found in the Parliamentary leadership and the leader's office. In the 1970s and early 1980s Labour's NEC contained a powerful left-wing faction which was hostile to polling and reception of MORI's work was affected by the endemic rivalry between the party's left and right wings. In 1979 Norman Atkinson, the party Treasurer, informed the NEC, 'Twenty members of my general management committee and I can do a better job [than polls] of assessing public opinion'. (A young fellow left-winger, Neil Kinnock, interjected, 'Norman, why do you need the other twenty?')

A second difficulty has lain in the potentially explosive consequences of some of the poll findings. They have usually, although not always, been depressing for the left, and party leaders from Gaitskell to Blair have used survey evidence to promote policy changes unwelcome to it, for example, on public ownership and defence. Long-standing critics of polls, like Tony Benn, have claimed that by reporting opinion as it is – largely moulded by an anti-Labour mass media – rather than as it might be after a campaign, the polls impart a conservative bias to politics and are used to put the left on the defensive. As chairman of the NEC publicity committee, Benn instructed MORI in 1973 to discontinue questions about the popularity of politicians (he was unpopular). Harold Wilson told the pollster to continue and convey the findings to him alone.

Finally, Labour's pollster has also had to cope with the party's traditional suspicion of all polling (and advertising). In 1960 a Labour frontbencher condemned the Conservative use of public relations as introducing 'something into our political life which is alien to our British democracy', and others claimed that it was pandering to the voters' materialism and abdicating a party's role in leading and educating public opinion. After all, it was the job of professional politicians and party activists to 'know' what voters really wanted – even if the latter were not always able to know or express their 'real' preferences. Other critics have claimed, variously, that the private (like the public) polls report the obvious, do not measure 'real' attitudes, are too expensive, or are not as reliable as the traditional sources for tapping grass-roots opinion. An extreme example of this kind of thinking was the remark of the party's General Secretary in 1981 that if he wanted to know what the public thought he would consult the agenda of a trade union meeting. Some of Robert Worcester's post-election reports to the party on the polling convey this sense of frustration. In a post 1979 election report he complained that MORI, 'was unable to fulfil its function of tracking and analysing British public opinion for the Labour party – to the same degree that was possible during the two 1974 campaigns'. After the 1983 election he referred again to the limits imposed on the pollster's potential usefulness 'because of the late start . . . in working for the party during the run-up to the elections . . . . An expenditure of the *same amount spread over the year and a half before the election* would have been money well- and much better-spent . . . money [was] used as an excuse by those who don't want *any* research *at any price*' (Butler and Kavanagh 1984: 146: original emphasis). The situation improved for the 1987 election.

But the Labour party in general and the leadership in particular were certainly receptive to polls in the aftermath of the 1983 and 1987 election defeats. Survey evidence and election results showed that the party had drifted so far from the views of its potential supporters that it was a matter of urgency to bring the two into some kind of convergence.

Until the mid 1960s Central Office advocates of polling faced a mixture of opposition and indifference which, according to a study of the 1966 election, 'stemmed from a lack of understanding, partly from a diffuse sense that for a political party to commission surveys would be somehow immoral. The feeling that there was nothing new to be learned by these means was also widespread' (Butler and King 1966: 66). But since then the party has been more consistent in support for private polling. The elitist party structure gives the leadership great authority to decide strategy and if the pollster has the leader's ear then this helps the task. The party's support for public relations and absence of strong left/right ideological factions have also made it more receptive to survey research than Labour. Harold Macmillan displayed a disdain in public for opinion polls but in private was keenly interested in them. In the late 1950s he wrote a memo to the party's Research Department asking, 'Who are the middle classes? What do they want? How can we give it to them?'*

Polling organizations submit programmes of research and budgets to party headquarters. Labour's pollster (and the party leader) has usually had to battle for funds from the NEC and until 1987 usually got them very late in the day. An exasperated Harold Wilson raised private funds in 1974 to pay for private polling by MORI (Falkender 1983: 163), something which no successor has been prepared to do, and Mr Callaghan was denied funds by the NEC in 1978. During the 1987 election campaign Conservative and Labour each spent about £120,000 on polls; during the 1992 campaign the Conservatives spent about £250,000, Labour £200,000. Had the Conservatives continued with the Wirthlin research (see below) the costs would have increased considerably. Apart from their private work for the parties all these polling organizations have specialists who conduct other political polling (mostly for the media). Most of their market research is for

---

* But a reader of the memo thought that Macmillan's questions were partly rhetorical: 'I think he expected us to produce arguments to demolish the then current demand for concessions to the middle-class. He was such a complex character that it is impossible to be sure' (Douglas interview).

commercial clients and political polling is only a small part of their total survey operations. But polling for the parties, particularly a winning one, had been prestigious and may attract business from elsewhere. ORC achieved fame as the only polling agency to predict a Conservative win in 1970, and MORI was given a commercial boost by its association with Labour in the two 1974 election victories. In the United States political polling is a bigger business. Clinton's polling adviser, Stan Greenberg, claimed to have spent over $125 million on surveys and focus groups in 1992 and that 'there was no limit to research spending' (Bauman and Herbst, 1994: 124).

Private Poll Uses

Private polls have several potential uses for a party. These include:

Election timing

In choosing the most advantageous time to call an election, Prime Ministers consider public opinion polls and such other data as local elections, by-elections, the state of the organization, economic indicators and specially commissioned private polls. It was only when large private surveys confirmed the handsome Tory lead in the public polls that Mrs Thatcher was prepared to call elections in 1983 and 1987. Polls may also dissuade a Prime Minister from calling one. A gloomy private poll in marginal seats in the summer, confirming pessimistic reports from party organizers, was a factor in dissuading Mr Callaghan from calling an election in October 1978.

But the message of the private polls is not always heeded. Ted Heath ignored polling evidence that he would win an election in January 1974 (see p. 55). Over the summer in 1991 it was widely expected that John Major was planning an election for October. An encouraging private Harris national poll and a survey of marginals in August 1991 were disbelieved by the Conservative Chairman, Chris Patten. His doubts were confirmed when the public polls soon showed a good Labour lead. In February 1992 private polls in the marginals showed that Conservative support had declined but Mr Patten advised Mr Major to go to the country; the government had, anyway, virtually run out of time.

Image building

A party's image is a matter of public perception. Do voters view it as being united or divided, having strong or weak leadership, standing for one section of society or for all classes, being more concerned about unemployment than inflation or vice versa, being 'strong' on defence and law and order or 'caring' on social issues? The image is largely the product of a party's record and the voters' experiences over a lifetime, but it can also be shaped by communications. Polls are an important guide to the voters' perceptions. In 1966 Conservative private polls showed that the party was regarded as old-fashioned and out of touch, following thirteen years in office from 1951 to 1964. These findings were used to support the decision to concentrate publicity on the party's new policies and leaders (Edward Heath had replaced Sir Alec Douglas Home in 1965). When the Shadow Chancellor, Iain Macleod, complained that the party was burdened with too many policies, Edward Heath replied that the opinion polls 'show that people think we have run out of ideas' (Ramsden 1980: 252).

Private polls were important for Labour in educating the leadership about the reasons for its negative image and why it performed poorly in the 1987 election – fears about unilateralism, the trade union connection, the 'loony left' image of some Labour local authorities and worries that a Labour government would lead to higher inflation. Changes in policy and communications strategies were designed to improve the image.

The messages prepared by a party's advertising group are more likely to be influenced by qualitative than quantitative research. Advertising agencies prefer to conduct qualitative research with small 'focus groups' to gain a deeper understanding of the voters' mood and ideas for messages. Before the 1992 election Labour's Shadow Communications Agency relied upon such discussions with floating voters in marginal seats to prepare strategy and again to analyse the reasons for the party's defeat. Philip Gould, the Agency co-ordinator, said after the election: 'Underneath the voting figures there was no enthusiasm for Labour, even when we were in the lead. I think they were never going to vote Labour. The focus groups conveyed a different message from our daily polls. I think many people were never going to vote Labour, even when they said they were' (interview).

Policy

British parties insist that policy-making is separate from publicity and that polls are used to help in presentation not formulation of policy. In the United States the distinction is not so hard and fast and a pollster's assessment of public opinion may influence the policy positions of the candidate. In Britain the politician's authority is jealously guarded. Humphrey Taylor, the Conservative party's first pollster, described his task as 'a communication of already decided policies and the presentation of the party itself' and he claimed 'only a marginal influence on the Conservative Party'. According to Robert Worcester:

> I characterise the responsibility I have as one of bringing witness to the ripples, the waves and the tides. If the Labour party leadership wants to swim against the tide of public opinion, that is their responsibility. I see my role as telling them which way the tide is running and how strongly, and then I stop. (1977: 8)

It is probably wise for a pollster who wishes to have a long-term relationship with a party not to drop names, claim influence or be closely associated with a faction in the party. The standing of the politician in Britain may also depend on not being seen to follow the polls.

Taylor's private polls, however, certainly contributed to the Conservatives' decisions between 1970 and 1973 to increase old age pensions and introduce pensions for the over-80s and, despite the opposition of many party activists, accept local authority proposals for comprehensive education in state secondary schools. The sale of council houses to tenants did not start with Mrs Thatcher in 1979. Private polls for the Conservatives in Greater London Council elections in 1967 found that the idea was popular and the Conservative ruling group implemented the policy. Labour's private polls have usually been a force in encouraging leaders to soft-pedal nationalization and to be 'moderate'. At the very least, the surveys should inform a party about its agenda – which of its policies the public supports and it should project, and which it should try to defeat. In elections since 1979 Labour's favoured issues have been social welfare and unemployment, its weak areas tax, leadership and economic management. The

Conservatives have trailed on social issues, particularly health, but usually scored in the areas of leadership and the economy. One Conservative has succinctly described the two main parties' image: 'Conservatives, hard head and a hard heart; Labour, soft head and soft heart'. Since 1979 it has paid electoral dividends to be on the hard-headed side.

Tracking

Until 1983 both parties conducted daily polls during election campaigns, largely to warn them of potential weaknesses or point to opportunities. The Conservatives discontinued daily polls in 1983 on the grounds that the findings were not properly absorbed under the pressures of an election campaign. In the 1992 election Labour was the only party still monitoring the changing salience of issues and themes during the election campaign. They do this by regularly monitoring replies to 'which party is best at handling . . .?' for a range of issues – 'What has impressed you favourably or unfavourably about each party's campaign?' – as well as asking questions about the parties' images, which one is 'slanging' or making 'promises the country can't afford' and election broadcasts. Conservative daily polls in the 1970 election asked 'If there is an economic crisis, which would you want to handle it – a Labour or a Conservative government?' The Conservatives faced a 5 per cent deficit on the question at the beginning of the campaign, drew level a week before polling and moved into a lead of 4 per cent two days before the election. The trend was one source of Ted Heath's public confidence. Before and during the 1992 election Labour's campaigners wanted to fight on the health and education issues. But they also knew that it was crucial to narrow the Conservative leads on economic competence and leadership. In the last three days the party's private polls showed that there was a significant slippage in the number of voters agreeing that Labour was competent, would make people better off or provide a better future.

The daily surveys are too small (around 500) to be reliable guides to voting and the emphasis on speed means that the number of questions has to be limited. In the 1992 campaign the Conservatives commissioned four large polls which were available for the weekend strategy meetings of senior politicians and campaign managers. Regular questions were asked about the NHS, taxation, leadership and tactical voting (Conservatives were worried about a Liberal upsurge) if the election was likely to be close. But rarely are busy campaign managers and hard-pressed politicians able to do much about these findings.

Targeting voters

Surveys are important in identifying the interests and concerns of the targets of campaign broadcasts and advertising. Before 1964 the parties had tended to concentrate propaganda on their 'solid' voters. Subsequent surveys were important in showing how many voters were volatile and potentially detachable from the two main parties. Private surveys are now used to divide the electorate, broadly, into 'ours', 'theirs' and 'uncertain'. Both parties usually concentrate on potential 'floating' or voters who may switch. In 1992 Labour drew heavily on focus groups of potential floaters and weak Conservatives to identify the key issues. Conservative strategists similarly sought to recapture those 1987 supporters who had or were thinking of defecting.

Changing the party

Private survey findings may be used in internal party politics. They were important in easing the Labour party's acceptance of Neil Kinnock's move towards the political centre after the 1987 general election defeat. Although other events, particularly the series of election defeats, were more important in opening the minds of party influentials to the need to change policy, the surveys were useful as an educative tool *vis-à-vis* critics or for supporting an already chosen course of action.

Values

Labour and Conservative have been moving towards surveying the values of the electorate – another example of Britain following the USA. Sophisticated computers have helped researchers to apply complex multivariate techniques of analysis to the data. But the expense involved in conducting a large number of lengthy interviews has limited the development of such work. From late 1990 to the dissolution of Parliament in 1992 NOP provided Labour with quarterly surveys of the voters' values and their perceptions of the party's strengths and weaknesses. At the same time, the Conservatives drew on the advice of President Reagan's former pollster, Richard Wirthlin, to prepare an ambitious study of the electorate's values. He claimed that although a voter's preferences about the personalities and policies of the day might fluctuate, his or her underlying values were more stable. A party that could understand and, to some extent, shape these values, would be well placed to develop an effective communications strategy. The research required a large number of time-consuming (and expensive) in-depth interviews in which a panel of voters talked about their values and major concerns. The panel of voters could be re-interviewed periodically and changes in values and issue preferences tracked. Once the data was available campaign strategy could take account of changes in values and, at a more modest level, the research could suggest persuasive phrases and themes for speeches and party communications.

The Wirthlin connection developed out of contacts between senior Conservatives and Republicans in the Thatcher–Reagan period. In the US Wirthlin's research enabled him to categorize voters into different value groups, so that the campaign communications could target voters more precisely, according to their location, social status, religion and other characteristics. Conservatives hoped he could do something similar for them. Mrs Thatcher encouraged the work and sat through some Wirthlin presentations in 1988 and 1989. But when in 1990 she resigned as leader and Baker was removed from the chairmanship of Central Office the research lacked strong support from people in key positions. Some Cabinet ministers and the new Chairman, Chris Patten, thought that the work stated the obvious: 'It's a waste of time telling a busy Cabinet minister that he must give people "hope" or a sense of "belonging". And how do you do it in a recession?' (interview). In 1990 ministers were too preoccupied with political difficulties, particularly the unpopular poll tax, rising inflation and the threat to Mrs Thatcher's party leadership, to concentrate on the electoral implications of Wirthlin's research. There were also complaints that it cost too much (nearly £1 million in 1990 alone) and that it was too American-centred for use in Britain. Patten terminated it in early 1991. The episode is an illustration of a difference in outlook between some British politicians and most American candidates.

Brendan Bruce, whose departure as Director of Publicity from Central Office coincided with the termination of the Conservative party's contract with Wirthlin, remains a believer in the American's research. He has written that 'the party that first grasps the true importance of Wirthlin's work and applies it to the British political process will win an enormous advantage over their opponents, and greatly increase their chances of gaining power' (Bruce 1992: 86).

Influence of the Pollsters

The influence of the private pollster on a party's campaign is contingent not constant. Compared to regular members of the party machine, the pollsters are outsiders who are recruited for their expertise in a particular area – monitoring and interpreting public opinion. This is a source of both their strengths and limitations. At meetings they bring some objectivity to what is essentially a partisan and in-group gathering. Mark Abrams reminded Labour leaders before 1964 about the materialistic aspirations of the party's working-class supporters (e.g. for home ownership), Robert Worcester in the 1980s told campaign strategists of how many voters were alienated by the party's unilateral defence policy, and the thrust of Humphrey Taylor's surveys before 1970 reminded Conservative leaders and officials to appeal 'not to their own ilk but to the mass of ordinary people who might be expected to vote Labour' (Butler and Pinto-Duschinsky 1971: 197).

The closeness of a pollster to the party's strategic thinking is likely to vary with whether the party is in government or opposition. Ministers are busy and tend to be more concerned to implement and justify existing programmes than to test the popularity of new policies. The party machine – to whom the pollster reports – also tends to take a back seat when the party is in government. Although other factors affect the closeness of the relationship it is interesting that the Conservatives mounted their most ambitious survey programmes in the two periods of opposition since 1966, and did little polling between 1970 and 1974. Labour's major use of polls was during the opposition periods 1962–4, 1972–4 and 1987–92. Little was done for the 1966 and 1970 elections and only a modest amount for 1979, when the party was in government.

One can certainly point to cases where the private polls have had some influence in affecting the balance of a campaign decision. Survey research was used after 1987 to educate the Labour Party on the need to change its policies and image for the 1990s, and this paved the way for the major review of policy. Mr Kinnock was also encouraged by private and public opinion polls in 1991 to edge Labour towards electoral reform. Labour's decision to campaign on health and accuse

the Conservatives of attempting to 'privatize' the NHS was reinforced
by survey evidence, as were Conservative attacks on Labour on tax and
spending and the decision to target Neil Kinnock's leadership. But the
surveys were not decisive.

It is possible to exaggerate the influence of the private polls and of
private pollsters in British elections. Often they are not well integrated
into a communications campaign, certainly less than appears to be the
case in the United States. The expensive Wirthlin research did not
convince Conservative Cabinet ministers who were primarily concerned with running their departments and it was not systematically
linked to government communications. Presented in spring 1991 with a
MORI poll which showed public support for proportional representation (PR) John Major rejected it. And when the other parties favoured
greater self-determination for Scotland and, according to the polls, so
did the public, he again was not impressed. He calculated that on both
issues many voters did not have considered views and would respond to
a clear dismissal of them. Early in the 1992 campaign NOP found that
46 per cent of voters favoured the introduction of PR, with 20 per cent
against. But exit polls for both the BBC and ITN showed that more
voters now preferred the status quo than a change to PR. Mrs Thatcher
had similarly rejected survey evidence which showed the unpopularity
of many of her privatization measures, health reforms and the poll tax.
Indeed, private Harris polls showing the unpopularity of the poll tax
were dismissed by the party Chairman, Ken Baker, as 'unhelpful'
(Waller interview). MORI private polls (like public polls) showed
Labour leaders throughout the 1970s how unpopular were the trade
unions; the public perception was that the unions were run by
extremists and were damaging the country. It all fell on deaf ears.

No pollster in Britain has ever achieved the political influence of the
Americans, Pat Caddell, Richard Wirthlin or Stan Greenberg, pollsters
who were involved in the details of their Presidential candidate's
campaign strategy and subsequently moved into the White House to
help shape the President's communications. Caddell's research and
advice were important in stimulating President Carter to give fireside
chats on television, and make a televised address about America's
'national malaise' and 'crisis of confidence' in 1979. American pollsters
are really campaign consultants to many candidates and expect to have
an influence on the campaign, deciding which issues and themes are to
be promoted and how the candidate is presented. Indeed, candidates
are often kept at arm's length from campaign decisions and only

marginally involved in strategy. According to Luntz, 'Dependent on professional consultants, candidates have become less involved in decision-making in their own campaigns, sometimes appearing more like spectators than participants in the electoral process' (1988: 14).

Reflecting on her experience as a speechwriter to Presidents Reagan and Bush, Peggy Noonan complained:

> Polls are the obsession of every modern White House and every political professional. In every political meeting I have ever been to, if there was a pollster there his words carried the most weight because he is the only one with hard data . . . I felt that polls are now driving more than politics, they are driving history. (1990: 249)

Far from developing into a campaign consultant like his or her American counterpart, the pollster in Britain has if anything been marginalized over the past 30 years. The explanation lies in large part in the different contexts in which the pollster operates in Britain and the United States, particularly the more programmatic and disciplined character of British political parties (see chapter 10). In the United States most of the private polling is done for candidates who are much freer to take independent issue positions. The broadcasting medium in the United States is also a spur to polling: it allows candidates to buy time and much survey research is geared to the creation of television advertisements. Moreover, in Britain party leaders, their assistants and party officials are much less willing to be seen to be influenced by opinion pollsters and advertising agencies; they also jealously guard their 'turf'. Mark Abrams in 1964 was closely involved in the preparation of the Labour party's campaign publicity, as was Humphrey Taylor for the Conservatives in 1974. This has not been true of any of their successors in either party. Direct access to the party leader is limited. No pollster for Labour has been part of the key strategy group around the leader since Robert Worcester in 1974; thereafter, he was rarely part of the inner core of campaign decision-making. He pointed out his inadequate access to the leader and lack of information about the party's campaign plans and the limits these imposed on his usefulness. No Conservative pollster since Humphrey Taylor last polled for ORC in 1974 has had much access to the party leader. In the 1992 election, NOP's material was reported first to Philip Gould who then presented it to Labour's campaign committee, and Harris's findings were presented to John Major by Chris Patten.

During the 1992 election campaign the head of the NOP, Nick Moon, did not meet Neil Kinnock, and Robert Waller of Harris met only twice with John Major, on both occasions as part of a large group. British politicians jealously guard the decisions about campaign strategy and 'most politicians anyway think they have a direct line to the voters' (Patten interview). Pollsters in Britain are not campaign consultants; they are on tap, not on top.

Pollsters have their own personal and political baggage and this can be a hindrance in a factionalized party. Mark Abrams's access to Wilson was limited because he was seen as having been close to the late Hugh Gaitskell and after 1966 the communication team wanted a pollster who was detached from the party. Robert Worcester, a registered US Democrat, suffered in part because some Labour officials and politicians were simply jealous of his high profile as a pollster and media commentator. Personal relations are also important; suspicions that a pollster is boastful or indiscreet will exclude him from the party's inner circle. In the United States few well-known pollsters work with either party; most strongly prefer to work for a candidate whose ideology they find congenial (Luntz 1988: 51). No British pollster has yet worked for more than one party, although Robert Worcester, once his relationship with Labour ended, informally advised some Conservative managers on polling and strategy before the 1992 election. Earlier, in 1981, at a time when it was not clear that he would continue to work for Labour, he had also had discussions with some Conservative officials about working for the party. ORC and Harris have always worked for the Conservatives since 1965. Since 1962 Labour has employed four different agencies to conduct its private general election polling.

The message of the private polls is more likely to have an impact if it is consistent with other signals about public opinion, is reinforced by events or supports the party's existing policies and values. Politicians are more likely to be persuaded if the polls confirm their other sources of information and their own prejudices. Richard Crossman was surely not alone when he confessed that he believed the polls only when he agreed with them. One of Labour's communicators claimed that 'Polls seldom tell you something that your conscience does not tell you. But they can be useful when people disagree about public opinion. We needed them to put the Bennites in the party on the back foot' (Barry Delaney interview).

Understanding of opinion polls varies among politicians and officials. Of party leaders since 1966 perhaps only Mr Foot and Mr Callaghan have shown indifference to the parties' standing in the polls during an election. Mr Wilson, Mrs Thatcher, Mr Kinnock and Mr Major were particularly keen to learn the latest voting figures. In 1992, Mr Kinnock was also an avid reader of the 'verbatims', the comments made by voters in the course of focus group research. 'That way I can get behind the figures' (Kinnock interview). Some judge the private pollster after the election according to the accuracy of his prediction – even if he did not make one. Some still demand, literally, 'good news', or get excited in the campaign over small and statistically insignificant shifts of opinion. However unfairly, the private polls, like the party machine and political leadership, often become enveloped in the recriminations following election defeat. This has regularly been the fate of Labour's pollsters. Yet the identification of electoral weaknesses is surely crucial to learning the lessons of defeat. Labour's qualitative research into the 1992 election defeat was pretty damning. Lengthy interviews with 'soft' Tories in the south-east (a key target if Labour is to win next time) showed that the party had failed to overcome the alienation that had grown over the previous two decades; it was regarded as hostile to 'success', 'getting on' and to people realizing their material aspirations.

Politicians and officials also differ in their expectations of the pollster. Some expect to receive just the polling figures, while others look for the figures to be accompanied by suggestions about what to do on the basis of the findings. The difficulty for the pollster is that his or her clients are not always consistent in their expectations. Many politicians appear to regard polls as background information, something to read like a newspaper article, and most of them have their own theories about electoral behaviour, which may relate to the weather, the feeling of prosperity, ideology, time for a change and so on. Mrs Thatcher and Mr Kinnock were more likely to be affected by personal experiences than by survey findings. After the election, Mr Kinnock claimed that he had sensed defeat in the last days of the 1992 election – 'it was just a feeling' (interview). Mrs Thatcher, according to her political secretary, was more impressed by a constituent's letter or personal account of a problem than a poll (Sherbourne interview). And many politicians still refer to the size or warmth of an audience at a public meeting as an indicator of public mood. In both parties one still encounters some suspicion about the whole business of sampling and professional communications, as well as politicians who prefer in the end to trust their own judgement of the voters' mood. Such scepticism may increase after the performance of the polls in 1992.

Yet sustained exposure to the private poll presentations has probably contributed to an improved understanding of electoral behaviour among politicians and officials – which was an aim of some of the advocates of the polls thirty years ago. The pollster, with the perspective of an outsider, may remind the committed partisans of how remote many of their concerns are to the ordinary voter. Strategists may now use evidence where they once relied on hearsay and other impressions. Reports from the grass roots are also more likely to be considered with a more discerning, even sceptical, eye.

Conclusion

Private polling is now a fixture of elections. Politicians and campaign managers need research to devise an effective communications strategy and to monitor it. After defeat they need good evidence of what has gone wrong electorally. In both parties the growing reliance on opinion polls, private and public, as indicators of the public mood has undermined the importance of feedback from constituency agents and activists. At a time of declining membership in both parties party activists may be increasingly unrepresentative of voters.

There are, however, several reasons why private polls sometimes fail to be absorbed into the campaign machinery. Campaigns certainly have their elements which are planned and co-ordinated; yet from the inside they can also appear messy and rushed, with many actions resulting from accidents and failures of communications. One suspects that a lot of private polling material simply gets 'lost' in the overload of information (this may also be true of policy-oriented research). The other problems apply to surveys in general. They may show that voters want policies which are inconsistent or which a party finds politically 'impossible', or they may be compatible with quite different interpretations and programmes of action. Here is a limit on the party's ability to act on the basis of polling – the lack of a tried and tested model of effective campaigning. If a party's favoured issue is of low salience, one may as readily interpret this as a basis for emphasizing it as for ignoring it. If a party's policy is unpopular should one campaign to make converts or not talk about it? As one frustrated politician commented: 'The polls may give us information about problems but they do not tell us how to solve them'.

7

USES AND LIMITS OF POLITICAL MARKETING

The previous chapters have shown how during the last three decades professional communication methods have gradually been adopted by the major political parties. One indicator of the acceptance of professional communications is that no major British party would now dream of entering an election campaign without a communications strategy and advice from professionals. This chapter considers the implications of these changes for the conduct of elections and for the parties. In particular, it considers:

1 The many claims and counter-claims advanced about the political effectiveness of the professional communications approaches.
2 The claims that negative or 'attack' campaigning is successful and has increased as a consequence of the new methods.
3 The predictability of campaign strategies, as the 'logic' of modern campaign methods means that the parties are able to anticipate the themes raised by their major opponents.
4 The relationships and tensions between communications professionals, party officials and British politicians. Have the pollsters and advisers achieved the kind of influence that their counterparts enjoy in the United States?
5 The effects of the new campaign approaches on the parties.

Effectiveness

It is possible to exaggerate the electoral impact of the package of polls, broadcasts, speeches and advertisements, compared to political factors, events or economic conditions. One has to acknowledge at the outset that professional communicators have a vested interest in encouraging the media to highlight their contribution to a campaign, not least to persuade parties that they have received value for money. An election campaign provides great visibility for a polling or advertising agency and association with the winning side can be good for business. Saatchi's advertising for the Conservatives in the 1979 election made it the most famous agency in the country and MORI's polling for Labour in 1974 greatly enhanced its visibility as a polling agency.

There is also an audience for the claims. The mass media are increasingly interested in behind-the-scenes stories about the parties' campaign strategies and techniques, the role of 'private' polls and advertising and how the parties handle the media. The interest in the process as much as the substance of the campaign usually results in the impact of the communicators being exaggerated, with journalists often attributing too much to them for a party's success or failure. This is marked in the US but noticeable in Britain also. One needs to recall, however, that the political position of the Conservatives was so strong in 1959, 1979, 1983 and 1987 that it is difficult to imagine that the party would have lost the elections even had it not campaigned at all. During 1992 the Labour campaign was widely praised by the media and the Conservative one widely criticized – until the result was known! The warning of somebody who was closely involved with Conservative election communications between 1968 and 1974 is salutary:

> My general impression is that hindsight is now applied so vigorously and quickly to everything that takes place in the professional communications world that if there is such a thing as reality and truth, it is almost immediately obscured, if not buried, through interpretation, by those who stand to gain in terms of ego or, dare I suggest it, materially from the record. (Letter to author)

Some politicians are sceptical of the communicators' claims that their techniques shift many votes or decide elections, perhaps regarding them as a comment on the politicians' own prowess. Other politicians reject the techniques on the grounds that they talk down to voters, over-simplify the issues and pander to popular prejudices. Many commentators, however, particularly in the United States, express concern that some politicians, in spite of their disclaimers, connive at being sold to voters like a bar of soap (Nimmo 1970; McGinniss 1970; Gold 1986; Spero 1980; Schnudson 1984). What is the truth of the many claims made for and against the impact of political advertising?

In spite of the research we still do not know how effective political advertising is (e.g. Broadbent 1981). Studies of television political advertisements in the United States suggest that they have some effect on heavy viewers, the less partisan and the more apathetic (McClure and Patterson 1974; O'Shaughnessy 1990: 61–2) and in elections which have a low turnout. The problem, however, in any such measuring exercise is that there are several other influences on the outcome, many of which have nothing to do with the campaign; surveys of voters also have limitations because voters themselves may not be able to articulate fully the reasons which have led them to their decisions or be reluctant to admit the influence of an ad. Barry Delaney, who has written television scripts for Neil Kinnock and ads for Labour, claims 'You can't measure its influence. It's part of an overall communications process and you can't isolate the effect of an ad' (interview).

One advertising agent with some experience in political campaigns claims that his colleagues usually exaggerate their achievements:

> because they do not understand the broad forces that affect political behaviour. You cannot claim that electoral success is due to advertising. All the basic points about a product or the party must be in good shape. And even then the reasons for the voting decision may be due to history, personal experiences or perceptions of the records of the government and the opposition. Advertising men are not always very sophisticated about politics. (Tim Delaney interview)

Others are more modest. According to John Bartle:

> Advertising can be a catalyst but it has got to be picked up by the press, has to go with the grain and ultimately depends upon the nature of the product. On its own it can do very little . . . Much advertising is self-cancelling. There is disillusion with politicians and this is compounded by negative advertising. As more is spent the advertising is probably less effective. (Interview)

Sir Tim Bell echoes this theme: 'As I look back on the campaign ads I have worked on, I do not think we changed anything. All we could do was reinforce a mood' (interview). David Kingsley, having advised Harold Wilson in three elections, agreed: 'I always said we could not invent attitudes. But we could take attitudes already there in the electorate and try to enhance them. That is why "Thirteen wasted years" or "Yesterday's men" worked' (interview).

Communicators, understandably, look for proof that their campaigns have, if not delivered victory, then at least helped in achieving it. Sometimes they point to their party's improvement in the opinion polls, more often the evidence is in the form of anecdote, say praise from a top politician or a journalist. In 1987 and 1992 Philip Gould, of Labour's Shadow Communications Agency, claimed that Labour's communications initiatives had driven the Tories onto the defensive, in 1987 forcing them to spend more money on press advertising, and in 1992 keeping the Tory tax campaign off the front pages of the press for several days, because of the Jennifer's ear broadcast.

Survey evidence suggests that some scepticism is in order about the claimed power of political advertising. The Labour campaigns in 1987 and 1992 gained high marks and the Conservative campaigns low marks from commentators. Voters, perhaps influenced by the media, agreed. After the 1987 election the magazine *Campaign* commissioned the research group, Mass Observation, to report on voters' assessments. It found that voters thought that Labour provided the best election broadcasts and the Conservatives the best press and poster ads, although most could not recall any party advertisement at all. A MORI survey in the *New Statesman* (24 July 1987) found poor scores for all the Conservative communication efforts and good ones for Labour. Yet such a fine campaign, which attracted applause from the commentators, added less than 4 per cent to Labour's share of the vote compared to the disastrous 1983 campaign. Neil Kinnock's much praised election broadcast produced a marked short-term improvement in his own standing but not in the party's electoral support. Labour's image, particularly its association with strikes and left-wing extremism, was something that the party's communicators wished to change, and opponents to exploit. But that image was the product of history, particularly the voters' experience or perceptions of the 1970s and the winter of industrial disruption in 1979. By 1992, after a Parliament in which the Conservative party had been visibly divided over Europe and the poll tax and experienced a traumatic leadership contest, voters still perceived Labour as being the more divided party. In spite of the economic recession voters still regarded Labour as less economically competent than the Conservatives. After the 1987 election Labour's Philip Gould said: 'We could change their minds, but not their votes; that takes four years not four weeks' (interview). After 1992 he realized that even four years was not enough (see p. 107).

It is also possible to lose sight of the ultimate purpose of all campaign communications – to win votes. Communicators can point to more indirect benefits of their efforts – such as changing perceptions of the party, improving the morale of party workers, getting the voters to think well of the party, dominating the agenda and providing a demonstration to contributors of how their money is used. But in the polling booth people do not vote on which party or leader has campaigned best or which party has run the most attractive advertisements – indeed only 1 per cent and 2 per cent of voters admitted that they had been influenced by press ads or posters in 1983 and 1987 respectively. John Sharkey, who handled the Conservative campaign in 1987 for Saatchi, commented: 'Advertising is meant primarily to be a persuasive act and should actually achieve a change in people's voting, buying or thinking patterns' (interview). He echoes an American's blunt statement that a political campaign, unlike a commercial one, culminates in a 'one-day sale' and that an advertisement that does not gain votes 'simply isn't a good ad' (Sieb 1987: 152).

The weakening of political partisanship, the less efficacious socializing role of parties and social changes have increased the scope for effective campaigning. The effects, in terms of reinforcing or, more rarely, changing political attitudes and behaviour, may be significant in a close-run contest. Uncertainty is a great stimulus to effort and innovation. But the extensive literature on communications effects, and the interviews cited in this book, suggest that the electoral impact of political communications is modest. Election campaigns are rarely able to overcome the prevailing climate of opinion; on the contrary, they must work with it.

The Case of the Liberals

The Liberal party presents a test case of the effectiveness of the new techniques, for it largely does without them. In the House of Commons its handful of MPs (a postwar high in 1983 of 23 out of 650 MPs) means that it has little presence or opportunity to exercise influence in

Parliament, and between elections it receives minimal media coverage. Shortage of finance in turn precludes any ambitious opinion polling or advertising. The party headquarters operates on a shoestring and has little control over the constituencies. Such relative poverty and lack of an infrastructure make the party an unattractive client for any major polling or advertising agency. Moreover, an agency knows that it is not going to be associated with a winning Liberal party.

Some part of the Liberal appeal has of course been that it is unlike the main parties; out of office for so long it can hardly be held responsible for national failings, and it can voice a principled distrust of political power. Many local Liberal activists and councillors tend, understandably, to be more interested in local than national politics and are more concerned with particular causes than with achieving power at Westminster. Most Liberal MPs have been elected as prominent and independent local personalities in their own right. This in turn limits their incentives to respond positively to campaign instructions from the national leadership.

The shortcomings of such an approach were apparent in 1987, when the party tried to fight a national campaign. The Liberals had formed an Alliance with the Social Democrats and entertained realistic hopes of overtaking the Labour party in popular votes. But the lack of discipline was seen in the way in which the two separate party leaders, David Steel and David Owen, went their own ways in the election campaign, frequently contradicting each other and ignoring strategic instructions from the centre. The Alliance campaign was the least orchestrated of any party's. The leaders made no attempt to set the agenda, there was no clear definition of the purpose of the Alliance and the organization was, in the words of one of its leaders, 'a shambles' (Pardoe 1989). The advertising agency employed for the election found the experience dispiriting and one of the publicity team referred to 'the Alliance's non-advertising campaign' (Carroll 1989: 91). Indeed, neither of the agencies employed in 1983 and 1987 'would willingly undergo such an experience again. The briefings were cloudy and confused; the budgets were too small and uncertain; the politicians meddled with the creative work; and everything was done too late, too hurriedly, without a guiding strategy or vision' (Fletcher 1990).

Yet, in spite of such disadvantages and an inability to employ modern campaign methods on anything like the scale of the other parties, the main third party has managed to attract an average share of 20 per cent of the vote in the last six general elections. Since 1959 it has seen its share of the vote, according to the opinion polls, increase during every campaign, other than October 1974 (when it started at a high level) and 1987. It receives virtually no media coverage between elections and then, because of the rules about party balance, a sudden boost for the four weeks of the campaign. Free television coverage has been virtually the only 'modern' resource which the party has drawn on. Harrop's warning that 'the limited electoral impact of press advertising is suggested by the growth in support for the Alliance during the [1983] campaign, despite the complete absence of any Alliance advertising in the national press' (1984: 212) may apply to other techniques as well.

Negative Campaigning

The media coverage of campaigns regularly deplores the politicians' alleged neglect of great issues – for example, the slight attention paid to the environment, starvation in the Third World, Britain's role in the European Union – and the reduction of many issues to party knockabout. 'Parties fail to rise to the challenge' is a frequent theme of editorials. The negative campaigning or 'knocking copy' communications is often condemned as yet another undesirable import from the United States, although in that country it is largely directed against the 'character' of opposing candidates (Sabato 1981: 265–74). Surveys also show that voters claim to dislike negative campaigning.

But such campaigning may work in the right circumstances e.g. for a party or candidate trailing in the polls, or for an incumbent candidate or government party with a less than impressive record. A striking example of such a campaign was the 1988 American Presidential election, when the National Security Political Action Committee ran the infamous Willie Horton advertisement for the Republicans. The television ad stated that the Democratic candidate Michael Dukakis had, as Governor of Massachusetts, allowed a convicted rapist, Horton, out of prison on parole, and on his release Horton raped again. It addressed public concern over law and order, was designed to show that Dukakis was 'soft' on crime and has been credited with transforming Bush's position in the polls. The proportion saying that the government was not 'tough enough' on crime and criminals rose from 23 per cent to 61 per cent between July and October, while the proportion saying that Dukakis was not 'tough enough' rose from 36 to 49 per cent. Marjorie Random Hershey's conclusion on the Horton ad campaign was 'It would be hard to find more convincing proof of the efficacy of attack politics. The campaign did make a difference' (Pomper 1989: 96).

Such messages gain in potency because the controversy they generate ensures that they are frequently carried and discussed in news programmes. They become a 'newsad' – a 'segment of news that might as well have been paid candidate advertising' (Jamieson 1992b: 133). They are also likely to affect the tone and language in which the issue is discussed – in turn, reflecting the values of the ad. A good example of this was seen in Britain in the 1980s when the Conservatives and sympathetic tabloids publicized some of the more controversial activities of local authorities controlled by Labour's left wing; the label 'loony left' was widely associated with the local parties and councils.

The most celebrated negative advertisement to date has been the so-called Daisy spot run by the Johnson campaign in the 1964 Presidential election against his right-wing Republican opponent, Barry Goldwater. In the advertisement a little girl is picking petals from a daisy and miscounting '. . . 4, 5, 7, 6 . . .'. As the frame freezes on her face and closes in, her voice is replaced by a military one, counting down, '10, 9, 8, . . .'. At the stroke of zero an explosion is heard, a mushroom cloud appears and President Lyndon Johnson's voice declares: 'These are the stakes: to make a world in which all of God's children can live, or to go into the dark'. The advertisement reminded viewers of Goldwater's reputation (although it did not mention his name) as an impulsive, trigger-happy man who might destroy the world. It proved to be so controversial that it was withdrawn voluntarily, but not before it had given massive publicity to the Democrat charges that Goldwater was a warmonger.

The effectiveness of any campaign, negative or positive, depends in the end on the voters' willingness to accept the message, which in turn depends on their predisposition. Tony Schwartz, the creator of the Daisy ad, commented: 'Commercials that attempt to tell the listener something are inherently not as effective as those that attach to something that is already in him' (cited in Gold 1986: 148). Without Goldwater's warmongering reputation and public concern about the nuclear issue, the Daisy advertisement would not have been so effective. Without the public concern about law and order and stereotypes among some people about blacks, the Horton message would have had less impact.

To date, British parties have not indulged in personal attacks or emotional appeals to anything like the degree of American campaigns, largely because they calculate that public opinion would reject such an approach. In 1970 Labour's Denis Healey strongly objected to his party's use of the 'Yesterday's men' poster attacking Conservative leaders (see p. 83), on the grounds that it broke a long-standing understanding between the parties to shun personal attacks. In February 1974, Conservative leaders immediately regretted running a hard-hitting election film broadcast (see p. 55). In 1979 Mr Callaghan rejected suggestions by staff that he attack Mrs Thatcher, which he thought beneath his dignity (see p. 88). In 1983 Roy Jenkins, the Social Democratic leader, vetoed the use of hard-hitting ads attacking the two main parties ('Don't you think there's a better choice?') by the party's agency. Roger Carroll, who helped with speechwriting for Labour's Jim Callaghan and then for the leader of the Social Democrats Roy Jenkins in 1983, commented wistfully: 'Senior British politicians are uneasy with negative campaigning' (interview).

The refusal of the British broadcasting authorities to carry the 20- or 60-second 'spot' advertisements – which in the US are the vehicle for most of the personal attacks – is another important barrier. Short ads can convey only simple messages and such a format may lend itself more easily to attacks than positive policy statements. In the United States the parties do not promote sharply defined national programmatic choices and primary contests within the party are almost inevitably personalized; hence the personal nature of many of the 'spots'.

In 1992 the Conservative campaign was widely criticized in the media for relentlessly attacking Labour's taxation proposals, rather than promoting the party's own policies. The Conservatives in 1983 and 1987 had been criticized for their attacks on Labour's defence and economic policies. All three campaigns were also unpopular with the public and, in 1987, with Mrs Thatcher, who felt that the campaign was not 'positive' enough, that it did not highlight her government's achievements (see p. 63). Conservative campaigners have two lines of defence against charges of negativism. The first is to blame the media for its reporting of the election, for portraying the election as a 'battle', in which the parties attack and counter-attack. Campaign leaders in Britain seem to believe that a 'positive' approach, e.g. reporting a list of a party's achievements or proposals for future policy, receives scant media coverage. In other words, the media influence the style of campaigning. According to Chris Patten, 'In 1992 we started off with training and education and then the next day the manifesto and got no coverage. When we attacked Labour we got coverage and were criticized for being negative' (interview). According to Neil Kinnock, 'After our experience in 1992 I'm sure that negative campaigning works' (interview).

Research into media coverage of campaigns in the United States shows that it is the negative advertisements and attacking parts of a candidate's speech that are most heavily reported (Jamieson 1992b). Analysis of the media coverage in the Nuffield studies of the last three general elections and work conducted in 1992 by the Communications Research Centre at Loughborough University suggests that this is true also for Britain. Some 40 per cent of the media coverage of the Conservative campaign was devoted to attacking the other parties, compared to 37 per cent of Labour's coverage and 43 per cent of the Liberal Democrat coverage. The television headlines were rarely positive; reports of speeches 'warning', 'accusing', 'attacking' or 'rejecting' comfortably outstripped those 'promising' or 'offering' (Harrison 1992: 162).

The second defence is that the Conservative campaigns worked in 1983, 1987 and 1992 because they tapped existing unease about Labour. According to Labour's Communications Director for the 1992 election, 'The negative campaigns only worked because we had so much baggage from the past. We had supplied the Conservatives with a lot of ammunition' (Hill interview).

In the absence of similar evidence for earlier elections we cannot establish if there is a trend towards more negativism. But campaigns in the past have hardly been models of reasoned discourse. Before the extensions of the suffrage and the introduction of laws against corruption in the late nineteenth century British elections were marred by intimidation, bribery and outrageous personal attacks. In this century the forged Zinoviev letter in 1924 was a classic anti-Labour scare. During the 1931 election National Government ministers ruthlessly whipped up fear of Labour. The Prime Minister Ramsay MacDonald waved a fist of worthless German paper marks before an audience as a warning of what inflation would do, and a colleague claimed that a Labour government would raid the savings of Post Office depositors. In 1945 Churchill broadcast his famous 'Gestapo' warnings about what life would be like under Labour. In 1951 the *Daily*

Mirror powerfully evoked Winston Churchill's warmongering reputation by asking on its polling-day front page 'Whose finger on the
trigger?' over a photograph of a man with a cigar, in half-profile. An
analysis of the speeches of party leaders in the 1970 election reported
that Harold Wilson devoted 75 per cent of his script to attacking the
other parties, 20 per cent to defending his government's record and
5 per cent to proposals for the future. For Mr Heath, the opposition
leader, 70 per cent was devoted to attack and 30 per cent to the future
(Robertson 1971). All this may suggest that negative advertising is
the old campaign tactic of adversary politics packaged in modern
communications technology. But in commercial advertising, however,
there has been a general dislike of knocking ads. Richard Rose's study
of the subject observed that 'the maxim of the advertising world is that
advertising should concentrate on the positive virtues of the client'
(Rose 1967: 51).

Labour's 'Jennifer's ear' broadcast in 1992 was probably the most
emotional political broadcast yet made in Britain and Chris Powell, a
Labour communications adviser, suggests that such ads might be the
way of the future. 'It was interesting and emotional. It took a nerve end
about the health service, people's fear about the universality of the
NHS, and twanged it' (interview). The broadcast was designed to
contrast the different treatments given to families able to afford private
health care and those relying on an underfunded National Health
Service. But Labour's charges of 'unfairness' and underfunding were
soon overtaken by the media questioning about the truth of the claims,
reporting the identity of the little girl suffering the ear infection and
speculating over who leaked her name to the press. The story was
transformed from health to the ethics of the broadcast (see p. 182 for
press treatment) and Labour appeared to be the loser.

What is interesting, however, is that Labour's big poll leads on 31
March occurred four to five days after the furore had faded. The polls
also showed that the salience of health as an issue increased, stories
about health and waiting lists dominated regional news broadcasts
and regional newspapers and, for a time, the issue prevented the
Conservative tax attack from dominating the news. A campaigning
objective for a party is to use broadcasts and advertisements to
generate a major controversy on its own agenda. Defenders of the
broadcast argued that what was needed to retain the initiative was a
follow-up in the final week. There was a plan that Robin Cook, the
Labour spokesman on health, would bring the issue to the fore again by

launching a 'scare', based on a true-life health scandal. But Mr Cook chose not to do so. He was unhappy about the broadcast (notably the failure to gain the prior agreement of Jennifer's two parents) and the row that followed, and felt that Labour was losing public support. The communication specialists and, apparently, Mr Kinnock favoured the follow-up; other Labour politicians and officials did not and their rejection of attacking campaigning carried the day.

Some of the criticism of negative campaigning misses the point. In any campaign, be it in politics or commerce, the communicators have to strike an effective balance between attack and defence. An important part of a communications exercise for a political party is to put a negative gloss on the record of its rivals and point to their past mistakes and incompetence – a tactic that has not until recently been allowed in commercial advertising. Campaign managers want to focus on the political alternative as defined by them rather than by the rival party. A party also understandably wishes to emphasize the contrast – to its advantage – between itself and the other political parties.

What emerges from my interviews is the belief among campaign managers that negative campaigning works. In the United States this has become part of the lore of professional consultants. One verdict is that 'They argue that since the ultimate goal of any campaign is to win, any strategy that seems to work well should be used; if negative campaigning is to stop, then the electorate must stop responding more readily to negative than to positive messages' (Foster and Muste 1992: 20). Many advertising executives think that in politics the necessary succinctness of an advertisement means that it is easier to promote a negative message about the opposition than a positive one about their own side. British advertising executives point out that the most memorable ads in recent elections have been negative, e.g. 'Yesterday's men', 'Labour isn't working', 'Labour's double whammy', 'Labour's tax bombshell', 'Vatman'. They also complain that many politicians who criticize negative advertising do not understand it. According to Sir Tim Bell, negativism is not new but is an application of one of the two basic models in political advertising:

> One is 'Time for a change' in which you try and heighten dissatisfaction with the government of the day. The other is 'No time for change' in which you ask people not to trust the opposition. We have to understand that in real life most people don't take risks. Often they are making negative decisions, be it about not changing jobs or not changing houses

because it will cost them. This is not so much disillusion with politics as a realistic outlook on life. (Interview)

Winston Fletcher, who helped the SDP with its advertising, also did not regard negativism as new. But it was effective: 'Positive advertising does not work because all parties favour the same goals – peace, prosperity, better welfare services, safe streets and so on. The challenge is to say *how* they will achieve and that is too complex for an advert' (interview). But others claimed that political communications have changed in recent years. According to Chris Powell:

> Knocking adverts work. People are so disillusioned with politicians that you can't convince them of your good points. But they are prepared to believe that the other lot are worse. . . . political advertising has got to show that things are going to be worse under the other side. People are so fed up with politics that you are now pushing at an open door. If they have doubts about the other side you have to make people hold them even more strongly. (Interview)

John Sharkey, who ran the Saatchi campaign for the Conservatives in 1987, spoke in a similar vein:

> Politics is of low interest to people. That is why you cannot be positive. People are not interested in following the complicated claims that politicians make to defend their record. Voters will follow their instincts and discount a party's claims about its achievements. You have to address voters' fears. You cannot persuade voters that they live in a nirvana or that politicians can deliver it. Essentially, you say 'Vote Labour and all hell will break loose'. People can understand this. (Interview)

An interesting post-election survey finding in 1992 was the response to the following question by MORI: 'Thinking about the way you voted, which was stronger, your liking the party you voted for, or your dislike of the other parties?' By 55 per cent to 37 per cent people said that it was dislike rather than liking that decided their votes in 1992. Here, perhaps, is a large part of the answer to the question posed by Ivor Crewe: 'Perhaps someone might explain . . . why the best advertising is negative when opinion polls consistently report that people say they want an end to slanging matches' (Crewe and Harrop, 1989: xv).

But why this popular disillusion with politicians and parties? Compared to the past is there more disappointment with the outputs of government? Are politicians now regarded as less trustworthy or less effective shapers of policy and outcomes? Is the tendency towards more negative attitudes in news reporting cause or consequence of the public disillusion, or a bit of both? There is evidence in the United States that exposure to 'negative' or 'attack' advertising increases voters' cynicism about politics and the electoral process (Ansolabehere, Iyengar, Simon and Valentino 1994). Investigative journalism, which was boosted in Britain as well as the United States by the Watergate scandal, is constantly on the lookout for political scandals, real or imagined. In both countries party managers' more blatant attempts to manipulate the media have produced a reaction among reporters. In the US the reporters appear to be more critical of the main candidates as a means of demonstrating that they are not beholden to them (Graber 1989). Journalists may also assume a 'disdainful' approach to the parties, seeking to expose for readers and viewers the media strategies of the parties. The effect of such 'unmasking' may be to increase cynicism among voters. In other words, 'negative' campaigning by the parties is complemented by negative election reporting by journalists (Patterson 1993). Barry Day, who worked on the 1970 and two 1974 Conservative campaigns, elaborated:

> The media are now elevating so many people and then try to debunk them when they are over-exposed. This is happening to sports stars, soap personalities, the Royal Family and politicians. Clinton, for example, is now being destroyed in a way that Kennedy would never have been. The heavy coverage of celebrities means that they have a limited shelf life; people become bored more quickly. Moreover, the media knows that bad news makes headlines in a way that good news does not. Negative political advertising is also easier. You can see that the other side is making a mess of it. (Interview)

What was not recognized in my interviews was the possibility that the political advertising, by accentuating the negative, may be contributing to a general disillusionment with politics.

Anticipatory Campaigning

The parties take elaborate precautions to maintain the security of their campaign plans. The Saatchi team in 1992 had special locks fitted to doors and safes in the top-floor offices of their headquarters in Berkeley

Square. Agencies and volunteers assure the party that work on its campaign is limited to sympathizers with the party; copies of strategy documents are numbered and marked 'Personal and Confidential'; and a low profile is usually assumed by those working on the campaign. (The low profile also reassures politicians that they are in charge and that the communicators do not get ideas above their station.) Each party is pretty successful in maintaining security, in the sense of preventing leaks about its plans. But it has had little or no success in preventing the opposition from correctly anticipating its communication strategies.

Both Labour and Conservative communication teams routinely research their own and each other's weaknesses, when exploring the reasons why people will or will not vote for a party. After all, the opinion polls and focus groups are telling all parties the same thing. 'To write about your own side's image weaknesses means that, in effect, you are writing your opponent's strategy', commented one Labour communicator. Most governing parties project one essential message, asking voters to let them carry on, to finish the job, not to risk change. This was the explicit appeal of Labour governments in 1950, 1966, 1970 and 1979 and of the Conservatives in all elections since 1979. The tactic is hardly new. It was also reflected in Baldwin's 'Safety first' campaign in 1929 and Churchill's ('Help him finish the job') in 1945. The opposition invariably says that it is time for change. In 1964 Labour fastened the 'thirteen wasted years' label on the Conservatives, just as in 1979 the Conservatives pinned 'the winter of discontent' on Labour, and both oppositions exploited the mood for change. Incumbents play on a mixture of satisfaction and fear of change among voters, oppositions play almost entirely on dissatisfaction. Each side therefore has a good idea of the other's hand and how it will be played.

This was clearly seen in 1992. Both Labour and Tory campaigners regarded the key voters as 'soft' Conservatives or those who had voted Conservative in 1987 and defected. Labour could not win without attracting a large number of them and the Conservatives would win if they could regain a substantial proportion. In 1987 and 1992 both teams knew that taxes, economic management and defence were weaknesses for Labour and that health, education and 'fairness' were weaknesses for the Conservatives. Each anticipated with reasonable accuracy the lines of attack the other party would develop.

Some of the similarities in the parties' private planning documents are remarkable. In May 1991 Saatchi & Saatchi found it difficult to write an advertising strategy for the Conservatives. By appearing to accept Labour's criticisms about the limits of markets the government was fighting on Labour's ground. The agency argued that rather than compete with Labour in projecting a 'caring' image the Conservative party should return to its traditional strengths – in economic management – and link this with improving public services. At the same time Labour's communications team was writing: 'There is clear evidence that the electorate believes that the post-Thatcher Conservatives have lost direction and consistency. Shifting to the 'middle ground', while paying lip service to the Thatcher revolution has led to an impression of government indecision and muddle'.

Research by both parties into the reasons people offered for not voting Conservative in the general election showed that many feared that a further term of Tory rule would result in a 'privatization' of the NHS. This charge had been effectively made by Labour in the Monmouth by-election in June 1991, when health rose in salience as an issue and Labour captured the seat. Conservative denials of any such agenda were not believed, according to surveys, and Labour continued with this line of attack before and during the general election. In late 1991 when Saatchi floated the idea of demonstrating the government's commitment to the NHS by earmarking one or two pence of the standard rate of income tax for the health service, Chris Patten dismissed it as a gimmick. Yet, at the same time, Neil Kinnock was privately urging a similar policy on John Smith. Saatchi wanted to protect the Conservatives on health, Kinnock to advance Labour's lead on the issue (see above, p.103).

Conservatives regularly cost Labour's programmes – based not only on the party's manifesto (which in 1992 deliberately limited its spending plans) but also on party conference resolutions, statements from Labour's frontbenchers and party policy papers – and then ask, 'Where's the money coming from?' In 1987 the total spending plans were costed at £34 billion which, it was calculated, would involve a 50p standard rate of income tax. In January 1992, in spite of Labour steps to deny opponents any opportunity to attach a price tag to many of its proposals, the Conservatives repeated the exercise and produced the 'Tax bombshell' advert, claiming that the proposals would cost the average family an extra £1,250 a year in income tax. Labour responded with an effort to cost the amount of money stemming from the government's policy mistakes but this gained little media coverage.

In November 1991 the Conservative Communication Director,

Shaun Woodward, included in his strategy document for party leaders a discussion of what he called *Labour's Election Surprise*. He forecast that Labour would, in the closing stages of the campaign, declare support for proportional representation. Woodward referred to polls earlier that year which indicated that such a step would be worth an extra 2 or 3 per cent of the vote for Labour. Indeed, Neil Kinnock had already received private polling advice to this effect and was slowly edging the party towards such a step – which he took in the last week of the campaign (see above, p. 105). Conservative strategy documents also claimed that Labour would run a human interest or tragic health story in the campaign, as they had in 1987, and ministers and party officials warned friendly newspaper editors against this. Labour acted as expected in the campaign.

Within a few days of John Major replacing Mrs Thatcher as Prime Minister, Labour's Philip Gould predicted that the Conservatives would now be able to satisfy the voters' desire for change. The Conservative campaign would run on the slogans of 'You can't trust Labour. You can trust Major' and 'We have made the change', and on the themes of choice, ownership, low taxes and decent public services. Labour's communications team also anticipated the kind of attack the Conservatives would launch on Kinnock and Labour and the costing of Labour's programmes. They would claim:

'Labour is the party of high taxation.'
'Labour's team does not have the experience.'
'Labour would be run by the trade unions.'
'Labour is economically incompetent.'

Tensions between Politicians and Communicators

Professional communicators sometimes co-exist uneasily with politicians and party machines. Their advice, like that of civil servants or party officials, can be taken or ignored by politicians. Just as private pollsters are often kept on the outside, or apart from direct contact with the party leader, so also the communicators are often kept at a distance. In both parties, all advertising copy and most election broadcasts (because of disorganization at the centre, Labour's in 1979 were an exception) are subject to high-level political approval, sometimes involving the party leader. Campaign advisers to Harold Wilson and James Callaghan had no doubt that final decisions were made by the party leader. Wilson vetoed the publicity plans on the eve of the 1970 election and in 1979 Mr Callaghan refused to deliver the hard-hitting speeches his office had prepared. One speechwriter recalled: 'His wife said to him, "You have built up a reputation over thirty years. Don't let these young men destroy it". He was convinced he would lose and wanted to do so with dignity' (Carroll interview).

Speechwriters often commented in interviews about party leaders rejecting drafts as unsatisfactory. 'It's not me' was one Thatcher form of rebuff to speechwriters. Mr Kinnock complained of having to write much of his own speeches because drafts 'however good in themselves, were not me' (interview). Barry Day welcomed this attitude: 'It is when politicians do not have beliefs that the consultant fills the void, as in America. My view is that if the best thing Ted could say was the best thing that I could write, then we were in trouble' (interview). Ted Heath and Margaret Thatcher had their own views about election broadcasts and, in the latter's case, advertisements in 1987 (see p. 63). In 1983 a Saatchi advertisement, featuring Michael Foot as an old age pensioner, was dropped on grounds of taste or political calculation, and Labour leaders vetoed a proposed advertisement in 1979 (see above, p. 89). According to Sir Tim Bell, Mrs Thatcher was uneasy about jokey advertisements: 'She did not want politics reduced to entertainment. If you are too jokey you might trivialize the message. And she would sometimes veto an advert, just to let you know who was in charge' (interview).

Communications specialists may have an expertise like that of a dentist or engineer. Politicians, however, are more likely to challenge the advice of the former than of the other professionals, largely because they consider themselves also to have some expertise in communications. An index of a communicator's importance is his or her access and proximity to the party leader. The party leader determines the relationship and it depends on the perceived usefulness and friendship of the communicator. Tim Bell had regular access to Mrs Thatcher in 1983, and he and Sir Gordon Reece did so in the 1987 election, even when they had no formal position in the party's campaign structure. Both were personal friends as much as advisers. For example, Mrs Thatcher relied on both in her leadership election campaign in 1990 and they warned her that she would have to do something about the poll tax. On the other hand in the 1987 election Saatchi personnel had no direct meetings with Mrs Thatcher ('Everybody was terrified of her. Only Tebbit could see her, and even he was terrified', said one Saatchi

Director), although in 1992 Maurice Saatchi was a regular member of the small Conservative daily strategy group, which John Major convened immediately after the party's morning press conferences. Harold Wilson regularly relaxed with his communications advisers (see above, p. 82). But of Labour campaigns since 1974 only in 1987 did the communications team have close contact with the party leader, although the key link then was Peter Mandelson. Many members of the Shadow Communications Agency were frustrated throughout 1991 at the lack of interest in their work shown by senior Labour politicians, and by Mr Kinnock himself.

It is a ritual for politicians to declare that they will not be 'packaged'. For many it offends their sense of professionalism. Ted Heath rudely told his publicity advisers in 1969, 'I have better things to do than rehearse for television'; Neil Kinnock abandoned a video training course and often rejected draft broadcast speeches; and John Major early on signalled his determination to be himself by declaring, 'What you see is what you get'. During the campaign he frequently complained about the photo-opportunities which his staff had prepared. Communications advisers employed by the Social Democratic Party in 1983 found it frustrating, partly because of the involvement of many committees and partly because 'The SDP leaders suffered from a seemingly irresistible urge to rewrite other people's copy' (Fletcher 1990).

But politicians also think that publicity about their reliance on such help is bad for their image. To be seen to receive assistance with presentation may provide ammunition for charges that they lack principles and convictions and are being 'packaged'. The cynicism reported in McGinniss's (1970) account of the 'selling' of Nixon by advertising men in the 1968 Presidential campaign has left its mark. The politicians' line is that what they do and say is their own work. It is almost an extension of ministerial responsibility and the myth in British government that all initiatives come from the minister. The lesson therefore for modern Presidents, according to Nixon, is that they 'must try to master the art of manipulating the media not only to win in politics but in order to further the programs and causes they believe in; *at the same time they must avoid at all costs the charge of trying to manipulate the media*' (Nixon 1978: 354, emphasis added). When, in 1964, it was revealed that Sir Alec Douglas Home was being helped by speech-writers, Harold Wilson boasted that he wrote his own speeches, and Mr Callaghan scoffed, in private, at Mrs Thatcher's image-making.

This may explain why autobiographies by political leaders usually relegate the role of publicity advisers and speechwriters to a footnote. In his 1,000-page memoir of the 1964–70 government Harold Wilson (1971) makes no reference at all to his communications advisers, 'the three wise men'. In her 960-page memoir of her years at Downing Street Lady Thatcher (1993) gave four perfunctory references to Sir Ronald Millar, who helped her with countless major speeches, including all her party conference speeches, and only three to Saatchi. In interviews which David Butler and I have had with party managers and politicians over twenty years, the number who have acknowledged the importance of the professional communicators in elections can be counted on the fingers of one hand. A Conservative campaign planner advanced a number of reasons for the exclusion of Sir Tim Bell from the 1992 campaign, including: 'Tim's too high profile, he attracts too much attention. That was OK under Mrs Thatcher. Because John Major is a more retiring person Bell is not suitable' (interview).

The art of successful public relations may now turn on not being seen to be too packaged. In his contest with Kennedy for the Presidency in 1960 Nixon acknowledged that he had neglected public relations. He probably went to the other extreme in 1968.

In British parties the communicators have also been caught up in internal disputes and political rivalries. Criticisms of Conservative communications advisers in the February 1974 election stemmed from opponents of Ted Heath's policies and groups who felt that their campaign advice was ignored. But the advisers also felt that Heath was uncooperative. Geoffrey Tucker recalled:

> It is a very difficult task to deal with a party in government. Heath enjoyed being a Prime Minster and statesman more than he enjoyed being a party man and a television personality. He slipped back, he became more attached to the civil service than to the party and his television appearances showed this . . . The warmth and the contact died. Public relations in all its aspects took a backseat. When he called a snap election in February 1974 we were all unprepared. (Interview)

In 1986 and 1987 the Saatchi & Saatchi agency was a casualty of tensions between Central Office and Downing Street, which was receiving advice from rival agencies. Mrs Thatcher rejected the advertisements which Saatchi had prepared. 'She panicked', said one Saatchi executive. 'She behaved unprofessionally', said another. In 1992 Conservative party grass-roots critics of John Major and Central

Office complained of the expenditure on polling and advertising – 'we could have told them that', 'we live in the real world', were the reactions of some constituency agents and party workers.

Labour's advisers have more often been caught in battles between the party leader's office and the party headquarters and NEC. This occurred periodically for most of the elections held between 1959 and 1987, notably in 1970, 1979 and 1983. They have also had to contend with hostility to advertising among some members of the NEC. After the 1992 election defeat Labour's Shadow Communications Agency and private pollsters were bitterly attacked by left-wingers – 'beautiful people' in John Prescott's sarcastic phrase. The Agency was accused by NEC members and officials of taking over the campaign, deciding the polling questions, interpreting the findings and then deciding the subsequent communications strategies. In this case, some of the attacks were a lightning rod for dissatisfaction with Kinnock's policies, authoritarian style and marginalization of the left. 'Modernization' of the party, involving the dilution of many left-wing policies and an emphasis on professional communication methods, was regarded by critics as 'selling out' the party's values at the behest of the pollsters and advisers. Critics who had felt excluded by the leader and the unelected people around him, particularly in his private office and the Agency, now felt free to speak out. They were also emboldened because Labour had lost the election. Within 18 months of the election, the party had a new leader, had disbanded the Shadow Agency and turned to an advertising agency for its campaign needs.

Money adds to the tensions. Yet it can hardly be argued that the parties are financially exploited by pollsters or agencies. A party's budgets for polling and advertising are dwarfed by those of a big company. Saatchi & Saatchi have regularly provided a number of cost-free services for the Conservative party (in 1992, the agency did not charge for the services of its three senior executives who helped with the campaign) and the contributions of most members of Labour's Shadow Agency were given free. But for a party the cost is considerable and it looks at an agency's proposals and invoices with a suspicious eye. In 1983 the then Conservative party Chairman, Cecil Parkinson, cancelled a blitz of final weekend press ads, saving the party some £2 million and Saatchi forfeited a substantial sum in commission. There followed a protracted dispute over who should bear the costs of cancellation. In October 1991 the agency submitted two campaign budgets, one for £9.3 million (including £7 million for press ads) and one for £6.5

million (£4.1 million for press ads). The then Chairman, Chris Patten, doubted the usefulness of press ads (a source of continuing tension between him and the agency during the campaign), knew that the party had little cash, and in the end provided a budget of just £5 million. This was not big business for Saatchi, fighting its most difficult election campaign for the party. It might be compared with the £20 million publicity campaign for electricity privatization in 1990. In contrast to commercial clients the Conservative party has been slow to settle its bills with the agency; two years after the 1992 election it was still paying off the costs in instalments. 'Deep down, they (the party) probably think we should do it for nothing', said one Saatchi executive. The gains for the agency have to come as a 'spin-off', in the form of publicity, praise and prestige from being on the winning side.

Both politicians and professional communicators share an interest in persuasive communication. That may be one reason why there is often mutual suspicion between them. The professional communicators are usually more single-minded about defining objectives and proposing the most effective methods to achieve them. The advertising men that I interviewed thought that few politicians shared this outlook. Jeremy Sinclair, a Saatchi executive who has worked on all Conservative campaigns since 1979, says 'I am aware of this discipline when I go away to do a poster. I might have four words or perhaps ten words to say something. That teaches the art of condensation. Few politicians have this' (interview). According to Tim Delaney, who has worked with Labour:

> Politicians do not think in marketing terms. They like to think that it is their personal charisma or their speeches on a one-to-one basis or before an audience that decides elections. In contrast, advertising people objectivize the whole process, they ask what the objective is and then how we can achieve it. This means that the skills of the politicians are not so unique or special as the politicians believe. (Interview)

The professionals do not regard the politicians, as a class, as good clients. They often express disillusionment at politicians who regard themselves as communication experts ('For a politician a good party broadcast is one in which he appears. They are so egocentric'), and at the defensiveness of party officials who fear that their 'turf' is being invaded. With the exception of 1979 Stephen Sherbourne has worked at the centre of every Conservative general election campaign between 1970 and 1992. From 1983 to 1987 he was Mrs Thatcher's political secretary, moved to public relations and in 1992 he returned to work temporarily in 10 Downing Street for John Major. He suggests that all communications professionals have problems with politicians: 'because politicians think that they are the experts. They have stood for election, won votes, knocked on the doorstep. They may acknowledge that people like Bell and Reece are good, but they haven't done it like the politician has' (interview).

Barry Day has noticed a change over the past twenty years. Politicians may have accepted the need for communication skills and instant analysis 'but they resent it and they wish it were not so' (interview). Winston Fletcher agrees:

> Politicians are persuaders. They started out on the stump. Even when they follow the script of an advertising man, they resent it. They do not like being told what to say and how to say it. I wrote a broadcast for Roy Jenkins, when he was leader of the SDP. He had not reached the third sentence, before his pencil was out, editing it. Far from being profoundly influenced by image makers, the SDP leaders listened to them and usually ignored them. Often, with good reason, it must be added' (interview).

Barry Delaney observed at close quarters Neil Kinnock's reactions to advice: 'Once you become leader you are surrounded by image makers telling you how to win. But the leader will say to himself, "If I'm so bad, how did I get to be where I am now?"' (interview).

Another factor that makes for difficulties is that parties, particularly Labour and Liberal, are more likely than a business to involve lots of committees in making decisions. Fletcher claims that in the SDP 'The things that were achieved were done by individual politicians – by-passing the committees. This is the only way marketing can be carried out effectively by political parties – short lines of communications between the leaders and the doers'.

Lord Hollick, the businessman, was taken aback when proposals for Labour's campaign in 1992 were vetoed by politicians and officials on the grounds of 'not before party conference' or 'that's politically too difficult'. Compared with leaders in business or advertising he thought that too many politicians failed to focus on winning votes or to think strategically: 'Labour needs to become an efficient decision-taking body'(interview).

Politicians have their own complaints about advertising and polling specialists. One is about their political naivete. 'Advertisers are not always sensitive in recognizing what messages can blow you out of the water', said Shaun Woodward, the Conservative Communications Director in 1992. Some Saatchi advertisements for the party were rejected by Patten and Woodward in September 1991 as too hard-hitting. Policy suggestions by individual members of Labour's Agency in 1992 were also regarded by politicians as lacking political judgement, e.g. on taxation and electoral reform (see pp. 104–5) and health campaigning (see p. 105). Conservative Central Office was sceptical about the Saatchi agency's suggestions for last-minute press adverts in 1983 and again in 1992. Chris Patten resisted continued Saatchi pressure for a press advertising campaign, although some ads were eventually carried but paid with special subscriptions or heavily discounted by some friendly newspapers.

Some politicians deplore the emphasis upon soundbites, photo-opportunities, opinion polls and advertisements, claiming that they devalue the political process. Roy Hattersley complained after the 1987 and 1992 election defeats that Labour concentrated too much on the packaging rather than the product, and that the smart presentation in 1987 actually drew attention to the poverty of the product, i.e. policy. Labour, he argued, should devote more of its energies to being the party of ideas. Another Labour frontbencher after 1992 doubted that Labour's appeals to social conscience and calls for redistribution could be conveyed effectively by photo-opportunities and soundbites. In private, Chris Patten, John Major and John Smith have also expressed regrets about the trends. John Major, according to staff, would ask in irritation, 'Do I have to do this?', when photo-opportunities were scheduled in the 1992 election, and expressed unease about the negativism of the advertising. Patten would like to imagine a political world without polling, soundbites and advertising (interview). John Smith similarly was only a half-hearted convert to the new methods.

Sympathy and Commitment

In the United States, political consultancy is a business and, for many consultants, 'It's whoever gets to us first' (Sabato 1981). In contrast, British advertising agencies do not regard themselves as guns available for hire to the highest bidder. One reason why the BBH agency turned down the opportunity of handling the Conservative advertising account for the 1992 election campaign was because the directors found that not enough staff were sympathetic to the party.

As one considers the views of Sir Gordon Reece, Sir Tim Bell, Geoffrey Tucker, Maurice Saatchi, Philip Gould, Patricia Hewitt, Mark Abrams, Lord Lovell-Davis, Chris Powell and Tim Delaney one is struck by the extent to which they have all believed in the cause – political party or leader – they were working for. The idea of professionalism entails, in part, the advertiser's detachment from the client and the product being promoted. Detachment is necessary to consider evidence objectively, develop an effective strategy and react to events. But in election campaigns this detachment is usually combined with remarkable dedication and effort by the people involved in the communications. Professional communicators seem to regard elections as different from other campaigns, feeling that they can only work effectively in politics if they are true believers. They will work for one party, but not another one – that is almost like betrayal. This explains why so many give their services free or for a nominal fee. Sir Gordon Reece explained:

> You need to believe in a party. It is the only way that you can get other people in an agency to work so hard for it. At the end of the day you are leading them and therefore if you cannot convince them that you believe yourself they won't provide the necessary enthusiasm. (Interview)

For Labour, Les Butterfield recalled in an interview his despair after the party's election defeats in 1983 and 1992: 'I could either give up or become involved and do something about it, and decided on the latter'. He expressed his delight when in late 1993 his agency was appointed to handle Labour's communications. 'I'm doing the best job in the world – something I really believe in.'

In turn, each leader has his or her own favourite advisers. Mr Callaghan's team had no place for members of Mr Wilson's entourage, with the exception of Bernard Donoughue, the head of the Policy Unit. Peter Mandelson and Philip Gould, so close to Mr Kinnock between 1985 and 1992, were relegated to the background under John Smith. But they became key advisers to Tony Blair when he replaced John Smith as Labour leader in 1994. Similarly, Mr Heath and Mrs Thatcher had different outside advisers, even though key party officials and the polling company remained in place. 'We were Ted men and when he lost we were finished', said Barry Day (interview).

Consequences for Parties

What are the consequences for the parties of this professionalization of campaign communications? More bluntly, might the professionalization be part of a broader political agenda in which professional communication methods are a prelude to changing policy? Before tackling this topic it is worthwhile restating the *partial* extent to which the new methods have taken over the parties and politicians. The use of polling by parties remains modest, in comparison with the United States, has not grown impressively over the past twenty years, competes with other cues about the public mood and does not drive policy to nearly the same degree – though it certainly reinforced other pressures for Labour to ditch unpopular policies after 1987. The parties have become more self-conscious, even ruthless, in targeting their activities to the media (particularly television), although there are legal constraints on the extent to which the parties can gain access to television screens (see above, p. 12). Finally, the campaign suggestions of media professionals often have to compete with advice from other sources and take account of the values and traditions of the party, and the preferences and personalities of the party leader. We are therefore talking about a *partial professionalization* of election campaigning.

Some thirty years ago Otto Kirchheimer (1966) argued that in Western Europe *mass integration* parties were being transformed into pragmatic or *catch-all* parties. He claimed that the combined effect of social and economic changes, particularly growing affluence and secularism, and social and geographical mobility, meant that a party's support was being drawn less from strong adherents, voters whose partisanship was part of their social identity, often rooted in social class and religious allegiance. As the parties extended their reach in pursuit of voters across all strata, so the ideological and emotional ties between parties and their voters were being weakened. The trends were observable among parties of left and right – the Gaullist party in France, Christian Democrats in West Germany and Italy, the Conservatives in Britain, the Social Democrats in West Germany and a number of socialist parties. Among the catch-all features identified by Kirchheimer (1966: 190–1) were:

A reduction of a party's ideological baggage.
Attempts by the party leadership to strengthen its influence and autonomy *vis-à-vis* the mass membership.

A downgrading of the role of extra-Parliamentary bodies, such as the annual party conference.

A de-emphasis of specific group appeals by parties and a concern with promoting policies and themes that would appeal to the electorate as a whole, particularly the floating or less attached voters.

The use of opinion polls, advertising and promotion of the leader to enhance the party's electoral appeal.

A weakening of party – interest-group links.

These features are clearly at one with the 'end of ideology' literature at the time and echo Michels's analysis before 1914 of how electoral considerations led to the weakening of ideology and internal democracy in socialist parties (Michels 1962). Parties were beginning to commission electoral surveys in the late 1950s and finding a large number of voters who were detached from or weakly attached to the parties, had little interest in ideology and were more concerned with improving their standard of living. The changing style of party politics and the more consensual agenda were in part a response to social change, although the parties' methods and appeals in turn also encouraged the weakening of partisanship.

What has all this to do with British parties? There are several difficulties in testing the catch-all thesis and it is more usefully regarded as a vantage point for discussion, rather than as a well-developed concept. If we regard it as a vantage point we recognize that the Conservatives have long been something of a catch-all party. Party leaders often approvingly quote Disraeli's dictum: 'The Conservative is a national party or it is nothing'. Having captured most of the upper- and middle-class vote early in the century, leaders have reached out to the working class and shown great flexibility and even opportunism in doing what they regarded as necessary to win power (see above, p. 46). In the 1960s they certainly regarded the private survey findings as a means of educating local constituency organizers against the dangers of being a narrow middle-class party.

But the notion that there is a causal connection between a party's adoption of public relations and the decline of ideology hardly fits the Conservative party under Mrs Thatcher. Some of the Thatcher government's positions on trade union reform, immigration and law and order were certainly popular with the voters; surveys showed that they appealed to what political scientists have called populist authoritarian attitudes (Saalvik and Crewe 1983). The Conservative's electoral support since 1979 also fits in with the catch-all thesis, in so far as party support has been fairly widely drawn across the social classes, though geographically concentrated in the south-east. But many of the post-1987 policies, notably the reforms to the health service, poll tax and privatization of electricity and water services can hardly be said to have been driven by the opinion polls. The irony is that the high point in the use of public relations in British elections in the 1980s was exploited by the century's most ideological Prime Minister.

Labour presents a more complex case. In the beginning it clearly resembled the anti catch-all party. It had an ideology, appealed largely to one class and one interest and its constitution gave ultimate authority to the annual party conference, which represented the mass membership. The ways in which the Parliamentary leadership tried to escape from these constraints and emulate the Conservative party have been a matter of controversy (see Miliband 1961; McKenzie 1963; Kavanagh 1963). But since 1959 the changes have been, however unevenly, in the catch-all direction. Hugh Gaitskell certainly used surveys and analyses of the party's third successive election defeat in 1959 to force changes in policy, campaign methods and party organization. He was convinced of the need to educate all levels of the party to the electoral implications of social change and the bourgeois aspirations of the working class, and for the party to modernize itself. He took a number of steps in line with the catch-all thesis, including:

Questioning and weakening the authority of the annual party conference, on the grounds that it was unrepresentative of Labour voters.

Challenging the party's ideology, specifically public ownership, in Clause IV of the party constitution.

Placing more emphasis on electoral communications via the national media, rather than relying on detailed policy making and local activists.

Urging the need for the party to extend its electoral support beyond a diminishing working class.

His successor Harold Wilson continued, though less directly, with this approach. In the 1960s the authority of party conference declined steadily and the policy of public ownership was downgraded (Minkin 1980). During the 1970s and until 1983 the left and the conference regained influence and professional communicators were effectively sidelined. Neil Kinnock then embarked on a programme to modernize the party, one that gathered pace after the 1987 election defeat. The party made greater use of professionals in campaign organization, policies and communications were prepared with the aim of appealing to non-Labour voters, the leadership of Neil Kinnock became a key element in the communications strategy, increased reliance was placed on the mass media and public relations for communicating with the electorate, and the party edged towards a looser connection with the trade unions (Webb 1992). The evidence of survey research for the party throughout the 1970s and 1980s was that people wanted a party that they could trust, would improve their standard of living and was concerned with the interests of all people: class, ideology and the trade union connection, the buzz-words of the left, hardly figured. Surveys after the 1987 and 1992 elections echoed the message but also told the party the many things that people did not like about Labour. It had to move in the catch-all direction.

Conclusion

In spite of all their reservations and criticisms, politicians turn to modern communication techniques because they want to communicate more effectively with a mass electorate. Political campaigning has always adopted and adapted to the latest tools of persuasion. Using polls, television, advertising and public relations is just the latest stage. It is undeniable that politicians now campaign in a more orchestrated manner – re-stating, almost *ad nauseam*, the line of the day, the chosen phrases and particular themes – have a clearer idea of their target audiences and rely more on pollsters, consultants and media advisers. The journalists and producers covering elections for the mass media are professionals: they now confront politicians who are also assisted by professionals. The consequences of these trends for the mass media are considered in the next two chapters.

8

MASS MEDIA: THE PRESS

We have already referred to the important role of the mass media in earlier discussions of campaign strategy, communications and opinion polling. The press and television deserve some discussion in their own right, however. An election campaign encompasses a great variety of activities and events – speeches, rallies, press conferences, broadcasts, newspaper articles, opinion polls, party workers distributing leaflets and canvassing, and so on. To a large extent it is the mass media which integrates these diverse activities, defines the important issues and themes of the election, differentiates the positions of the political parties and assesses how well the parties are doing and, through the opinion polls, declares which side is winning. For most people the campaign is what is covered by the media. It has long been the case that the media are both reporters and actors in the political campaign. Politicians, however, appear to have become more sensitive than ever to the activist role of the media, particularly of television. Ministers in government, politicians in all parties, and pressure groups regularly use the media to promote policies and personalities, a process described by Franklin (1994) as the 'packaging of politics'. In this chapter we explore how the newspapers cover the campaign, the ways in which they set the election agenda, and, finally, how the parties in turn try to shape the coverage.

Covering the Campaign

General election campaigns are major occasions for the national press. Newspapers significantly expand their coverage of politics and the parties provide events for them to report and photograph. A general election for the political reporter is the equivalent of an Olympic Games for a sports reporter. A national newspaper will have specialist writers on the press conferences, media, opinion polls, a party or party leader, regional and constituency tours, as well as commentators who provide background and interpretative articles. It is difficult to think of any other topic that is guaranteed coverage, day after day, on the front page and several other pages.

Most political journalists follow a gruelling routine during an election. Many will rise early to scan the newspapers for reports and interpretations of the previous day's events and overnight developments. The reports may provide leads for the early-morning BBC *Today* radio programme and further stories and questions for that morning's party press conferences. In 1992 the Liberals held their conferences at 7.30 a.m., Labour at 8.00 a.m. and the Conservatives at 8.30 a.m. At the conferences politicians answer questions on the record; afterwards journalists try to speak privately to them and the campaign managers. The rest of the morning is often relatively 'quiet' as journalists catch up with a late breakfast, gossip and exchange impressions with other journalists, and check with their newsdesks on which reporter is doing which assignment. In the afternoon reporters may accompany a politician or travel on a press bus following the party leader on tour. Although the leaders' regional excursions are arranged primarily for the benefit of television cameras they also provide journalists with opportunities to mix freely with the leader and his entourage. Most non-front-page campaign stories for the morning newspaper are filed before 5.30 p.m., with the front page kept open for late developments and reports of the party leaders' evening rallies.

The broadsheets give much space to the columns of their political commentators. In 1992 Hugo Young in the *Guardian*, the late Peter Jenkins in the *Independent* and Peter Riddell in *The Times* regularly wrote think pieces about such topics as which party and politicians were doing well, which political issues were being ignored, what was the national mood and whether politicians were rising to the occasion. The academic David Butler was something of a pioneer commentator on polls in the 1960s, writing regularly for *The Times*. Today many broadsheets employ either academic political scientists or their own specialist reporters to write about the opinion polls.

Most papers take sides in the party battles and differ in their approach to reporting. A paper's support for a party does not, however, mean that it gives more space to that party. The trend among tabloids has been to devote more attention in features and editorials to the main party they oppose than the one they support. Of the pro-Labour *Daily Mirror*'s front-page lead stories and editorials in the 1992 election 27 were devoted to the Conservative party and only seven to Labour; for the *Express* it was 25 to Labour, 17 to Conservative; for the *Mail* 34 to Labour, 11 to Conservative; and for the *Sun* 25 to Labour and 13 to the Conservatives (Harrop and Scammell 1992: 188). The last three papers were all pro-Conservative. Most of the coverage of the opposition is of course 'knocking' copy. In 1964 and 1966 the pattern was very different. Then the *Mirror* gave twice as much coverage to Labour, the party it supported, as to the Conservatives, while the pro-Conservative *Express* and *Mail* devoted twice as much to the Conservatives as to Labour (Seymour-Ure 1968: 151).

It is interesting to note that press coverage of Presidential candidates in the United States has similarly shifted dramatically in tone since 1960, from a 'good news' coverage to a 'bad news' coverage. Although Vietnam and Watergate marked a stage when journalists turned against politicians, the news coverage has become progressively less positive with each election (Patterson 1993: 20–1). Has the trend to negative political coverage in the partisan national press paralleled the rise of negative advertising, or is the allegation about the growth of negative campaigning a judgement on how the campaign is reported?

The tabloids are the major vehicle for communicating the negative messages of both Labour and Conservative parties. Some idea of the relentless way in which the tabloids ran anti-Labour stories in 1992 is shown in table 8.1. Many of the stories reported charges made by Conservative ministers in speeches and press-conference statements but were carried in a more arresting style. A week before polling day Kenneth Baker, the Home Secretary, warned voters about the implications of Labour's policies on immigration and refugees. The following day the *Express* and *Mail* ran prominent stories on the issue and both papers returned to it on 7 April. Both also gave prominence to Baker's warning that proportional representation, which Labour was considering, would lead to political instability. Conservative Central Office had few problems in getting other themes aired in the tabloids, notably its attacks on Labour's tax plans or warnings that a Liberal vote might lead to a Labour government. Two of the *Express* front-page headlines in the final days echoed John Major's final speeches: 'Wake up Britain' followed by 'Don't throw it all away'. The *Mirror* was just as

Table 8.1   Negative press coverage of Labour (1992)

Date	Press coverage
16 March	
Express	Kinnock backs '83 manifesto
Sun	Kinnock admits he was wrong in the past
Mail	Kinnock backs '83 manifesto
26 March	
Express, Sun, Mail	Attack on Kinnock and Labour over broadcast
Sun	Will Kinnock ever tell the truth?
1 April	
Mail	Clive Hollick smear, Labour to increase taxes, Labour's CND cover up
Express	Labour's CND cover up, Labour and the unions, Labour's secret tax plans
Sun	Jack Straw three houses smear
2 April	
Mail	Beware the Trojan Horse, Labour and immigration, Labour poll lead shares slide
Express	Lib. votes will let Labour in
3 April	
Mail	Kinnock 'My errors', Labour tries to seduce Ashdown, 'Don't throw away the good life'
Express	Kinnock admits errors
Sun	Kinnock 'I've blundered', Harriet Harman's private school swimming pool
4 April	
Sun	'How Kinnock will crucify South-East'
Express	Major spotlights Kinnock's U-turns
Mail	'Car chiefs dread the cost of Kinnock'
6 April	
Mail, Express, Sun	All the papers lead with John Major's 'Wake up' call
Express	Six out of ten worse off with Labour tax plans
7 April	
Mail	Kinnock tax muddle and Heseltine: Lib. vote equals a Lab. government
Express	Baker's 'Migrant flood warning'
Sun	'Nazi riots in the UK'
8 April	
Mail	Mortgages threatened by Lab.
Express	Major warns of race riots, 'Mortgages up with Labour fear bosses'
Sun	'Trust Major', plus nine-page 'Nightmare on Kinnock Street'

much an echo chamber, notably on health, for Labour. Its eve-of-poll front page was headlined 'It's time for change' and the polling day front-page headline was 'Vote Labour'. But Labour and the *Mirror* could feel that it was an unequal struggle.

Tabloid coverage of an election campaign is distinctive in other ways. Compared with the broadsheets, tabloid journalism contains more entertainment and overt propaganda, relies more on bold headlines and presents simpler portraits of politicians as goodies and baddies. Seymour-Ure (1993) has shown how the tabloid papers simplify (often by ignoring, for example, minor parties, many issues and all but a handful of politicians); exaggerate (passing extreme judgements on parties and leaders); and make great use of graphics, particularly headlines. 'Headlines now sprawl over sparse text like beached whales', is Seymour-Ure's description of how developments in design and technology have driven words out of tabloids. Finally, the tabloids also indulge in personalization, a feature which is encouraged by exaggeration and simplification and thrives on graphics. In 1992 29 per cent of the *Sun*'s entire election coverage and 41 per cent of its photographs were devoted to the three party leaders.

Even the broadsheets report the campaign in adversarial or battle terms. Between a third and a half of the front-page lead stories about the campaigns in 1983, 1987 and 1992 in the *Guardian*, *Telegraph* and *Times* were highly adversarial. Many headlines featured terms like 'attacks', 'warns' and 'charges'.

Agenda Setting

For all the emphasis on television, the press remains important, not least as a source of stories for television which in turn may then be further developed by the press; the two media feed off each other's agendas. In the 1987 campaign three important stories developed as a result of the interaction of press and television and all harmed Labour (MacArthur 1989: 100–1). Neil Kinnock's television interview on defence with David Frost early on Sunday morning made little impact until it was picked up by the press in succeeding days. Some of the newspapers were tipped off by Central Office, which then exploited Mr Kinnock's stated refusal in the interview to use nuclear weapons in the event of a Soviet invasion. The Tory tabloids headlined the story for three successive days. On the Wednesday, the *Mail* front page ran

'Kinnock: the man with the white flag', and the *Express* had a virtually identical headline. Nigel Lawson, then Chancellor of the Exchequer, has reported how he provided analyses of Labour's tax plans for the *Daily Mail* and the *Daily Express* (see below, p. 191). These in turn were used by television interviewers to ask awkward questions of Neil Kinnock and Roy Hattersley, in different parts of the country, about how much extra income tax the average worker would pay under Labour. Their different answers were seized on by hostile newspapers. The *Sun* carried a front-page story about a private hip operation which the wife of Denis Healey, Labour's Shadow Foreign Secretary, had received several years earlier. The next day Healey was interviewed on TVAM and his discomfort was clear when he was questioned about Labour's attitude to private operations, a question which would not have been asked without the *Sun* story. His angry outburst to the interviewer when the programme was over was then carried gleefully by the Conservative tabloids.

The 1992 election provided perhaps the most dramatic case of the interaction of press and television, as both media followed up Labour's election broadcast about the NHS's delay in treating a little girl's ear complaint. For a day the main election story was how the *Express* and the *Independent* had acquired the name of the girl featured in the film. The press competed in interviewing the girl's parents, grandfather and consultant. This gave rise to major rows on the same day at Labour and Conservative press conferences, which were then covered in detail on television. In the same election a front-page story by the *Guardian* about the parlous state of public finances gave rise to some hostile questions at the Conservative morning press conferences and some coverage on television, but the impact was nothing like that of the stories in 1987. A problem for Labour in1992 was that any evidence of a potential economic crisis might be bad news for the government, but was not necessarily good news for Labour in view of its poor ratings on economic management. Party leaders and their media advisers complain in public and private that the Tory tabloids put them on the back foot.

'Pack' Journalism

Journalists are often in close proximity with political leaders and campaign managers. But they are in even closer contact with each other. They travel on the press buses which accompany the party leader and sit together at rallies and press conferences. This can encourage 'pack' or herd journalism among the pool of reporters (Crouse 1972). A kind of consensus is formed as they are exposed to the same speeches, interviews, press handouts and press briefings. The journalists also meet every morning at the parties' press conferences, talk with each other and compare their assessments. In spite of the competitiveness of journalists it is understandable that a certain view or 'story' emerges (Kavanagh and Gosschalk 1995). Writing about the 1964 election press conferences Butler and King (1965: 147–8) noted 'The assembly of the cream of the political writers every day in the same place produced something of an in-group atmosphere; the nuances of the campaign in Smith Square were far removed from the reality of everyday electioneering in the constituencies'. There is also a kind of 'safety' in a number of journalists broadly agreeing on a line. A journalist is sometimes pressed by his newsdesks to explain why his story or interpretation differs from other journalists'.

It is worth restating the crucial role of opinion polls in colouring journalists' assessment of the impact of a campaign. Until 1959 journalists reported the speeches of the party leaders and relied on a combination of audience reaction, visits to key constituencies and communications with party officials. But now the polls have become important in two respects. First, they are prominent items in the election news. In 1987 and 1992, although the polls reported very little movement of opinion, one fifth of all daily newspaper front-page lead stories during the election concerned opinion polls, more than the coverage for any other single topic. Second, they shape the 'line' among journalists of which party is ahead and inspire media analyses of the political implications of a party 'winning' or 'losing'. The leading party is described as 'confident', 'pulling ahead', the trailing party as 'struggling to recover ground' or 'falling behind'. Long before polling day stories are being written about who will succeed the defeated party leader, likely faction fighting and which heads are likely to roll because of the election defeat.

This phenomenon was seen clearly in the 1970 election when journalists accompanying Ted Heath were writing elegiacally about his campaign and about the brave but unconvincing way in which he dismissed the opinion polls. Throughout the campaign the message of the polls was bad for the Conservatives. At one stage the betting odds on a Labour victory reached 20–1 and the bookmakers refused to

accept any more bets. Questions at the daily press conferences and
much press comment assumed that a Labour victory was inevitable. In
turn, the journalists' expectations about the likely winner and the likely
loser affect their evaluations of the parties' campaign performance. The
leader is winning because he or she has addressed the right themes and
issues, been more skilful in the use of media, etc., while the loser is
losing because he or she is running a poor campaign. The Nuffield
study of the 1970 election reports a selection of commentators' verdicts
and they are presented here only to illustrate how universal were the
expectations of a Labour victory, largely because of the opinion polls
(Butler and Pinto-Duschinsky 1971: 165–6):

> Both party leaders are now recognising that only a bolt from the blue . . .
> can save Harold Wilson from becoming the first Prime Minister in
> British history to win three general elections in a row. (Nora Beloff,
> *Observer*, 7 June)

> Short of a miraculous turn-around in public opinion Mr Wilson is
> headed straight back towards 10 Downing Street, probably with an
> increased majority. (Ronald Butt, *Sunday Times*, 14 June)

> It will be no surprise to anyone to learn that I think [Labour will win] by
> a majority of 40 or 50 seats. (David Watt, *Financial Times*, 15 June)

> What will become of the Tories after a third successive poll defeat? Why
> is the Labour party winning with such apparent ease? (Peter Jenkins,
> *Guardian*, 15 June)

> It is too late [for the Conservatives] to recover lost ground. (David
> Wood, *The Times*, 15 June)

> Unlike the ORC, I am registered as a 'Do Know'. The Tories will have
> some gains but, as I have kept saying, Labour will certainly win. (Robert
> Carvel, *Evening Standard*, 18 June)

The same consensus was evident in 1992. The journalists' most
compelling election story is about who is winning and who is losing,
and this enables the opinion polls to have an almost hypnotic effect on
their assessments. The *Guardian*'s political commentator wrote 'It [the
electorate] looks like decreeing that now is the time for change'. The
Conservatives were behind in the polls; therefore, their campaign
strategy, organization, broadcasts and leaders were all poor; the
campaign was written up as lacking direction, energy or anything
positive to say. Shortly before polling day *The Times* and *Observer* asked
a total of 22 pollsters, commentators and academics to predict the

outcome. The great majority predicted that Labour would be the single largest party in a hung Parliament. Only two forecast a Conservative victory.

By the final week the polls pointed to a hung Parliament, with no one party having a clear majority. The story now concentrated on the consequences of a hung Parliament – the likely demands of the Liberals, the position of the monarchy, the precedents from previous hung Parliaments, what happens in other countries, what might be a Lib.–Con. or Lib.–Lab. programme, what circumstances would trigger a new election and so on. It was almost inevitable that Neil Kinnock's statement a week before polling day about extending the membership of Labour's working party on electoral reform would be analysed in this context and be widely interpreted as a 'bid' for Liberal support. On 3 April the *Mail*'s front-page lead story was 'Labour try to seduce Ashdown' and the *Sun*'s 'A vote for Paddy Ashdown is a vote for Kinnock' – an echo of Central Office propaganda. *The Times, Guardian, Independent* and *Financial Times* all led with Kinnock's 'hint' of a 'shift' to a PR deal with the Liberals. This was the new story and was followed by front-page reports of the demands Ashdown would make of Labour in a coalition, the boost which extremist parties would get from PR and the instability which a hung Parliament and fresh elections would cause. To Labour's frustration, the media were not interested in health, the poll tax or other issues which it wanted to raise. The media was now shaping the agenda, just as it had over Labour's health broadcast.

Press Influence

There has long been an imbalance in the partisan leanings of the press and it has increased since 1970. In that year the Conservative party was supported by papers which had 57 per cent of national daily circulation, Labour by papers which had 43 per cent. As shown in table 2.5 (p. 42) by 1992 the figures divided 70 per cent Conservative, 27 per cent Labour (cf. Seymour-Ure 1991). The switch of the popular *Sun* newspaper in 1974 to the Conservatives accentuated the imbalance. As long as 80 per cent of the working class read a tabloid, most Labour voters will be exposed to a Tory-supporting paper. It is worth noting that this bias against the parties of the centre left is found in many other countries, including the Scandinavian countries which have strong social democratic parties.

Figure 8.1 A montage of newspapers covering the 1951 and 1992 general elections shows a continuing concern to exhort the readers to vote for the favoured party.

Some research has cast doubt on the impact of the papers on voting behaviour. Early American studies of the press suggested that, like most communications, it operated largely to reinforce existing loyalties. Most readers of the press and listeners to radio were selective in their exposure to and perception and retention of political information; they used the media to confirm their partisanship. In the first national study of British voters Butler and Stokes (1969) also reported that people often chose newspapers to fit in with their existing party loyalties, i.e. they were selective in their media exposure. Martin Harrop (1986) doubted the effect that the press could have in the four weeks of a campaign and thought that on balance the support of the press was worth only a 1 per cent advantage (or some ten seats) to the Conservatives. He allowed, however, that over the long term the press could influence attitudes.

Recent research has been more willing to attribute influence to the press. At a time of declining loyalty to the main parties there is less scope for reinforcement and more for persuasion. In the six months prior to the 1987 election the Conservative recovery of electoral support was most marked among working-class readers of the Tory-supporting *Star* and *Sun*, papers which were particularly strident in attacking Labour and trumpeting good economic news (Miller et al. 1990). The questions of press bias and influence came to a head in 1992. After the election that paper proclaimed 'It's the Sun wot won it'. The *Sun* had campaigned ruthlessly against Labour and Neil Kinnock and on election day ran a nine-page special, with the front page reading 'Nightmare on Kinnock Street'. Its claim was endorsed by Lord McAlpine, a former Treasurer of the Conservative party, and by Neil Kinnock, who attacked sections of the press when he announced his resignation as Labour leader. McAlpine called the Tory tabloid editors 'heroes' because of their strong support for the party:

> Never in the past nine elections have they [the Tory press] come out so strongly in favour of the Conservatives. Never has the attack on the Labour party been so comprehensive. . . This was how the election was won, and if the politicians, elated in their hour of victory, are tempted to believe otherwise, they are in real trouble next time. (*Sunday Telegraph*, 12 April 1992)

In the first half of the campaign the Tory-supporting papers privately expressed impatience with the Conservative campaign. Some tabloid editors allegedly complained about the lack of a 'line' to follow from Central Office. But in the last few days the Tory tabloids threw aside doubts and pulled out all the stops in attacking Labour. The *Express* and *Mail* acted as little more than vehicles for Central Office propaganda; their stories about the Conservatives were largely Conservative oriented and initiated (just as Labour stories in the *Mirror* were largely supportive and often initiated by that party) and their stories about Labour were overwhelmingly negative (Curtice and Semetko 1994). The *Sun* was more inclined to wage its own campaign, although it regularly referred to a 'Kinnock government' not a 'Labour government', in line with Conservative tactics of emphasizing the differences between Major and Kinnock. The *Mirror*, by contrast, sought to emphasize the strengths of Labour's team (Seymour-Ure 1993).

Subsequent analysis has cast doubt on the *Sun*'s claims that it produced the alleged late swing to the Conservative party, although it may have slightly increased perceptions of Labour as being divided and extreme. The swing to Conservative occurred across readers of most papers and included readers of the Labour-supporting *Mirror*. A careful study of the subject concludes that partisanship, however attenuated, still operates, leading most voters to screen out unwelcome or divergent political messages. In other words, the old factor of selectivity still operates (Curice and Semetko 1994). But the continued imbalance in press partisanship and the diet of anti-Labour propaganda may have long-term effects, notably in making voters more resistant to Labour's themes, reinforcing negative images of the party and putting party spokesmen on the defensive by raising anti-Labour 'scares' during the campaign. And at a time of declining party loyalty, there is more scope for other influences, including the media. The debate on press political influence is far from over.

Parties' Management of the Press

A first task of campaign managers is to ensure that the leading party figures sing the same tune, adhere to 'the line'. They try to keep their more independent-minded MPs and potential dissenters off the television screens and away from newspaper reporters. Party spokesmen are urged to avoid commenting on a colleague's controversial remarks until they know exactly what was said, and be suspicious of seemingly innocent questions from journalists or requests for photographs, particularly from those employed on a hostile newspaper. It is far safer for party leaders to make contrived appearances for the cameras than to engage in spontaneous question and answer sessions with reporters and in the 1980s the Reagan and Bush Presidential campaigns were single-minded in doing this. Some journalists understand why this media access to leaders is so carefully controlled and limited. Neil Kinnock's staff in 1987 and 1992 were convinced that some anti-Labour journalists were determined to trap the leader into making unguarded remarks or losing his temper: the result was that he engaged in few spontaneous question and answer sessions with journalists and his staff formed a protective barrier around him when he was walking to and from the podium. According to Michael White, the political editor of the *Guardian*, 'You have to understand that if the politicians say something interesting it will get twisted. The safest thing is to keep your mouth shut' (interview). Elections have become something of a game in which many journalists try to trap politicians and the latter try to use the former.

Politicians and party strategists brief journalists on lobby terms, as they do between elections. This means that journalists may use the information imparted to them, as long as they do not reveal the source. At election time, however, the stakes are higher and the partisanship more intense than normal, for the election is about which party is to govern the country for the next four or five years. The parties' publicity and press officers act as 'spin doctors' (another Americanism) who are skilled at putting the most positive gloss on a story, or suggesting leads for journalists to follow. They give access and exclusive stories to friendly journalists and deny them to reporters on newspapers which are regarded as hostile. We have already noted that during elections the daily coverage in the *Daily Mirror* or the *Mail* and Express often bears the heavy imprint of Labour and Conservative party headquarters respectively. One Conservative official, describing how he had influenced stories in sympathetic newspapers, continued:

> They want to support us, but they regard themselves as newspapers also.
> They do not want to follow the same line, unless they can put a spin on it.
> They are, after all, competing with each other. Better still, they want you

to favour them with an exclusive, but we have to beware of offending other editors. (Lansley interview)

All the parties have their own early morning (about 7 a.m.) campaign briefing meetings, at which the early editions of the national papers are reviewed in the search for stories which they can turn to their benefit, or which might give rise to questions at the daily press conferences. In his years as Labour's Campaigns and Communications Director, Peter Mandelson acquired a formidable reputation as a 'spin doctor', as did Reece and Bell for the Conservatives in 1983, and to some extent in 1987. Each party has its 'line of the day', the theme, issue or interpretation which spokesmen are supposed to convey, and campaign managers try to co-ordinate the press conference, photo-opportunities and major speeches around it. The objective is to so manage the party's communications output that the media will have little choice but to carry what the party wants. Control is also exercised by politicians and managers referring journalists' queries to the party's official publicity spokesmen and by urging all candidates to follow the 'line'.

Nigel Lawson (1992: 703) has written of how, as Chancellor of the Exchequer, he briefed friendly newspapers and provided suitable quotes on Labour's tax plans in the 1987 election: 'On 5 June the *Daily Mail*, carefully briefed by Andrew Tyrie (his special adviser), and supplied with a suitable quote from me, led with "Labour's lies over taxation"'. A similar Lawson–Tyrie operation led to the *Daily Express* running a story headed 'Exposed: Labour's tax fiasco', the following day. In late September 1991 many commentators built up expectations that John Major would call an election for October. On 29 September, however, Major and the Conservative Chairman, Chris Patten, decided to scotch the election story, and gave another Cabinet minister, John Wakeham, the task of phoning the news to favoured political editors the next day.

The parties' research teams will provide handouts, statistical analysis and background briefings for friendly reporters. In 1992 officers in the Conservative Research Department fed exclusives to the *Daily Mail* about Labour's plans for public sector pay and the *Evening Standard* on the left-wing links of Labour MPs. 'Friendly' press proprietors and editors were frequently in touch with Mrs Thatcher's and John Major's office in the 1987 and 1992 general elections. The close links were again evident when Conservative Central Office contacted the *Express* about the consultant in the Jennifer's ear health broadcast. The expression 'Nightmare on Kinnock Street' was first suggested to John Major by a friendly political editor, used by Major in a speech on 20 March and then headlined by the *Sun* on the eve of polling day.

The parties' early morning press conferences are public attempts at management. They were started by Labour in 1959 and London-based journalists found them a source of useful copy. As Labour-initiated stories dominated the papers the Conservatives were forced to follow suit. Parties now devote increasing time to the conferences, ensuring that the leader and other prominent figures are present and employing visually interesting props for television coverage. Conferences begin with a press release on the theme of the day; this is the party's first shot at establishing its agenda for the day – and in 1992 the Chairman required journalists to confine their opening questions to the theme. Journalists expressed irritation at the frequency with which Conservatives announced that the day's conference would be on taxation or Labour that its conference would be on health. The theme is usually kept secret, to limit the opportunities for journalists to prepare or co-ordinate hostile questions. Another tactic which the platform used to disarm the prying journalists in 1992 was to deny them the opportunity to ask supplementary questions. But for all the parties' efforts the conferences were not very successful in 1992 in shaping press or television stories, except for the press conferences on Labour's health broadcast and they were a disaster for both Labour and Conservative parties (Kavanagh and Gosschalk 1995). By late morning in the final days the broadcasters were spurning the press conference stories and John Major was pressed into recording new interview material for the lunch-time news programmes.

Some idea of the interaction between journalists and politicians is conveyed by a BBC political correspondent's published diary of his encounters with party spin-doctors in 1992. Nicholas Jones reports a telephone conversation with David Hill, Labour's Campaign and Communications Director, about Neil Kinnock's controversial proposal to invite members of other political parties to give evidence to Labour's working party on electoral reform: 'He immediately asked me if I had seen *News at Ten*. "Did you see Neil being interviewed by Michael Brunson? That was Neil's best interview of the day. He took every question and ran with it. He got his message across every time."' Mr Jones realized that David Hill had tired of his questions about electoral reform and wished to switch the subject. He continues: 'The spin I was putting on Mr Hill's remarks was that Labour were finally realising that they must try to keep Mr Kinnock well away from proportional representation and get back to the bread and butter issues of the campaign' (Jones 1992: 112). Jones also reports a conversation with Tim Collins, the party press officer accompanying John Major, the following day. Collins

> assured me Mr Major was 'a very chirpy chappy' because MPs in the marginal constituencies were telephoning him to say their support was firm. They were finding there was considerable reaction on the doorsteps against Labour, and considerable criticism of the triumphalism displayed by Labour at their rally in Sheffield. (Jones 1992: 116)

The hope presumably was that these comments would influence Jones's reports for the BBC.

Not all the 'feeding' is from politician to journalist, however. Politicians also seek assessments privately from journalists about how the campaign is going. In 1992 playwright David Hare reports overhearing a conversation between John Major and John Simpson, the BBC reporter, in which the former asks for professional advice:

> *Simpson*: '. . . all seems a bit pointless . . . ways in which you could be better presented.'
> *Major*: 'I know. I know. What do you think I should do?'
> (Hare 1992: 199)

At an early stage in the election a so-called 'White Commonwealth' of sympathetic political editors was invited to meet John Major in Central Office to discuss the Tory campaign. (Such briefing is not confined to the Conservatives, for the phrase had been first employed in the late 1960s for Harold Wilson's regular briefing of sympathetic editors.)

While party managers try to influence or 'spin' the campaign coverage of journalists, of course the latter delight in uncovering disagreements, scandals and blunders. The 1970 and 1974 Tory campaigns were nearly hijacked by the dissenting voice of Enoch Powell and the intense media interest in him. Conservative press conferences were dominated by journalists' questions seeking Mr Heath's views about Mr Powell. In the end Mr Heath declared that he would take no more questions on the subject. Labour has also suffered from prominent politicians saying different things to the media. In 1974 Shirley Williams shattered party unity by declaring at a press conference that she would resign from a Labour government if a forthcoming referendum voted against Britain's membership of the European Community and in 1983 Jim Callaghan publicly disagreed with the party's official defence policy. Such frankness and indiscretion were a gift to journalists looking for 'interesting' stories and damaged the party's attempts to present a united front.

Press Advertising

The press is a significant vehicle for one specific form of party propaganda – advertising. Uncertainty among party managers about the legality of press advertising during a campaign meant that it was not used on a large scale until 1979. Now most of the press advertising is concentrated in the campaign period and more money is spent on it than on any other item. The Conservatives in 1979 concentrated press advertising in the national press in the last few days and did so on a greater scale in the 1983 election, spending over £1.2 million. Labour spent less than a third of this. In 1987 the Conservatives increased their outlay to £3.6 million, including 11 full pages of advertisements in most national papers over the last four days of the campaign. Labour also increased its efforts but the total cost was a more modest £1.6 million (Harrop 1988: 177). In 1992 the Conservatives cut back and Labour actually spent more. The Conservative Chairman Chris Patten was sceptical about the electoral value of such communications and resisted pressure from the party's advertising agency, supported by some tabloid editors, to finance them. Some ads were eventually run on behalf of the party and paid for from other sources (see above, p. 73).

The press advertisements are largely negative. A good example, in 1987, was the Conservative ad 'Labour's policy on arms' – a young soldier with his arms raised (see p. 208). 'The tone of press advertising was strongly negative, indeed more so than in earlier elections. Bombs, rockets and boxing gloves were favourite metaphors' (Harrop and Scammell 1992: 206–7). The Conservatives in 1992 used a picture of a flying bomb to highlight the effect of Labour's spending proposals in their 'Labour's tax bombshell' advertisement. Martin Harrop's judgement was that the adverts increased voters' cynicism about the political parties, promoted their awareness of the differences between the parties but did not affect their votes (Harrop 1988: 178). Supporters of such advertisements claim that they are good for the morale of party activists and reassure them of the commitment of the leaders in London. In view of the restrictions on buying time on radio and television the press is the main advertising medium which the parties can use. One Labour advertising man, Barry Delaney, thinks that although it is impossible to measure the impact of advertising the case for ads is that

> They are the authentic voice of the party. In all the claims and counter-claims, advertising is distinguished as the message that the party wants to convey in a tone of voice and style that it determines – unperturbed by Jeremy Paxman, unsullied by the comments of the *Sun*. (Interview)

Conclusion

Print journalists cannot compete with the broadcasters in carrying the latest campaign news. The lengthening of the campaign day, the campaign managers' interest in gaining television coverage and their desire to provide new stories for the broadcasting outlets have all increased the pressures upon print journalists. The tight central control imposed by the parties over reporters' access to the party leader and at press conferences – excluding more than one question per journalist and insisting that early questions be confined to the party's chosen theme of the day – emphasis on photo-opportunities and the ticket-only rallies, are attempts to relegate the print and broadcast journalists to the role of transmitters of the party's message.

One press response, particularly in the broadsheets, to the dominance of television has been to try and create a distinctive role by commissioning and interpreting opinion polls, inviting independent experts to audit the parties' spending plans, analysing issues, parties' campaign strategies and media coverage (particularly television's) of the campaign. The *Guardian* in 1992 ran regular analyses of media coverage from Loughborough University's Communications Research Centre. Another is for reporters to create stories by conducting their own research into, for example, the records and claims of the parties. One casualty in the change of campaign focus has been a decline of reports of constituency contests and of politicians' speeches (Harrop 1986: 143).

There is a distinction between the press culture of *reporting* and observing an election campaign, on the one hand, and *participating*, on the other. Politicians in all parties frequently complain that the press is moving more and more from the first to the second. For their part, the more investigative and thoughtful reporters and commentators chafe at the constraints of managed campaigns. Like television reporters, they may adopt a posture of 'disdaining the news' by calling the readers' attention to the ways in which politicians use photo-opportunities and image-making (Levy 1981). The thinly veiled message in such background articles is that politicians and their communications advisers are trying to manipulate the voters and that presentation is often done at the cost of substance. This in turn infuriates the vigilant members of the party's media monitoring units. For what it is worth a Gallup survey (September 1993) into the public's assessment of the honesty and ethical standards of professions found that journalists scored the worst (61 per cent thought them low or very low) and MPs were only just ahead of them.

9

MASS MEDIA: TELEVISION

This chapter explores the role and effects of television in election campaigns. It examines how television reports elections, the approaches of the parties to the medium and, finally, the effects of political television on voters and the political system. The starting-point for any analysis of this subject is to recognize the interdependence of politicians and broadcasters, particularly during election campaigns. Politicians rely on television for their case to be carried to the public and try to influence the coverage by a mixture of accommodation, persuasion and pressure. The broadcasters in turn resent the attempts to manipulate them, yet are also conscious of their obligations to be fair and balanced in their treatment of the parties. Both sides know that most people regard the medium as the main and most trusted source of news.

Television Coverage

Many politicians assume that television is so important that what is on the screen *is* the campaign agenda. For party managers election campaigns now are largely about setting the television agenda. They expect to choose who appears for the party on programmes and sometimes also demand a say on who appears for other parties, topics to be covered and, if in government, to have the last word. They also make suggestions or even demands about the political 'balance' and running order of topics in news and current affairs programmes. Parties have for long, at least implicitly, thought in terms of agenda setting. What is new is the intensity and coordination with which they are oriented to television; virtually all of a party's communications – speeches, photo-opportunities, press conferences, election broadcasts and posters – are designed for television. Broadcasters have become more aware of these pressures and acknowledge as a fact of life the 'heavy breathing', or not too subtle guidance and comment on their reports, from the headquarters of all parties (Simpson 1992). Over time the balance of power in deciding what is covered has shifted from the politicians. Until 1959 they virtually controlled the limited television coverage – which was confined to party election broadcasts (see below, pp. 206–7).

Tensions between the politicians and journalists stem from the fact that 'the objectives of campaigners and reporters are incompatible' (Arterton 1984: 108). If many journalists view political communication as an opportunity to enlighten and educate voters, politicians are more likely to regard it as a means of persuading voters to their point of view (Blumler and Gurevitch 1981). Few journalists share the campaign managers' desire for the reporting to be predictable, repetitive and orchestrated, but want to report events on the basis of their news-worthiness. Television, like other media, is interested in the new, unexpected or unpredictable, in contrast to the party managers' wish to have their campaigns reported as they planned. Personal attacks, signs of internal party disagreements, mistakes, or sudden shifts in the opinion polls or in a party's strategy are sure to be covered intensively. Table 9.1 shows that news bulletins, like the press, present the campaign in battle terms. Between a third and a half of lead stories in the main evening news programmes are based on attacks by the parties. The Loughborough team's judgement on the television news coverage

Table 9.1   Negative television campaign coverage 1983–92

Year	BBC	ITV
1983	7	8
1987	10	9
1992	9	6

Note: The above figures refer to the election lead stories in the main evening news programmes which figured such terms as 'warning, attacking and criticizing'
Source: Successive Nuffield Election Studies

in 1992 was that the three main parties were more often reported attacking opponents than presenting or defending their own policies (cited in Harrison 1992: 162).

The media also like to report the polls, however static they are, as showing public opinion in flux (Crewe 1982: 122). Polls are given maximum coverage if they indicate a sharp rise for one party (e.g. Labour on 1 April 1992) or a sudden surge for the third party (e.g. the rise of the Alliance in 1983 and the prospect that it might displace Labour as the second party in 1987).

The parties have their own ideas of what the election should be about. Labour usually wants to talk about social issues, pensions, welfare and, in recent elections, unemployment. Conservatives prefer to concentrate on the tax increases which they claim Labour will impose to pay for its spending promises, as well as law and order and defence. Interviewers may find themselves in the position of asking Labour politicians the questions that the Conservatives want to raise but Labour wants to avoid, and vice versa. In turn, this stance may make politicians more resentful, as they compare how 'toughly' they are treated compared with opponents and even break off the interview. In the 1979 election the Prime Minister, Mr Callaghan, abruptly terminated an interview with an ITN reporter because he objected to questions about industrial relations and strikes – a subject on which his party was vulnerable, following the winter of discontent. On the day of Labour's 1992 manifesto launch the party's campaign spokesman, Jack Cunningham, complained about a question on the party's policy for privatized utilities on the Radio 4 *Today* programme, on the grounds that the question had not been agreed beforehand: 'Your viewers [*sic*] ought to know that you are introducing an agenda I was not informed about'. It is not surprising that political interviews, however brief, are often preceded by complex negotiations between campaigners and broadcasters over 'the rules of engagement' (Franklin 1994: 145), the time, interviewer and questions. In the last resort, a dissatisfied party may simply refuse to supply a spokesman for a programme.

Objective or balanced coverage has also come to mean that commentators usually present a 'pro' and 'con' report on a party's activity or that a statement by one party spokesman is matched by statements from other parties. Reporters try to protect themselves from accusations of bias by quoting so-called 'informed sources', e.g. 'Party leaders claim that', or 'One of John Major's staff told me that', or being even-handed, e.g. 'On the one hand . . ., on the other . . .'. Interviews

with 'experts' can also be a means of conveying evaluations of the
different claims of parties – as well as a source of imbalance. Opinion
pollsters, academics, political journalists, interest group spokesmen
and City economists are regularly interviewed to comment on opinion
polls, campaign developments, parties' policies and economic statistics.
In 1992 the Loughborough Communications Centre's assessment of
the political leanings of the 'experts' and organizational spokesmen was
as follows:

Anti-Labour	39
Anti-Conservative	8
Pro-Labour	3
Pro-Conservative	40

Labour leaders complained about the anti-Labour implications of the
narrow economic perspective applied by the City economists who were
interviewed.

In some respects television may be too responsive to the parties.
British television, compared with the press and US television, has been
more disposed to cover the activities and statements of politicians,
notably from the party leaders. In the 1983 election, for example,
soundbites from party leaders accounted for 20 per cent of television
campaign coverage compared with only 2 per cent in the *Sun* and
3 per cent in *The Times* (Semetco et al. 1991). The BBC appears to be
more accommodating to the parties than ITN; in 1992 BBC news
bulletins were twice as likely as ITN's to report party-initiated stories,
e.g. press conferences and rallies; ITN was more likely to initiate its
own stories, particularly on the polls, and report and analyse campaign
plans and strategies and 'state of play' (University of Loughborough
1992). Too compliant a coverage of the agenda of the parties exposes
broadcasters to the charges that they are reporting the equivalent of
junk mail – the photo-opportunities, the unveiling of posters and the
walkabouts that are specially staged for the media – rather than
exercising their own judgement and reporting the election according to
strict news values. A damning verdict on television coverage of the 1992
election was:

> Mostly, these nightly packages were not only repetitive, boring and
> uninformative. They were unacceptably complaisant. Travelling day-by-
> day with the candidates and their minders, only the more experienced
> and strong-minded could maintain both their distance from the
> reporting pack and from the party spin doctors and some reporters came

uncomfortably close to simply relaying what the party they were following wanted conveyed at any given moment. (Harrison 1992: 167)

Yet radio and television producers have taken some important initiatives in election coverage. Phone-ins, which allow ordinary voters to question politicians, sessions in which party spokesmen are questioned by an audience or debate with each other, and major interviews with party leaders have helped to link the parties' campaigns and promote debate. Increasingly, as journalists carry challenges, responses and counter-challenges between politicians, they have forced the parties to address each other. Politicians rarely welcome this for they want to stick to their self-interested scripts. A dilemma for broadcasters, as their role has expanded, has been, *'how to make significantly independent contributions of their own to the campaign, without intruding improperly into what should be a choice for voters between whatever the political parties were offering in their own terms'* (Blumler, Gurevitch and Nossiter 1995: emphasis in original).

Another important feature of television coverage of the campaign is the interview with senior politicians. Early political interviews were heavily staged events, in which deferential interviewers elicited stilted answers from the politician. Nowadays, party leaders can expect to submit themselves to at least two or three lengthy televised inquisitions during the election. Campaign managers have mixed views about the interviews. They may welcome the publicity and the opportunity for the leader to expound the party's case, display his or her strengths and disarm critics. But the politician has no protection against a hostile interrogator – something provided by the Speaker at Question Time in the House of Commons – and there is always the danger of being wrongfooted or committing a 'gaffe'. In 1964, in answer to one viewer's question about pensions, the Prime Minister Sir Alec Douglas Home mentioned giving 'donations' to hard-pressed pensioners, a reference quickly exploited in the speeches of the Labour leader, Harold Wilson. Neil Kinnock came unstuck in an interview on defence with David Frost in 1987 (see pp. 181–2) and again in 1992 when he told the same interviewer that he still regretted Labour's defeat in 1983 (on its most left-wing manifesto in 50 years). The Tory tabloids and politicians contrasted this defence of extremism with his new moderation ('The Kinnock mask slips', the *Daily Mail*). In the 1987 election Mrs Thatcher, in an eve-of-poll interview with David Dimbleby, dismissed 'people [who] just drool and dribble about poverty'. Conservative managers were relieved that the interview was not broadcast until late on polling day.

The major political interview now appears to have had its day as a vehicle of getting politicians to answer questions directly. Sir Robin Day, an experienced interviewer, has complained that modern leaders, particularly Thatcher and Kinnock and their communications advisers, have 'hijacked' the interview. The leaders arrive in the studio, armed with buzz words, statistics and soundbites which they deliver and repeat almost regardless of the question. Faced with an awkward question they usually give an answer which is evasive or irrelevant. Bill Jones (1992) argues that the political interview has become less an opportunity for an exchange between the interviewer and the politician than a vehicle for the latter to deliver the party message. Party leaders are more willing to appear on chat shows and light entertainment programmes and probably have an easier time. Mrs Thatcher was carefully steered by Gordon Reece to such programmes (see above, p. 59). According to Reece, 'Everything was geared to the floating voter. Some Conservatives hated any use of the *Sun, News of the World* and light television and talk shows. But I was aiming at a particular type of audience that read those papers and watched those programmes' (interview). Jones (1992: 64) notes, 'There were obvious gains to be made by avoiding the fast bowling of Sir Robin Day and hitting easy sixes off the likes of Michael Aspel and Jimmy Young in front of much bigger audiences'.

Parties and Agenda Management

The increase in recent years in the number of television and radio outlets provides more opportunities for politicians to communicate their messages and for the campaign to be mediated by television. The influence is more marked in the United States where, 'Being on television is the most effective form of campaigning' (Ranney 1983). Walkabouts had been introduced by Harold Wilson in 1970, expressly for the television cameras. Mrs Thatcher, guided by Gordon Reece, carried the photo-opportunity idea further, usually taking pains to ensure that photographers and film crews got their pictures. In 1979 she held a new-born calf for over 15 minutes in a field in Norfolk for the benefit of cameras and was, according to one study, 'a mistress of the pre-planned, carefully packaged appearance' (Cockerell et al. 1984:

91). Mr Kinnock also proved himself adept at exploiting the new media opportunities in 1987 and 1992. Mr Heath, Mr Foot and Mr Callaghan, however, perhaps because they were reared in an earlier age, were less comfortable with photo-opportunities.

Image makers have become more important actors in preparing the televised speech. According to Brendan Bruce, 'Every element that will appear on screen is now considered beforehand by experts. The speaker's appearance (facial expression, clothes, body language), performance (humour, delivery, rhythm, pitch and tone) and environment (background, platform, surrounding colleagues, audience) is a body of data designed to persuade' (Bruce 1992: 132). Just like a screen actor or actress, the politician is advised by professionals about 'body language', dress and speech delivery. Television coverage has meant that speechwriters and party leaders have to think carefully about the message they wish to get across. Because television shows only a fraction of a speech, political reporters are important in interpreting and 'contextualizing' the speech for viewers. A party's press officers can brief the lobby journalists beforehand about the main points of a leader's speech, fill in background facts and correct misconceptions and factual errors (Bruce 1992: 133). A more active role is played by spin doctors who suggest phrases and passages for publication or airing and generally coax the reporter to cover the speech as the politician wants. Politicians also realize that the message has to be concentrated in a few key sentences if it is to be carried on television. Harold Wilson was the first leader to time the delivery of his evening speech to coincide with television news broadcasts; he would also switch to the quotable parts of his evening speeches when he saw that the lights of television cameras were switched on for live coverage. But excerpts from political speeches now make up only a small part of television coverage of the campaign; in 1992 the average television election soundbite for party leaders was down to 18 seconds. Not surprisingly, party leaders in Britain now address fewer rallies and those that they do are arranged primarily for a clip on television.

This trend is another symptom of Americanization. In the US the average length of television soundbites for Presidential candidates had fallen over twenty years from 42 seconds to ten seconds in 1988 (Patterson 1993: 160). The networks promised to provide more time in 1992; in the event the 'bite' averaged less than ten seconds. The average length of candidate quotes in American newspaper articles has also fallen by a half between 1960 and 1992 (Patterson 1993: 76).

Television has had the effect in the US, and to a lesser extent in Britain, of providing campaigners with fewer and fewer opportunities via the media to elaborate reasoned arguments, discuss complex problems or develop anything but rather simple ideas. The speech has given way to the soundbite and both are giving way to the photo-opportunity.

Much research has shown that pictures usually make a more powerful impression than words and in the American viewer's home television pictures speak louder than words. Doris Graber's *Processing the News* (1987) shows that in the US the perception and retention of messages and images from television is higher for visual images than verbal communications. Similar trends are evident in Britain. Just as the parties' press releases are timed for newspaper deadlines and couched in an arresting style, so the political leaders' speeches and activities are timed to meet television deadlines and provide 'good pictures' for television. In 1970 the Conservatives had a specially designed blue background for Mr Heath's speeches, which accompanied him on his travels. Other parties have followed and in 1992 the Conservative party spent over £500,000 on John Major's set. Parties also carry their slogans, logos and pictures as a backdrop at their press conference – again to benefit from 'free' television coverage.

In 1979 Conservative Central Office began to mark up maps which showed how long it would take for news films to reach television studios from different parts of the country. By 1987 use was made of ENG equipment (electronic news-gathering), which allowed lightweight video cameras to be used with portable video recording facilities to send pictures directly to newsrooms. Parties are virtually guaranteed coverage of their early morning press conferences on the lunch-time news broadcasts. The afternoon is usually devoted to photo-opportunities, such as leaders' visits to factories or hospitals or schools, and these will be covered by regional television and early evening news broadcasts. In the evening the leaders address major rallies which will be carried by the main national news programmes. The campaign day reported by the broadcasters follows the order of the party leaders' day.

Campaign managers do not wait passively for television coverage, but try to ensure that it covers the party's agenda by reporting its planned speeches, press conferences and photo-opportunities. The tactics adopted by party managers to influence television to cover the party's chosen theme include:

Holding a number of press conferences on the same topic on the same day.

Putting forward only one or two major speakers on the hustings, to discourage cameras from reporting party figures who do not voice the chosen issue of the day.

Coordinating a leader's activities during the day so that the same theme is reflected in what he or she says and does.

Forcing the rival party on to the defensive, by raising a series of provocative questions for journalists to take up.

Declining interviews on subjects not on the party's agenda (Blumler et al. 1989).

Another management tactic which appears to have increased recently is backstop editing by politicians. They subject the broadcasters to constant pressure about the political coverage – the choice of topics, running order of stories, selection of personalities and extracts from speeches. The BBC has been a particular target for complaint; in 1945 Churchill was convinced that it was staffed by Communists, in 1966 Wilson that it was staffed by Conservatives. Sometimes the political pressure seems to take the form of a pre-emptive strike before the election, to induce caution in the broadcasters. In 1986 the Conservative Chairman Norman Tebbit complained about BBC bias and set up a monitoring unit within Central Office. Chris Patten, a later Chairman, protested about its political coverage in 1991 and urged Conservative viewers to jam the BBC switchboard in protest. In February 1992, with the pre-election campaign in full swing, the Home Secretary Kenneth Baker warned the BBC 'to be very careful over the next eight to ten weeks'. The corporation did not need reminding that the Home Secretary would be deciding the size of its licence fee (and therefore its income). The complaints from the Conservative party continued right until election day.

Labour has also felt aggrieved with the broadcasters, not least because it is already outgunned in the tabloid press. Harold Wilson frequently complained of the BBC's anti-Labour bias and claimed in 1970 that its political reporters took their questions from the Tory press (Cockerell 1988: 132). After the October 1974 election the party commissioned a report into BBC bias from a Labour-supporting academic – which happened to absolve the corporation from charges of bias. In 1987 some television stories about taxation, extremism and Kinnock's leadership shortcomings reflected the agenda of the Tory tabloids.

Even if politicians accept that the broadcasters are even-handed most of the time, or at least strive to be, they may now calculate that it is in their interest to cry 'foul' or 'bias'. Press officers in government departments and in the parties' headquarters try to influence what is broadcast. One broadcaster, quoted by Melanie Phillips, complained: 'It's relentless and it's coming at us from all sides . . . They're all trying either to kill a story or spin us a line' (Phillips 1992). Shortly before the 1992 election Labour's Campaigns and Communications Director, David Hill, remarked 'It's a rare day when we don't complain about radio or TV' (Phillips 1992). It would be surprising if the sheer frequency of the complaints did not put some broadcast journalists on the defensive (Blumler, Gurevitch and Nossiter 1995). One study of the broadcasters at work during an election has noted how the struggle to set the agenda divides many newscasters from many politicians. For the newscasters 'communication was a tool of public enlightenment; to the latter [politicians], a weapon in a two-way struggle – against rival parties *and* professional journalists' (Blumler et al. 1989: 157).

In common with the practice in many other states, the British broadcasting authorities provide free air time at elections for the parties. Party broadcasts on radio started in 1924, on television in 1951. These provide the one opportunity for parties to put their own case as they wish on television and radio and to shape the media agenda. Before each general election a committee of broadcasters and party representatives agrees the shares of election television and radio broadcasts for the political parties. In allocating broadcasts the committee takes account of a party's political support, measured in votes or seats, at the previous election. In 1959, for example, the television companies allocated the broadcasts on a 5:5:2 basis between Conservative, Labour and Liberal. As third-party support grew, the committee agreed to increase the Liberal share to three in1964, four in October 1974 and then five for the Liberal/SDP Alliance in 1987, falling back to four for the Liberal Democrats in 1992. The proportions are important because they apply also to party shares of news coverage during the campaign. The arrangements are constrained by an *aide-mémoire*, drawn up in 1947 and slightly revised in 1969, which provided for second-for-second balance between the parties. In 1992, however, ITN abandoned the 'stop-watch' criterion and stated that it would report the campaign according to newsworthiness.

Although they have declined in importance (in 1983 the authorities ended the simultaneous transmission of party broadcasts on all channels) parties still devote considerable time to the preparation of election broadcasts and they do help voters decided how to vote (Miller

1991). At first the broadcasts were 20–30 minute sessions in which senior politicians spoke directly to camera. In recognition of the allegedly shorter attention span of modern voters the broadcasts have become briefer as well as more technically sophisticated, using soft focus, romantic or ominous music and other devices of contemporary filming. Politicians are featured less and more scope is given to actors and voice-overs. In 1970 the Conservatives modelled their broadcasts on news and documentary programmes and the style of advertisements was borrowed from American practice. Barry Day recalls: 'We realized that the audience was more visually sophisticated as a result of what they saw on TV. They would no longer tolerate the talking heads. You had to get to the point quickly' (interview).

The film biography of the party leader is another import from America. In 1987 Hugh Hudson, director of *Chariots of Fire*, co-operated with the writer Colin Welland to make a film of Neil Kinnock and in 1992 John Schlesinger, director of *Midnight Cowboy*, made *The Journey*, a film of John Major's odyssey from Brixton to Downing Street.

A student of the election broadcasts must be impressed by the sheer persistence of many substantive themes and images. In 1979 a Conservative broadcast used film of the recent winter's disruption of public services – the rubbish piled in the streets, airports closed, graves undug, schools closed and hospitals picketed. In the subsequent three general elections the party's broadcasts have always found some way of reminding voters of that winter. In both 1987 and 1992 Conservatives featured broadcasts on Labour's defence policies and on Neil Kinnock's alleged political weaknesses and inexperience. In 1979 a Conservative broadcast portrayed a so-called Olympics prosperity race in which the British runner was shown burdened with weights, labelled high taxes, high inflation and high unemployment, all the fault of the Labour government. In 1992 a broadcast featured a blacksmith chained to three iron balls, marked 'Taxes up. Prices up. Mortgages up', to warn viewers of what would happen under a Labour government.

Yet the politicians' attempts to shape the agenda often come unstuck. In 1970 the Labour government was boasting about its success in converting a balance of payments deficit into a surplus. To its consternation the monthly trade figures announced three days before polling showed a £31 million deficit, and lent support to Conservative warnings of an impending economic crisis. In February 1974 Mr Heath's government attacked the National Union of Mineworkers for 'holding the nation to ransom' in pursuit of a wage claim that broke government guidelines

Figure 9.1 Saatchi & Saatchi's poster in the 1987 general election which took advantage of Neil Kinnock's admission in a television interview that he would not repel a Russian invasion of Britain with nuclear weapons.

and asked the electorate to endorse its pay policy. But, a week before polling day, an official body reported that the miners were apparently paid less than the national average. Although the figures were subsequently recalculated the story called into question the justification for holding the election and gave the impression that the government had mishandled the dispute.

Similar upsets occurred in the 1987 and 1992 elections. In 1987 Labour's defence policy was a source of division within the party and unpopular with voters; party leaders wanted, as far as possible, to ignore the issue. These hopes were destroyed by Neil Kinnock's television interview with David Frost. When asked how Britain, having relinquished her nuclear weapons under a Labour government, would repel an invasion by a foreign power, Mr Kinnock said that the people would resort to guerrilla warfare. The reply was a gift to Conservative and tabloid accusations that a Labour government would leave Britain defenceless. The Saatchi agency capitalized on the interview by hurriedly writing a memorable advertisement which portrayed a British soldier with his hands held high in a gesture of surrender, and the headline 'Labour's policy on arms' (figure 9.1). On the other side, Conservative claims in 1992 that the economic recession was ending and the government's policies for recovery were succeeding, were contradicted by the frequent press and broadcast headlines of bankruptcies and job losses which dominated the first week of the campaign. The economy was generally regarded as a Conservative issue, in so far as voters regarded the party as more competent than Labour. But coverage of the gloomy statistics, factory closures and job losses reminded voters of the government's mismanagement of the economy and the recession. Conservatives wanted to talk about the economic recovery, Labour about the recession, and the coverage helped Labour.

The parties were also thrown off their stride by the row over Labour's party election broadcast on health in the second week of the 1992 campaign. The broadcast on 'Jennifer's ear' was a party-initiated event, but thereafter it was the media which set the agenda. To recap, the broadcast dealt with the cases of two young girls, both of whom suffered from the same painful ear illness and were waiting for an operation. The parents of one were able to afford private health care and she was treated quickly, the other, Jennifer, relied on the NHS and had to wait several months for treatment. The broadcast was designed to illustrate claims about the underfunding of the NHS and how this had led to long hospital waiting lists; it also warned of the emergence of a two-tier service, with those people able to afford private treatment getting a better health deal. Labour claimed that the film was based on a real-life case but withheld the girl's name for fear that the media would harass the family.

These issues rapidly got lost in the furore that erupted when Jennifer's name was revealed, the disagreement between the parents about the truthfulness and ethics of the film, claims that the story had mixed fact and fiction and the role of press reporters in discovering the names of the family and medical consultant. At daily press conferences the journalists had already become increasingly irritated with the parties' campaign strategies. The Conservatives were concentrating on tax, Labour on health, the opinion polls were pretty static and journalists were looking for something 'new'. At last an issue appeared over which the parties had no control and which for a few days evolved almost hourly. At one stage journalists and broadcasters were interviewing each other. Indeed, as the media concentrated on the alleged dirty tricks of the two parties over the broadcast, the parties found it difficult to get the media to report anything else. Labour wanted to talk about an NHS under threat, Conservatives about Labour's unethical use of a sick child. In a revealing radio interview Michael Heseltine pleaded with an interviewer 'to give us the chance to get on to the issues . . . we depend on you, there is no other way we can get over what we want to say' (*The World This Weekend*, 28 March 1992).

As television covers the campaign so it becomes part of the campaign. Media coverage itself becomes an issue, part of the agenda. The parties now routinely make charges of bias, e.g. over the amount or tone of coverage, the order in which stories are presented and the choice of allegedly 'neutral' commentators. All the parties (and the broadcasters) now conduct a stop-watch analysis of coverage, to ensure that they are given at least their agreed shares of airtime, as well as monitoring output for 'fairness'. The broadcasters similarly try to achieve a proportionate distribution of lead stories between the parties, while trying to balance the claims of newsworthiness with 'fairness' and proportionality. In the 1992 election the Liberal Democratic leader Paddy Ashdown was scheduled to be interviewed on Channel 4's main news bulletin on the day his party's manifesto was released. When the programme makers decided to make the interview a second lead, behind an item on Labour's shadow budget also released that day, the Liberals cancelled the interview on the grounds that they had unfairly been deprived of the lead story. The broadcasters judged that, in terms of news values, Labour's shadow budget was more significant.

Resentful broadcasters can also fight back by 'disdaining' what they report, e.g. showing a poorly attended rally, an unflattering film of the leaders or adding a less than admiring commentary. This was illustrated in a commentary of Channel 4's political editor in the 1992 campaign: 'Mr Major went to the Ideal Home Exhibition today for a photo-opportunity. Presumably to show that he shares the aspirations of ordinary people' (University of Loughborough, 1992).

Television Effects

Early academic research on the political impact of all media suggested that they operated more to reinforce than change views. Political surveys in the United States showed that many voters followed the media and interpreted messages *selectively* to *reinforce* existing loyalties. Later study of television effects adopted what was called a *uses and gratifications* model, emphasizing how the voters' values and expectations led them to use the media for, variously, information, reinforcement of values, guidance and entertainment (Blumler and McQuail 1968). Both perspectives have been challenged more recently. One view is that at a time of declining partisanship, fewer voters have firm party loyalties to reinforce and the media therefore may have more scope for forming and changing views. Neo-Marxists and radicals have also argued that the media, including television, reflect the assumptions of dominant groups in society and are biased against parties of the left and trade unions which question these assumptions; the media shape the political agenda (Dunleavy and Husbands 1985; Glasgow University Media Group 1976; 1980).

Any discussion of the media's political impact should distinguish between effects on individuals and effects on the political system. Surveys have provided some evidence about the effects on individuals. Over half of voters claim that they learn a great deal or a fair amount from television and a significant minority claim that it helps them to decide which party to support. As with television advertising in the United States (see p. 150) persuasive effects have typically been concentrated among the less involved, informed and interested members of the electorate. This may help to explain why Liberals have often been the main beneficiaries of election campaigns and the increased television exposure they give the party (Blumler and McQuail 1968).

The survey evidence about the reaction of voters to political television consistently fails to support the politicians' concerns about bias. Some three-quarters of viewers detect no unfairness in election coverage and, when asked to compare the election coverage of various media outlets, more people mentioned television as the most informative and interesting (Harrison 1988: 159). Surveys have shown that election broadcasts of both Conservative and Labour helped viewers' knowledge of the parties' policies but had little or no effect on voting intention or turnout (Wober, Svennevig and Gunter 1986). They may also have other as yet unquantified effects, such as boosting the morale of party workers (Wober 1989).

Voters have other complaints about coverage, not least the withdrawal of popular programmes because of extended television coverage of an election. After all, only one voter in six claims to be very interested in politics and the great majority much prefer to watch sport, soaps or comedy programmes. Studies by the BBC Audience Research report a steady rise in complaints about the excessive amount of election coverage. The proportions complaining of 'far too much' coverage have risen from 17 per cent in 1970, to 31 per cent in February 1974, to 40 per cent in October 1974 to over 60 per cent in 1992. It appears that it is the nature of the activities covered (e.g. the walkabouts, polls, photo-opportunities and adversarial tone of the discussions and debates) that alienates viewers. But our knowledge of the effects of political television suggests that the parties are wise to concentrate on agenda-setting rather than on trying to influence voters. Television can (a) influence the salience of issues in the minds of viewers and (b) indirectly influence thereby the standards they apply when deciding which party to support.

Claims that television has assisted *the growth of Presidentialism*, or more leader-dominated elections should be treated with caution. In a pre-television age Gladstone, Disraeli, Lloyd George and Neville Chamberlain were dominant figures. And popular or dominant leaders have not always delivered election victory for their parties. According to the opinion polls Wilson in 1970 and Callaghan in 1979 ran ahead of the Conservative leader of the day, yet Labour still lost the election. People cast their votes on many grounds, including their assessment of the leader. But the last is not a major factor compared to the relative strengths of the parties' images and records and this was so in 1992 (Crewe and King 1994).

Yet there has been a Presidentialism in the sense of television focusing more on the activities of the party leaders in an election campaign. The party's messages are carried through the leader and voters find television useful for judging the party leaders (Blumler and McQuail, 1968). Outside of the election period the party leaders account for one third of the politicians mentioned in TV news programmes and during the campaign for over half (Foley 1992: 125). The concentration is partly a consequence of television resources. Because television companies assign camera crews and major reporters to follow the party leaders each day and fewer to the secondary figures, the news broadcasts have more film of the leader. Such intense coverage of the leader can be inconvenient for a party which is trying to promote an image of a team, as Labour was in 1983 and in 1992.

Britain has not yet followed the US, France and Spain in holding a television debate between leaders; the parties' attitudes to a debate have been governed largely by electoral calculation. When a party's electoral prospects are poor and/or it believes that its leader is clearly superior it will issue a challenge or accept an invitation from the broadcasters. Thus Mr Callaghan wanted to debate Mrs Thatcher in

1979 and Mr Kinnock challenged her in 1987 and Mr Major in 1992. But a party securely in the lead has no incentive to make or accept a challenge. The election may be decided on a mistake in the debate or be dominated by the debates. Gordon Reece, the Conservative Publicity Director, persuaded Mrs Thatcher to reject Mr Callaghan's challenge: 'I wanted the election to be about the Winter of Discontent not about the debate' (interview).

Another effect of election television is that people with experience of the medium – as editor or producer – have become key figures in a party's communications structure, advising politicians on how to 'manage' the media, project a message, react to stories and generally get a good press. Peter Mandelson, Sir Gordon Reece and Shaun Woodward all had a background in television before assuming key communications posts with the major parties. Not surprisingly, the high profile of these people often excites jealousy among fellow party bureaucrats (see p. 000). Their experience enables them to offer informed critiques of the structure and organization of programmes. Experienced film directors like Hugh Hudson and John Schlesinger have been recruited to make election broadcasts for the parties. But in employing media expertise Britain still trails the United States, where Reagan in 1984 and Bush in 1988 and 1992 placed campaign strategists and media consultants at the head of their campaign organizations. Indeed, consultants played a key role in persuading George Bush to invite Dan Quayle to be his running-mate in the 1988 Presidential election. Over 90 per cent of candidates for Senate and state governor posts employ a professional media consultant and over 90 per cent of a typical candidate's campaign spending goes on purchasing television time.

More debatable is the claim that television has advanced the careers of politicians who are skilled at public relations and presentation. Physical appearance is important, for viewers make up their minds about people on television very quickly and the medium does reward politicians who are reassuring, friendly and able to encapsulate their main points in a few sentences. But again the claim should not be pushed too far. Michael Foot, Ted Heath and Margaret Thatcher became party leaders, and in the last two cases Prime Minister, in spite of lacking obvious television skills. Mr Foot was more at ease addressing open-air meetings, engaging with the audience and speaking without notes; the same style on television appeared as ranting and the expansive gestures of the public meeting appeared melodramatic. Mr Heath was regularly coached to be more informal, Mr Kinnock more succinct and Mrs Thatcher less harsh, and in each case with only partial success. In Britain politicians usually get to the top by displaying Parliamentary skills, gaining the approval of senior party colleagues and being acceptable to all or most groups in the party. Even in the United States, if Kennedy and Reagan were television 'naturals', this was less obviously true of Nixon and Bush.

Most politicians think they are good on television and communications specialists speak bitterly of the rows they have had with politicians who were determined to appear on television. Campaign managers have to tread carefully if they want to limit the campaign exposure of senior figures whom they regard as ineffective on television; witness the complaints of Nigel Lawson at his low profile in the 1987 election campaign and of Norman Lamont in 1992 (see p. 240). In collaboration with their publicity advisers Harold Wilson and James Callaghan took care to minimize the television exposure of colleagues who, according to opinion polls, were unpopular with voters (e.g. Tony Benn) and Mr Kinnock did the same with the unappealing John Prescott in 1987 and 1992. Poor television performances by senior Conservatives, Francis Pym in 1979 and John Wakeham in 1987 ('that man will not hold office again', Mrs Thatcher is alleged to have said), led to their rapid banishment from the centre of the Tory campaign. Presentational skills (being 'good on television') have probably become marginally more important in promoting British politicians, but certainly not yet to the same extent as in the United States.

The political impact of television is not confined to election campaigns. A feature of the more 'permanent' campaign is that a party's press and broadcasting officers and public relations advisers are constantly advising politicians about communications long before the election. The build-up to elections for the party leadership or for Labour's Shadow Cabinet and NEC, or to the annual party conferences, are also geared to television coverage. The government of the day has many opportunities to shape the news agenda before the official campaign begins – and rules of balance operate – simply by exploiting its use of office and using ministerial announcements, policy initiatives, the Budget and Prime Minister's Question Time to dominate the airwaves. Party conferences, like American party conventions, have increasingly become stage-managed for the televised projection of a positive party image and strong leadership. Traditionally, a party conference was largely a relationship between the platform and the floor. But intense media coverage has transformed that relationship into one between the conference as a whole and the viewer at home, as the party managers try to shape the impressions made on the viewers. When BBC cameras first covered the Conservative party conference in 1954 party managers arranged for the most attractive women to be seated behind the leader Winston Churchill during his speech. The Labour party, caught up in Bevanite rows, refused to permit the cameras into the conference hall at Margate but allowed them in the following year.

Today the conference managers devote great energy to constructing a good stage set, presenting an arresting slogan, selecting sympathetic platform speakers and shunting less compelling speakers or potentially embarrassing topics to early morning and late afternoon slots when there are fewer viewers. Stage management probably reached its apogee at the 1986 Conservative conference. Saatchi & Saatchi, the party's advertising agency, devised a conference theme, *The Next Move Forward*, was involved in planning and staging the conference and even suggested suitable themes and phrases for the speeches of some ministers. As ever, the conference built up to a high Mass for the leader on the final day. The Labour party has moved in the same direction, giving party spokesmen and particularly the leader a more prominent role at conferences. A major business or interest group might look enviously on the opportunity of five days' virtually uninterrupted television coverage to present itself.

A final effect has been the increase in the broadcasters' analyses of their own coverage of elections. Broadcasters and print journalists also write behind-the-scenes pieces about the parties' strategies and how the parties are manipulating the media and how the media in turn covers the political parties. The development of such 'meta-campaign stories' is occurring in other Western states (Blumler, Gurevitch and Nossiter 1995). The journalists judge whether a party's campaign is 'disciplined', 'integrated', 'smooth' and 'slick', and in part these judgements are shaped by the standing of the political parties in the opinion polls and in part by the 'performance' of party leaders. It is as if the parties' press conferences, briefings, election broadcasts and leaders' interviews are judged as theatre 'performances', with the journalists in the role of theatre critics. Roy Hattersley, Labour's Deputy Leader, was a critic of the emphasis on presentation and warned after the 1992 defeat, 'We must not be so obsessed with the glitz and glamour that the media become the message'.

Conclusion

How does one assess the impact of this massive television coverage of modern election campaigns? Clearly the increase in media outlets and the lengthening campaign day, starting with breakfast television, early-morning press conferences and continuing through to evening rallies and late-night interviews and analyses, have placed more demands on campaigners and reporters, and provided an incentive for the parties to use the skills of professionals. Politicians also have to be more cautious, for more of what they say and do is now recorded on film or sound and can be replayed to their advantage or disadvantage. Spontaneous actions (e.g. Kinnock's display of euphoria at the Sheffield rally in 1992) or casual remarks can be damaging. As politicians try to become more self-controlled and party managers seek greater control over public campaign activities, so reporters become more frustrated. Until recently the campaigns of the different political parties went their own ways, with little in the way of debate, or challenge and response. By their interventions at press conferences and interviews with politicians, journalists have managed to increase the debating function of modern elections and carry the argument between political parties. At times, to the intense resentment of politicians, the journalists may even break through the control of the political parties and set the agenda themselves (e.g. 'Jennifer's ear' in 1992).

There are several critics of television's role in modern elections. Compared with newsprint, television conveys only a small amount of verbal information. Television obviously gives many voters an opportunity to see their leaders in a way that was impossible before the spread of the medium. But party leaders rarely meet ordinary voters on their visits to shopping centres, largely because they are surrounded by a mob of 200 or 300 reporters, cameramen and technicians for a photo-opportunity. The *Independent*'s political editor, the late Peter Jenkins, suggested that the photo-opportunities contrived for TV did not bring people and politicians together and that the medium might actually have become a barrier between them: 'It must be plain enough to viewers that what they see on their screens is not politicians meeting the people but politicians meeting the media' (*Independent* 24 March 1992). Hugo Young in the *Guardian* mourned the death of the open public meeting, with questions allowed from the floor. At the televised rallies voters were being relegated to walk-on extras, 'passive receivers, no longer active participants in a dialogue nobody controls. These are the politics of permanent condescension' (25 March 1992).

Britain, however, has not gone as far as the United States in the televised transformation of elections. In the United States the medium is more clearly the message and Presidential campaigns are dominated by soundbites and visuals. Ronald Reagan in 1980 and 1984 and George Bush in 1988 proved themselves masters of the new techniques of communications. Michael Deaver and Roger Ailes realized the importance of 'good visuals' for television. They strictly controlled the locations and backgrounds of their candidates for the network evening news broadcasts and kept them away from the travelling newspaper reporters and, where possible, from tough or unwelcome questions. They were helped, according to Mark Hertsgaard, by network correspondents whose first question at meetings with Reagan was usually 'Can we get pictures?' (1988: 37). A *Wall Street Journal* editor commented, 'TV producers are like nymphomaniacs when it comes to visuals'.

Politicians and broadcasters seem fated to a tense relationship, with the potential for mutual frustration, resentment and a sense of betrayal peaking during elections. The imperatives of professionalism pull the two sides in different directions. The parties want favourable treatment for themselves and the broadcasters want 'good' television, which usually means excitement and unpredictability. It is understandable that parties want a say over television coverage, for it is the main medium through which they address the voters. It is equally understandable that programme makers chafe at how they are expected to sacrifice normal news values for the campaign and cover pseudo-events in the interests of some notion of political 'balance'. There seems to be no ready solution to the problem.

10

AMERICANIZATION?

Chapter 1 highlighted the main features of the 'professional' model of election campaigning, one which gives a prominent role to modern communicators and their techniques. Many of the features associated with modern campaigns – saturation opinion polling, parties' orientation to the mass media, particularly television, emphasis on the orchestration of communications to advance the party 'line' and media fascination with the election horse race – occurred first or have been developed furthest in the United States and exported to other countries. Hence the claim that there is an 'Americanization' of campaigning across many countries. As earlier chapters have shown, the trends are found also in British elections, so much so that it was claimed that the Kinnock and Thatcher campaigns in 1987 'marked the full migration of American political packaging techniques to Britain . . . [and] politicians were being sold like a new brand of detergent' (O'Shaughnessy 1990: 218).

It is certainly true that British campaigners closely follow developments in the United States and seek to learn lessons. Knowledge of American campaigning has been spread in Britain partly by the vast literature on the subject, partly by the intense international media coverage of Presidential elections and partly by the personal contacts between campaign advisers in both countries. Harold Wilson in 1963 and 1964 encouraged commentators to make comparisons between his campaign and John Kennedy's bid for the Presidency in 1960. Edward Heath's media advisers borrowed from the Nixon campaign's use of television in 1968, particularly the news format and *cinéma-vérité* approaches to party broadcasts. The Conservatives' approach to television and to political communications in general in 1987 also owed something to President Reagan's 1984 campaign. Labour's election broadcast 'Kinnock' in 1987 was inspired by an earlier Democratic party television profile of Hubert Humphrey, 'What Manner of Man'. Before 1992 Labour strategists drew informally on the advice of such American campaign consultants as Bob Shrum, Mark Mellman and Robert Doak, and the Democratic National Committee, while the Conservatives drew on the advice of the US pollster, Richard Wirthlin. After working on the Clinton campaign Philip Gould wrote a lengthy private memo on the lessons for Labour. He claimed that in the media age effective campaigning required:

A rapid response to opposition attacks, which in turn requires a good research base. Labour was poorly served in 1992.

A clear consistent message, as Clinton had with his themes of change, economic recovery and reforming health care. Labour lacked such a clear message in 1992.

Flexibility. Clinton's campaign dispensed with daily press conferences and his schedule was decided only a day in advance. Labour's was decided before the election started.

A party with a record of election defeats needs not only to make changes but to admit that it has changed. The Democrats did, Labour did not.

A campaign structure which is open, friendly and mutually supportive. Again the contrast with Labour's campaign was stark.

The American Model

Contemporary election campaigning in the United States is marked by the following features:

The rise of single-issue and more candidate-centred campaigning. Among the many causes of these trends are the declining allegiance to the political parties, growing campaign costs, localism and weakness of national parties.

The importance of money, particularly in the pre-nomination Presidential campaigns (after nomination some public funding is provided for candidates), largely because of the high costs of paid media advertising. A candidate's need for campaign funds has in turn encouraged the rise of political action committees of interest groups (PACs), which target money to candidates who support their causes. Professional fundraising, often using direct mail appeals, has also become more important since legislation has imposed a maximum limit on the size of individual contributions.

The growing importance of professional communicators, including media and public relations experts, opinion pollsters and fundraisers, all of whom make use of the new communications technology. These have taken over in some measure many of the tasks traditionally carried out by party workers. Consultants may be generalists, who advise the party or candidates on all aspects of the campaign, including strategy, or specialists who provide expertise in opinion polling, direct mail, fundraising or advertising.

The role of the mass media in giving name 'recognition' to candidates in the primaries and interpreting and evaluating the campaign performance of parties and candidates.

The weakness of political parties, a weakness that is both cause and effect of the above trends.

The growing public concern about the influence and activities of the consultants. They have been criticized *inter alia* for adding to the length and costs of campaigns, exploiting negative and emotional themes to the neglect of substantive issues, promoting candidates who fit in with the new technology rather than the requirements of office, and narrowing the focus of elections.

Anglo-American Differences

Apart from the importance of television and contributions of pollsters and communications professionals the above list has little relevance to Britain. One can point to some emerging similarities in campaign methods on both sides of the Atlantic, as the British have followed the US. These include the increasing use of soundbites, photo-opportunities, more sophisticated techniques in political broadcasts, focus groups, direct mail, values research and negative campaigning. But as yet each is a pale imitation of the transatlantic original.

The political, legal and cultural differences between Britain and the United States remain significant in distinguishing the campaign cultures in the two countries. Perhaps the most important difference lies in the structures of the political parties and the campaign ethos that they encourage. British political parties are stronger than the American – they are more disciplined, programmatic and the national leadership has more control over local nominations and campaigns. Parties in Parliament still make and unmake their leaders and Prime Ministers and it is there that political reputations are primarily made. The leader is first and foremost a leader of the party in Parliament. In the House of Commons the conduct of business lies in the hands of the party leaders and whips and the overwhelming majority of MPs (99 per cent) vote in every Parliamentary division for their own parties.

Because British candidates stand on national party programmes, handed down by the leadership, there are limits on the kind of distinctively local or personal electoral appeals that they can make. If they are denied nomination by the party headquarters their candidacy is sunk, for people largely vote for a national party label. Over 90 per cent of people regularly vote at general elections in line with their party identification, in contrast to the United States where only two-thirds admit identifying with a party and split-ticket voting is but one indicator of the fragile nature of partisanship. Because the bulk of British campaign spending (over 65 per cent) and the thrust of campaign communications are decided by national party head-quarters, the election campaign is a 'national' one. Strict limits on the amount of spending in the constituencies mean that apart from some telephone canvassing and direct mail, the new techniques have largely by-passed local candidates. The strength and centralization of national political parties in Britain may be less apparent today than thirty years ago, but they stand out when compared to parties in the United States.

American political parties are weakened by the division of powers and separate elections for the White House and Congress. The ideology of the Republican and Democratic parties also differs from state to state. These features divorce the party standard bearer in the White House from his nominal followers in the legislature and reduce the role of elections as contests between rival parties bidding to govern the country. One sign of this divorce between Presidential and Congressional elections in the minds of voters has been the growth of split-ticket voting, where the voter endorses a candidate of a different party in the Congressional election and a candidate of another for election to the Presidency. The President has many responsibilities but no guarantee of a Congressional majority behind him and no Cabinet consisting of heavyweight party colleagues. He finds himself having to use the media – 'going public' as Kernell (1986) describes it – to build popular support and form policy coalitions in Congress. He has his own campaign team, which is separate from party headquarters. Its members are primarily loyal to him and the team will probably have been built up from earlier stages in his political career. President Nixon's Committee to Re-Elect the President for 1972, for example, had its own advertising agency and direct mail operation, quite separate from the Republican party. A Presidential candidate may even rise from outside the ranks of the political party, as Eisenhower did in 1952.

Senators and Congressmen are usually elected on their own merits and records, particularly of constituency service, in so far as they manage to publicize them. The weakness of the party provides incentives for the politician to 'make his own name', to run almost as an independent if he is to be nominated, elected, re-nominated and re-elected for his constituency (Cain, Ferejohn and Fiorina 1987). As nomination and election are not in the gift of the party leadership, Congressional and Presidential candidates have to be political entrepreneurs. With only a two-year term as a member of the House of Representatives, success in an election is followed almost immediately with preparations for the next primary and election. Congressmen amass their own campaign funds to employ consultants and pollsters and build up a personal staff, many of whom are directed back to the constituencies to provide services for voters. It is not surprising that state and local party organizations are losing influence to the candidate's own organizations. According to Foster and Muste (1992: 11) 'candidates have been campaigning less as representatives of party organisations and more as individuals offering their personal political expertise to voters'. Funding of candidates by political action committees also increases the candidate's independence from the national party and broad programmes. If campaign finance nationalizes and centralizes election campaigns in Britain it decentralizes and fragments them in the United States.

The lack of meaningful party programmes and the significance of local political issues enables the candidate to contradict the national party leader without adverse consequences. Members of the House of Representatives will often adopt policy positions according to the preferences of significant constituency groups and they have more opportunities than MPs to influence legislation and spending pro-grammes. They are also able to use the generous Congressional facilities, particularly free postage, to mail constituents with informa-tion about their record. The local press and television stations constitute a genuinely local or regional mass media and are more willing than their British equivalents to publicize the local Senate or House member.

There are also significant differences in the national media arrange-ments of the two countries. Britain has a partisan national press but a broadcasting system that bans political advertising and covers politics as a serious activity. The elite culture in Britain is more 'closed' than the American, partly because of the Official Secrets Act, partly because politics has traditionally been a high-status occupation – more so than journalism or advertising – and partly because politics is centred in

Parliament. The British media devotes more time and space to national and Westminster politics than the US media does to Washington – no US daily paper summarizes proceedings in Congress in the way the British broadsheets do for Parliament (Butler and Ranney 1984: 220). In the United States the commercial television networks cover politics as entertainment; election news is heavily personalized, often portrayed as a game or horse race, with opinion polls and analysis of campaign strategy forming the main part of reports; the words of the candidates are carried in soundbites which have become briefer over the years. An interpretative style of reporting with its emphasis on the 'why' more than the 'what', as demonstrated by Patterson (1993: 80–1), increases the influence of the reporter over how the election is reported. These trends have become more evident in recent media coverage of elections in Britain, particularly on independent television (see p. 200). The British media may be more intrusive and more disdainful of politicians than twenty or thirty years ago, but it is markedly less so than the media in the United States.

Reforms in the American nomination process since 1968, particularly the expansion of Presidential primaries, have further weakened the recruitment role of the parties, while increasing that of the media. With the decline of party leaders and conventions as decision-makers and brokers, commentators have come to be a more significant intermediary between parties and voters and at times they act as a 'screening committee' of potential Presidential candidates. It is the reporters' judgements on whether candidates have 'under-' or 'over-performed' in election primaries which decide who 'wins' and who 'loses'. The bench-marks for the candidates are set by the expectations of the reporters. Candidates, faced with elections and primaries, use the media to publicize their activities and promote voters' recognition of their names. As Thomas Patterson has complained in his book *Out of Order*, 'The road to nomination lies through the newsroom' (1993: 33). Television skills, particularly an attractive personality, a facility for speaking in soundbites and an ability to convey assurance, appear to be increasingly important for successful candidates. Walter Mondale, the defeated Democratic candidate for the Presidency in 1984, regretted his lack of television skills and doubted that it was 'possible anymore to run for the Presidency without the capacity to build confidence and communications every night' (Kernell 1986: 118).

One has only to compare this reaction with the prominence in recent British politics of people like Gerald Kaufman, Nigel Lawson, Nicholas

Ridley and Michael Foot to appreciate the lesser role in Britain of television in shaping a political career. It is true that a new generation of leading politicians, including Kenneth Clarke, Chris Patten, Gordon Brown and Tony Blair, are effective on television. But they also have a high standing in the House of Commons as effective debaters and politicians who can master the details of a policy brief. Impressing one's Parliamentary colleagues rather than television viewers is the route to the top. In Britain major political announcements and debates are still expected to take place in Parliament; in the United States they are more likely to be delivered at televised press conferences, interviews or debates, university commencement addresses, or on talk shows like *Larry King Live*.

Many factors help political consultancy to thrive in the US. One is the sheer number of elections; there are nationwide elections for the Presidency, Senate and the House of Representatives, as well as primaries, state and municipal elections, initiatives and referendums. Consultants' skills are given more scope because of the low voter turnout in many of these contests, the comparatively light regulation of television and the greater opportunities to buy advertising time on the large number of television channels. There is also a more aggressive commercialism in the United States – one sees it in sport and religion, for example – and greater acceptance of advertising.

These conditions have contributed to the rise of 'a merchandised politics' (O'Shaughnessy 1990: 38) and an important niche for the more than 5,000 political consultants in the United States. Such consultancy is often a source of political influence. Almost the first campaign decision a serious candidate takes is to appoint a pollster and a campaign consultant. W. Lance Bennett (1992: 106) quotes a consultant: 'Candidates now deal primarily with consultants. They seldom deal seriously with the parties'. Some consultants are media 'stars', lending credibility to a candidate if they work for him or her, and immense powers of political persuasion are often attributed to them by admiring candidates and commentators. The Presidential victories of Nixon in 1968, Reagan in 1980 and 1984 and Bush in 1988 were all portrayed to an important extent as victories for the image-makers. The consultants have also taken over many of the roles traditionally played by the parties and their volunteer activists in getting out voters, raising funds, polling, direct mail and writing speeches (O'Shaughnessy 1990: 128; Petracca 1989).

So far there has been nothing in Britain comparable to the corps of campaign consultants available for hire in America. If American candidates court consultants, in Britain it is often the pollsters and advertising agencies who seek out the parties. Whereas consultants can make a good living from political campaigns in the United States, such groups as Saatchi, MORI, Harris and NOP derive only a small part of their revenue from political work (no more than 5 per cent even in an election year), and do it part-time, in contrast to the fulltime political commitment of US consultants. In Britain it is a case of commercial communicators turning to politics every four years or so, compared to the American case of professional political communicators operating continuously. The British parties are not big spenders compared to commerce, and the relatively small amounts of money spent on campaigning limit the degree to which public relations and advertising can 'Americanize' British elections.

It is also worth noting the confines within which the professionals have had to operate in Britain. Until recently the only campaign tools available were election broadcasts and posters. Only in 1979 did the national press begin to carry party political advertisements on a large scale during the campaign and parties still cannot buy time on broadcast outlets. British parties do not grant the polling or advertising agencies the same authority that American candidates give to such consultants as Joseph Napolitan, David Garth, Richard Viguerie or Robert Squier. The latter play a more influential role in political strategy and tactics than their British counterparts. Many British politicians resent their dependence on the communicators and take a dim view of any suggestion that they are being 'packaged' for the voters (see above, p. 171). Party pollsters and advertising people who claim credit in public for election victory in Britain will not last long. America is hardly a uniformly positive campaign model for British politicians.

Many British politicians are ambivalent about the new trends, seeming to regard opinion polling and the whole business of public relations as an 'add on' or 'background', something that they can do alongside traditional campaign activities. For the most part they still decide for themselves what they will say, relying on intuition, drawing on the lessons of experience, responding to advice from other people or doing what they feel comfortable with. Perhaps to a greater extent than their American counterparts, they still believe that campaign communications should centre on substantive issues and policies, and are sensitive to accusations of indulging in vulgar, unethical or gimmicky practices – the kind of personal attacks seen in the US televised 'spot' advertisements. To quote one observer, 'An American is struck by the absence of personality or even the mention of personages in the [British] ads . . . the concentration is . . . on the issues, with the *party* differences starkly and distinctly etched' (Sabato 1981: 128).

Many American political commentators have expressed concern about the consequences of the campaigning trends in their country. They complain that the types of media coverage, notably the emphasis on the horse race, the reduction of politicians' statements to soundbites for television and short excerpts in the press, the importance of finance and the negative advertising, combine to weaken the citizenship-enhancing role of elections. The emphasis on continual campaigning, a product of the lengthy road of the primaries and then the election for the President, also has costs in terms of the time which Presidential candidates can devote to developing government-related skills. A Presidential candidate learns more about campaigning and the requirements of the media: as Richard Rose argues, 'Today, campaigning is part of the job description of the President' (1988). He adds, however, that going public works against going government. A British Prime Minister, before his or her arrival in Downing Street, will have learnt more about governing because of his or her experiences in Parliament, Cabinet and Whitehall. Restoring political parties to better health may be one way of promoting clearer electoral choice to American voters. But the parties' decline is a symptom of many other forces and their's has been a long and largely fruitless cry in the United States (Ranney 1955). Indeed, many of the reforms have only further weakened the parties.

Conclusion

Britain is different from America and British campaigns have not yet been Americanized. As other societies become more 'American', in terms of levels of affluence, life style and communication technologies, so there is a growing similarity in the campaigning techniques adopted. America is also widely regarded by British politicians as a source of innovation in campaign techniques. But a comparison of the United States and Britain shows that the results of these trends are shaped by distinctive national political cultures and institutions. The British parties, specifically their leading politicians and officials, are still more significant actors in deciding campaign strategy.

11

CONCLUSION

This concluding chapter discusses different ways of measuring the effectiveness of election campaigns and asks what difference, if any, all the planning, professional communications and intense activity make. It then analyses the barriers to effectiveness. Finally, it assesses the extent to which modern campaigns contribute to the quality of representative democracy.

The first problem to confront is the notion of the campaign itself. Reference to the campaign conveys an impression of a single-purpose organization engaged in a concentrated activity in which candidates, party workers and party officials work together towards agreed goals. There is certainly a greater concern now by parties to manage the campaign agenda, exploit more professional methods of publicity, use polls to track the mood of voters and insist on spokesmen adhering to the strategy, to the 'plan'. Few participants or well-placed observers, however, would ever impute such a businesslike approach and actual implementation of well-considered election strategies to British political parties. Any realistic account of a campaign has to acknowledge the part played by *ad hoc* decisions, accidents, routines and inertia, and flashes of individual intuition – as well as blunders. Chris Patten, the hard-pressed manager of the Tory campaign in 1992, reflected: 'You have no time for making strategic decisions. You are on a toboggan and try to cope' (interview).

Analysis also has to take account of the sheer individualism of many senior politicians who want to do their own thing. In 1970 Tony Benn attacked Enoch Powell as a racialist – to the fury of Prime Minister Harold Wilson, who believed that the attacks gave further publicity to Powell and increased his popularity among some Labour voters in the West Midlands. In 1983 Jim Callaghan publicly disassociated himself from Labour's defence policy and Denis Healey made unguarded remarks about Mrs Thatcher 'glorying in slaughter' in the Falklands; Neil Kinnock made remarks in a similar vein, although the party's campaign planners had agreed to avoid references to the Falklands campaign. Leading politicians are usually difficult to discipline. Recall the Conservative insider, quoted on p. 169, who claimed that he did not have a clue about the party's strategy in 1987 and 1992 and doubted that, apart from the advertising, there was one: 'In an election, people are too busy to think about strategy. For advertising, yes, for the rest, no. It is a case of busy ministers going on television and saying what they like. Nobody tells Major, Hurd or Lamont what to say' (Sherbourne interview). Another Conservative Cabinet minister claimed that, in his experience, political Cabinets (often concerned with election preparations) were 'a shambles':

> They were a shambles because Cabinet ministers had become used to addressing a problem, with papers on it, and then taking a decision. But when talking about election strategy, every minister has his own view, speaks from a different viewpoint and the meeting is too large anyway. (Interview)

There are countless examples of senior politicians departing from the campaign script. One readily thinks of Kinnock's televised interview with Frost in 1987 and then his display of euphoria at the Sheffield rally in 1992, Mrs Thatcher's television interview with David Dimbleby in 1987 (see p. 201), the Labour and Conservative parties' handling of the 'Jennifer's ear' broadcast in 1992 and Major's speech in defence of the Union on the final weekend in 1992 ('What the hell was he saying that for?' said one Central Office official, 'We are supposed to be concentrating on tax'). One could go on.

Measuring Effect

Measuring the effectiveness of an election campaign or a particular tactic is no easy matter, for an election result will be shaped by many factors, many of which cannot be individually measured. An increase in a government's popularity may follow an advertising campaign, but it may also follow a rise in living standards, a change of leader or policy, errors by the opposition, or a shift in public mood which is due to other factors. One effect, many possible causes. Some measures of campaign impact are relatively straightforward, e.g. surveying the percentage of households which have received party leaflets or been canvassed by party workers. For advertisements, posters and election broadcasts surveys can test levels of recall or appreciation among voters. But these are campaign outputs not outcomes, they do not tell us about effects on voting. One can also analyse opinion poll trends about party leaders and issues to get some idea of impact. If advertising agencies measure the effectiveness of their commercial campaigns in, for example, increases in sales figures or market share, they are usually less precise in talking about effectiveness in elections. They may point to such intangible effects as boosting the morale of party workers, impressing commentators, putting the other party on the defensive, winning the argument, preparing the ground for the next election, and so on. These claims may be true or untrue, there is no way of knowing. As noted on pp. 153–4, the party that has seen its share of support surge the most in recent elections has been the Liberal party, which is backed by fewer resources than the Conservatives or Labour.

Another measure of effectiveness may be in 'winning' the campaign itself, as distinct from the election. Commentators and opinion polls provide a verdict of sorts on the quality of a party's campaign. In 1983 Labour got a bad press, not least from its own supporters and, according to opinion polls, lost a quarter of its support during the election campaign (table 11.1). In 1987 Labour managers were determined to show that the party could conduct a competent election campaign – not least to demonstrate that the party had changed. Commentators in 1987, and again in 1992, judged the party to have done better than the Conservatives. In 1987 Gallup found that 47 per cent regarded Labour's as the best television campaign, 21 per cent the Conservatives and 17 per cent the Liberal Alliance. In 1992 when Gallup asked voters which party had campaigned most impressively the figures were Labour 36 per cent, Liberal 34 per cent and

Table 11.1 Changing perceptions of the parties (1983)

'Has your opinion of the (. . .) party improved, stayed the same or got worse since the start of the election campaign?'

	Lab. %	Con. %	All %
'worse'	46	28	14
'improved'	8	13	23

Source: MORI

Conservative only 10 per cent. Impact may also be seen in popular expectations of which party will win. Between the first and last weeks of the 1992 campaign Gallup found that the proportions expecting the Conservatives to win fell from 48 to 24 per cent, those expecting Labour to win rose from 31 to 47 per cent, and those expecting a hung Parliament rose from 5 to 18 per cent.

Finally, one may look at movements of opinion. In 1992 surveys reported that Labour enjoyed big leads on all the social issues throughout the campaign, and voters regularly ranked Labour's target issues of health, education and unemployment as the most salient, and health and education actually rose in importance during the election. But on the economic agenda, particularly on tax and inflation, Labour failed to narrow the gap with the Conservatives. A MORI final panel survey for the *Sunday Times* found that 70 per cent agreed and only 24 per cent disagreed with the statement 'Most people will pay more in taxes if Labour wins the election'. Large majorities also thought that under a Labour government taxes would go up for those on average earnings. A Harris ITN exit poll found that 49 per cent claimed that they would be worse off under Labour's tax plans and only 30 per cent better. The fact that these findings on tax and the economy co-existed with Labour still enjoying a lead on the voting-intention question has led some to doubt the importance of many of the issue questions as an indicator of voting choice. Even exit and post-election surveys found voters still claiming that social issues were the most important. The opinion polls – and much media commentary based on them – suggested that Labour had clearly won the battle for the agenda. Yet were these social issues as influential as views about economic management and living standards? Was a journalist correct in claiming 'We are a nation of liars'? (Harris 1992). Surely the economy was the central ground of the agenda and, in spite of weaknesses on virtually every other issue, the Conservatives managed to command this area.

Labour's campaign in 1992 also sought to pin the blame for the recession on the Major government; conversely, the Conservatives wished to stress the newness of John Major and the change from his predecessor. The Conservatives succeeded, Labour failed. Gallup in March 1992 found that 48 per cent blamed the world recession for Britain's economic difficulties, 43 per cent the Thatcher government but only 4 per cent the Major government. Labour's campaign also sought to reassure electors about its economic competence and Neil Kinnock's leadership; people could trust Labour, they could trust

Kinnock. Yet the NOP exit poll found that doubts on these were the two major reasons which voters gave for rejecting the party. The Conservative message, 'You can't trust Labour', worked.

Perhaps we need to modify our criteria of a 'good' campaign. To date commentators have drawn variously on the findings of opinion polls – though voters' evaluations of the campaign may also be influenced by reports of the polls – their own assessments of the public mood and 'performance' (usually presentational skills) of the politicians, and even on how efficient and co-operative the parties appear in conducting their media operations. Labour's election campaigns in 1987 and 1992 appeared to have 'mesmerized' many commentators into thinking that, because the communications were so impressive, the party's underlying image problems had been remedied. Chris Powell, a member of Labour's communications team in 1987 and 1992, reflected:

> Do election campaigns matter that much? Were we doing a disservice to Labour? A good campaign can preserve the hope of getting elected even if all the policies and personalities aren't yet sorted out. It may only take their minds off more fundamental problems and the need for radical changes – the 'one more heave' delusion. (Interview)

A party's analysis of its campaign may be marred by what has been termed a 'congratulation-rationalization effect' (Lamb and Smith 1968). This encourages winning candidates and managers to inflate their own contribution to the victory and praise the discernment and intelligence of voters. Those on the losing side, however, console themselves by minimizing their responsibility for the defeat. The latter are more likely to be nearer the truth in assessing impact. The burden of academic studies of voting behaviour in Britain and elsewhere is that enduring forces like the voters' social class, religion, party identification, the government's record and long-standing images of the parties are more electorally decisive. It is possible that, as voters are less committed to a party and campaigners develop more sophisticated techniques, these qualifications may be changing. And, of course, a poor campaign, like Labour's in 1983, can draw attention to a party's incompetence and lose votes. During the campaign the party, according to the polls, shed a quarter of its support. But most activities are still of marginal importance one way or the other in deciding the election outcome – although in close-run contests they can mean the difference between defeat and victory, and politicians are motivated by the possibility that their efforts *might* make the difference.

Causes of Ineffectiveness

There are many barriers to effective campaigning. In his pioneering study of election campaigning nearly thirty years ago, Richard Rose (1967: 195) concluded a discussion of 'obstacles to rationality', i.e. barriers to the systematic and effective pursuit of votes, by saying: 'the rational vote-maximising politician, acting with consistency and empirical justification in pursuit of the single electoral goal, is a myth. Campaigners are rational only imperfectly and intermittently'. The following eight points are among the barriers to effective campaigning.

Timing

Timing matters in an election just as in other communications campaigns. A government ideally tries to implement unpopular measures or tough economic policies early in the Parliament, so that electoral resentment is likely to have faded by polling day; conversely, it will try to deliver 'visible' economic benefits (e.g. tax cuts or increases in welfare benefits) just before the election, when voters' awareness is likely to be high. A government's control of the annual Budget also gives it an opportunity to distribute benefits and manipulate the economy to produce a feeling of well-being among many voters.

Labour, both in office and in opposition, has often found that a general election was badly timed for its campaign plans. In 1964 funds for its first extensive use of public relations were committed for a June poll, but the Conservative government delayed calling an election until October. Things were no better when Labour was in government. In 1970 the party's publicists had planned their communications for an election in October and were caught out by Harold Wilson's decision to call one in June.

The government has not always had a free choice over election timing (Kavanagh 1989). In the postwar period the 1950, 1964 and 1992 elections were held virtually at the end of the Parliament, the 1951, 1966 and October 1974 elections followed short-lived Parliaments in which the governing party lacked an adequate majority or any majority at all, and in 1979 Mr Callaghan was forced to call an election. This leaves only five postwar elections (1955, 1959, 1970, 1983 and 1987) in which the government dissolved in its own good time, was able to prime the economic pump and was reassured by comfortable leads in the opinion polls. Of these elections only in 1970, in a surprise outcome, did the governing party lose. But even when the government securely controls the timing other factors may spoil the run-up to the election. Industrial disruption, an international crisis or bad economic statistics may force a government into unpopular policies or spoil its message of success and competence. The poor balance of payments figures, just three days before polling day in 1970, were a blow for a Labour government which had invested so much political capital in improving the trade balance.

Conflict between electoral and other political goals

Not all politicians pursue votes as assiduously as the businessman allegedly pursues profits. Some claim to be motivated by 'higher' causes than winning elections. In 1960, Richard Crossman argued that the Labour party should not adjust its policies, particularly on public ownership, to so-called 'moderate' public opinion. Instead it should wait for the failure of existing Conservative policies and the inevitable economic crisis to emerge: 'Those who assert that the sole object, or even the main object, of the Labour Party today should be to regain office seem to me to misconceive not merely the notion of British socialism, but the workings of British democracy' (1960: 4).

All parties contain 'purists', activists who are committed to the advancement of particular policies and values, regardless of electoral support or what opinion polls represent as the public mood. At times, they suggest, it may be better for the party to lose an election and return to its 'first' principles in opposition: better to be right and lose the election than opportunistic and win it. They may also claim that a 'silent majority' is waiting to be mobilized by bold political leader-ship, by, for example, Labour offering more socialist policies, or the Conservatives pursuing more right-wing policies. In the United States, Barry Goldwater in 1964 and George McGovern in 1972 were classic cases of candidates who oriented their campaigns to conservative and liberal activists respectively, and which led to electoral disaster. Labour's left wing persistently called in the 1970s and 1980s for greater public ownership and unilateral renunciation by Britain of its nuclear weapons, in spite of surveys showing these to be sure vote losers. Its 1983 election manifesto was the most left wing for many years and the choice of Michael Foot as leader and the adoption of internal party reforms were all calculated to please activists. At the election Labour's share of the popular vote fell to its lowest since 1918. After the defeat the party's Research Director castigated the party's *'failure to prepare a manifesto and a policy programme which accurately reflected the concerns and needs of ordinary voters'* (Butler and Kavanagh 1984: 278: original emphasis).

Parties sometimes choose leaders who, according to the polls, are less electorally popular than other contenders – the Conservative choice of Lord Home in 1963 and Labour of Michael Foot in 1981 being notable examples. Each choice was influenced more by concerns for internal party unity than appealing to the electorate. In both cases the party lost the subsequent general election, the leaders' perceived short-comings were seen as a major cause of the defeat and both men resigned soon after. Loyalty to the new leader stood in the way of a vote-maximizing strategy. Prominent Labour campaigners in the run-up to the 1992 election remarked in private that Labour could not win as long as Neil Kinnock was leader.

At times a party leader may have doubts about the electoral appeal of a policy but decide to accept it for reasons of party unity. We have seen that well before the 1992 election Mr Kinnock was uneasy about the party's spending and taxation proposals. All the public and private polling evidence showed that voters were worried that Labour would increase taxes and be 'soft' on public spending. During 1991 he was gradually persuaded that the party's proposals for higher taxes could also damage the fragile economic recovery. He failed, however, to persuade John Smith, his Shadow Chancellor, to make changes and after a botched briefing of journalists (see p. 104) he did not pursue the matter. Why? One reason was that Mr Smith's standing in and out of the party meant that he was to be handled with care. He was a political heavyweight, a rival of Mr Kinnock and the most likely successor to Kinnock if Labour lost the election. He jealously guarded his Treasury brief, wanted to hold his hand until the government delivered a budget in 1992 and did not respect Kinnock's judgement. Another reason is that Mr Kinnock was also persuaded that to go back on the spending pledges might divide the Shadow Cabinet and damage party unity. The result was that Labour's electoral weakness – the perception that it would increase taxes for most people – remained.

Lack of sure knowledge

There is no science of political campaigning or voting behaviour, no body of knowledge which enables a campaign adviser to say to the candidate: 'Do this and you will win' or warn 'Do that and you will lose x number of votes'. Surveys may inform a party of its strengths and weaknesses, but they cannot prescribe how the weaknesses can be remedied. If opinion polls show that a party's policy or leader is unpopular this evidence may be used to argue in favour of down-grading the policy or the role of the leader or, alternatively, of a more intensive campaign on their merits. In the 1964 election the Conservative Prime Minister Sir Alec Douglas Home had an acknowledged expertise on defence and foreign affairs and the Conservatives enjoyed a large lead over Labour in the polls on both issues. On the other hand, the public was not greatly interested in them. But Sir Alec continued to talk about them. Lord Poole, a Central Office Deputy Chairman, said, 'Every PM has one issue he cares about more than anything else. Alec's is the bomb. He'd even be prepared to lose an election on it' (interview, Butler file). In 1991 and 1992 John Major was not impressed by survey evidence that his rejection of proportional representation or more independence for Scotland would be vote losers and he campaigned against them. Not only did he calculate that public opinion was 'soft' on the issues, but he was keen to emphasize policy differences between the Conservatives, as the party of the United Kingdom and constitutional stability, and the other parties. There is usually an element of personal judgement, intuition and hunch in the decisions politicians take.

Disagreement on campaign strategy and tactics

Campaigners may agree about the goal of electoral victory but disagree about how to achieve it. In the October 1974 campaign some of Mr Heath's senior colleagues and advisers argued that the party's 'national unity' appeal to voters would be more effective if he declared his willingness to stand aside in the event of his leadership proving a barrier to the formation of a 'national' government. He had already promised that if he won he would invite people from other parties to join his government but dismissed as a gimmick the suggestion that he declare his willingness to stand down. If some close colleagues regarded the 'national unity' appeal as a vote winner, other Conservatives, including Mrs Thatcher, rejected it as defeatist. In 1987 Mrs Thatcher and some of her advisers criticized the Central Office campaign and Saatchi advertisements for being too 'negative'; they wanted something more 'positive' that praised the government's record. The Saatchi agency and the party Chairman thought this was misguided and the differences eventually broke out in a major row on 'Wobbly Thursday' and a change in the advertising (see p. 64).

In spite of the campaign managers' insistence that leaders speak to 'the line', disagreements often emerge. A manifesto may fail to resolve deep divisions over policy or may provide insufficient guidance to cope with subsequent questions. We have already referred to Labour's embarrassment in the October 1974 election when the pro-EC Roy Jenkins and Shirley Williams announced at separate press conferences that they would not remain members of a Labour government which, as a result of a referendum, took Britain out of the Community. The Labour party and Cabinet were hopelessly split over British membership of the EC and the referendum was a device to paper over the cracks. In 1987 Mr Kinnock and his Shadow Chancellor gave different answers to questions about the income levels at which Labour's tax proposals would bite (see p. 182). In the same election Mrs Thatcher and her Secretary of State for Education, Kenneth Baker, gave contrasting answers to journalists' questions on whether schools which opted out of local authority control would be able to charge fees and re-introduce academic selection. The Alliance campaign in 1987 was marred by open disagreement between the two leaders, David Steel and David Owen, about their willingness to co-operate in a hung Parliament with a Conservative party led by Mrs Thatcher. Political opponents and their supporters in the press eagerly exploited such divisions. Disagreements on policy within a party are not unusual. But in the feverish atmosphere of an election campaign and under the relentless scrutiny of the media, they are often blown out of proportion.

Shortcomings of actors

A regular feature of British election campaigns is that politicians in both parties privately complain about the inefficiencies of their party officials and officials in turn reciprocate with a list of the politicians' failings. Strategy is one thing, implementing it is another. Win or lose, Conservative party leaders usually decide that Central Office has failed. Sometimes the criticisms are deserved. After the February 1974 election defeat Mr Heath criticized a sub-standard performance from Central Office and made several changes in personnel and strategy for the election later that year. Election defeat usually gives rise to criticisms of a party's campaign; what is striking is that the same fate accompanied Conservative successes in 1987 and 1992. After the election the new party Chairman, Sir Norman Fowler, who had accompanied John Major on his travels on the campaign bus, bluntly told Central Office staff at his first meeting with them: 'The election was won on the bus, not in Central Office'. The performances of staff at Labour headquarters are also regularly criticized by the leaders and their staff, even when the party wins. Bernard Donoughue, working with Harold Wilson in 1974, recalls that arrangements for the leader's election meetings and press conferences 'were often appalling' (1987: 43) and that the party machine was riven by 'petty jealousies and internal squabbling' and was 'of almost unbelievable inefficiency' (1987: 44).

The personalities and skills of party leaders are important in the projection of a party's message. According to the opinion polls and much anecdotal evidence neither Mr Heath nor Mr Kinnock were electoral assets to their parties and they were presented as members of a 'team' in their final campaigns as leaders. According to the polls the first was regarded as too 'cold' and a poor communicator, the latter as verbose and indecisive. Mr Kinnock's party leadership qualities were admired by many members of the Shadow Communications Agency, but it would be difficult to find more than a handful who thought he was not an electoral liability.

Distrust between key campaigners

Senior campaign staff may differ in their reading of election developments. The different views may be a consequence of their different responsibilities or vantage points as well as political or organizational rivalry. Party leaders are aware that their colleagues are ambitious and hope to advance their careers, whether the party wins or loses. The sense of rivalry encourages them or their staff to wonder why some colleagues adopt high profiles or low ones; commentators also play the game. Party officials or campaign advisers have their own 'turf' to protect, be it as treasurer, advertising agent, pollster, media adviser or constituency organizer. A leader's entourage may look at the campaign differently from party officials, the former being more oriented to the interests of the leader, the latter to the party. The careers of the former are bound up with the success of the leader, the careers of most party officials continue regardless of the election outcome.

In the case of Labour, the problem of having different power centres in the PLP and the party headquarters has been exacerbated by long-running factionalism between left and right. There were continuing tensions between the Wilson and Callaghan governments on the one hand, and the party's research department and NEC on the other, and both leaders left the party machine in the dark about their thinking on election timing and strategy in 1970 and 1978. According to one study of the 1970 election 'There were continual complaints from senior Transport House officials that Mr Wilson did not take them into his confidence, but he felt that they did not "get things done" and leaked any information he gave them into the gossip columns' (Butler and Pinto-Duschinsky 1971: 61).

The political differences between the Labour leadership and party machine continued for much of the 1970s and 1980s. During 1991 and even during the 1992 campaign there was a lack of mutual trust between key members of the Shadow Communications Agency and party officers, between the latter and members of Kinnock's office and, for a time, among members of Kinnock's staff. Some important campaign meetings were kept 'private', and were attended by the party's Campaign and Communications Director Peter Mandelson but not by other party directors, although the latter's co-operation was necessary if decisions were to be implemented. Mandelson's successor as Director was not on speaking terms with either his deputy or with Neil Kinnock's press officer. These problems weakened the party's ability to fashion and implement an effective communications strategy before the election.

The tensions boiled over in acrimonious post-election exchanges about the reasons for the party's fourth successive election defeat. Labour left wingers blamed the leadership and the Agency for downgrading 'traditional' (i.e. working-class) Labour values and left-wing policies, and complained about the influence of non-elected pollsters and communications volunteers in the Agency to the neglect of politicians and party officials. After the election one aggrieved senior party official complained in a memo to the NEC, 'Decisions must be taken by politicians, advised by professional staff with politics in their bloodstreams; who have experienced the battle at close quarters; and whom the party can hold to account'. All campaigns have 'insiders' and 'outsiders', with status defined largely by proximity to the party leader or the chief decision-makers. The memo quoted above is the perennial cry of the outsider.

Campaigns are also marred by disputes between politicians over who gets 'star' treatment (in other words, appearing on television and at press conferences) and who is excluded, because they are not regarded as good at 'presentation' (a favourite term of Mrs Thatcher). Nigel Lawson resented his exclusion from a more prominent role in the 1987 campaign and his memoirs quote, at some length, the favourable press notices he was receiving (1992: 701). Norman Lamont, as Chancellor of the Exchequer, was also unhappy about Central Office attempts to limit his media exposure in the 1992 election – on the grounds that he was no match for Labour's John Smith – and at one stage threatened to mount media initiatives of his own, without reference to Central Office. The Labour leadership similarly tried to marginalize the public role of Tony Benn and John Prescott in past elections, largely because of fears such outspoken figures might contradict the party's message.

Problems of coordination

The greater the number of units of a campaign structure to be co-ordinated the more opportunities there are for misunderstandings and failures in implementation. Compared to Labour the Conservatives have a relatively simple party structure, a consequence largely of the concentration of formal authority in the hands of the leader. The leader issues the manifesto, makes the key appointments at Central Office, and the annual party conference has only an advisory role on policy. By contrast, a Labour leader finds that his colleagues in the Shadow Cabinet are elected by party MPs; the annual conference and NEC provide an important input to the making of party policy; the NEC is formally a co-equal partner with the PLP in determining the contents of the election manifesto and controls the party organization. It was no surprise therefore that Labour election campaigns in the 1970s sometimes spoke with two voices – one from a more left-wing party headquarters and NEC and another from the more moderate Parliamentary leadership. Not only did this division contribute to the image of a divided Labour party but volunteers working on the party's election broadcasts and advertising were caught up in the internal party warfare.

Although Neil Kinnock concentrated much authority in his office, problems of coordination were still evident in the 1992 election. One problem was the aforementioned mistrust between key groups. Another was the plethora of different groups of decision-makers, often situated in different locations – the leader's office in the House of Commons, the party headquarters, the Shadow Communications Agency working from various offices, and the election campaign press conferences and strategy meetings which were held in a building in Millbank, near to the House of Commons. In a post-election critique written for the party Philip Gould admitted, 'the campaign was too compartmentalised, structurally and physically'.

Conservative campaigns have also had their problems. Because the party leader is often Prime Minister it is almost inevitable, in spite of joint meetings, that two decision-making sites develop – one in Downing Street, among the staff who habitually work with the Prime Minister, and the other in Central Office where the party bureaucracy is based. Differences between the two emerged in 1987 and 1992 (see above, pp. 64–5, 73). During the campaign the Prime Minister is absent from London on many days and much is left to the Chairman. But the latter is appointed largely on political grounds (including support for the leader) and it is not always apparent that organizational or campaigning skills are important factors in the appointment. The quality of party chairmen has varied greatly and some may be heavily engaged in campaigning for their own seats – as Chris Patten was in 1992.

Overload

The virtually round-the-clock mass media coverage of the election greatly increases the pressures on campaigners. They face demands to come up with fresh news stories and responses for breakfast, lunch, early evening and late-night news and current affairs programmes. The near 24-hour media coverage has led to a near 24-hour campaign. Central campaign participants are usually working 16 to 18 hours continuously for the four weeks of the campaign and often for several weeks beforehand, getting little sleep and eating irregularly. So many participants live near the edge – a reason surely for the feverish interest in and over-reaction to opinion polls, 'gaffes', media coverage and other events. It is an open secret that key campaign decision-makers occasionally drink too much alcohol or show other signs of wear and tear. The 1992 campaign was so gruelling that in private interviews Philip Gould compared the experience to fighting a war, Chris Patten to riding a rollercoaster and Shaun Woodward confessed afterwards that he needed at least six months holiday to recover. In the course of a hectic day at Central Office a Cabinet minister wondered 'How do you keep sane here?' Minor incidents in 1992, for example a 'revelation' that a Central Office desk officer advised Jennifer Bennett's consultant to get in touch with the *Daily Express*, or that Labour researchers incorrectly identified a couple of patients who were waiting for NHS treatment, were suddenly blown up into major stories by a frenzied press and dominated questions at press conferences. Both incidents revealed organizational flaws. An angry Chris Patten was not informed of the telephone call or an important letter from Jennifer's grandfather which was in party files. And Robin Cook, Labour's spokesman on health, was taken aback to discover that the party's broadcast had not received the approval of Jennifer's parents. Such flaws are inevitable given that so many people are working under intense pressure. It is perhaps surprising that people working under such pressures – way beyond those that could be expected or tolerated in other walks of life – do not make more mistakes and misjudgements. Temper tantrums, tears and drunkenness are understandable. Interestingly, the Clinton Presidential campaign in 1992 insisted on scheduled 'rest periods' for key staff.

Campaigning therefore falls short of full efficiency. Claims about professionalism and effectiveness are statements of aspirations rather than descriptions of reality. But this is true of most organizations. Campaigns have other functions for parties and candidates than winning over voters (Rose 1967; Kavanagh 1970). They provide politicians with a platform for expressing themselves, the parties with an opportunity for debate, activists with a sense of identity and purpose, and organizations with a test of their efficiency and morale. They may also convey a public statement about the nature of the party. After Labour's clear defeat in 1987, the party's Communications and Campaigns Director said, 'Running a good campaign was a means of showing that Labour was a competent party' (Mandelson interview).

Effects of Election Results

An election defeat often ends the career or weakens the authority of a party leader, particularly if he or she has already had a lengthy run in the post. Clement Attlee retired after Labour's second successive election defeat in 1955; Sir Alec Douglas Home did so shortly after the 1964 election defeat; Ted Heath lost the leadership contest in 1975 after two successive general election defeats in the previous twelve months; James Callaghan resigned in 1980 following his party's election defeat and Neil Kinnock after Labour's loss in 1992. In each case the view was widespread among MPs that the party was unelectable without a change of leader. Hugh Gaitskell's position was severely weakened for a time after Labour's defeat in 1959 and Harold Wilson's authority never recovered fully from Labour's loss of office in 1970. The accounts of colleagues and close friends, as well as their own testimony, reveal that defeat is often a heavy blow to the party leader, one that is felt all the more when it involves loss of the premiership as well.

Defeat also usually strengthens the hands of reformers in the losing party. Sometimes this results in the party moving to the ground occupied by the winning party. The outstanding case of such adaptation was that of the Conservatives after their crushing defeat in 1945. They came to terms with Labour's major policies – the National Health Service, extending welfare, full employment, public ownership and beginning the retreat from Empire. The Conservatives again revamped their policies following the election defeats in 1964 and 1966, to show that in spite of thirteen years in office the party still had fresh ideas. After the February 1974 election defeat on the 'Who governs?' platform the Conservatives prepared for another election and only had time to revise their electoral strategy. In the October campaign Mr Heath played a less prominent role, and the party advocated a government of national unity and rejected adversarial rhetoric. When Mrs Thatcher succeeded Mr Heath following a second defeat in 1974 she moved the party in a different direction again, but this time against the so-called middle ground.

After a third successive election loss in 1959 the Labour party quarrelled over policy, leadership and electoral sociology and political strategy. Revisionists argued that Labour should drop from its constitution Clause IV which pledged the party to extensive public ownership, should come to terms with the embourgeoisement and aspirations of the working class, and should become more of a catch-all party, appealing to all classes (see above, p. 175). The reaction to the election defeat of 1979 – and the Labour government's performance over the previous five years – was a sharp move to the left, involving far-reaching changes to the party's constitution and big shifts in policy. Subsequent election defeats in 1983, 1987 and 1992 saw the party move back towards the political ground defined by its opponents. It accepted that it had moved too far from the views of most voters, abandoned many left-wing policies, embraced modern campaigning techniques and loosened the party's trade union connections.

Campaign Effects

Businesses can measure the effectivness of their operations by increases in sales, profits or market share, a football manager by a team winning a match or gaining promotion to a higher division. For parties and candidates electoral effectiveness is most decisively measured in the result – victory or defeat. But this is hardly a fair indicator of the impact or added value of a campaign. Parties do not start an election on a level playing field. Some four-fifths of voters have already decided how to vote before the campaign has begun; for many their votes are the outcome of a lifetime of experiences (Rose and McAllister 1990). Some candidates or parties may realistically have more modest goals – aiming to improve on last time, maintain their share of the vote, or establish a bridgehead for a future election. Others seek consolation elsewhere. In 1983 Tony Benn discovered positive signs in Labour's worst election performance for over fifty years: 'for the first time since 1945 a political party with an openly socialist policy has received the support of over 8½ million people'. 1987 was Labour's second-worst defeat, but some campaign managers claimed to be consoled because they had beaten the Alliance for second place and Labour was firmly established as the only realistic alternative to the Conservatives.

For long the local campaign has been written off, largely by academics, as it appeared that voters responded to national issues and events, rather than to the quality of the candidate or the local party organization. Writing shortly after Labour's defeat in the 1959 election, Anthony Crosland claimed that the election showed that

> the élan of the rank and file is less and less essential to the winning of elections. With the growing penetration of the mass media, political campaigning has become increasingly centralized; and the traditional local activities, the door-to-door canvassing and the rest, are now largely a ritual. (cited in Minkin 1980: 276).

But evidence is now accumulating that in recent general elections the local campaign has counted for more than was acknowledged. Michael Steed and John Curtice in the Nuffield Election Studies have shown that there is an incumbency advantage of some 750 votes for MPs facing their second election – enough to be decisive in a close contest. This may be a reward for the active MP providing services for constituents or taking an independent but popular line in Parliament

(Pattie et al. 1994). Other work claims that, for local Labour parties at least, higher levels of political activity can increase the party's vote by between 1,000 and 2,000 (Seyd and Whiteley 1992; Denver and Hands 1992). In close general elections, as in 1950, 1964 and February 1974, the results in 20 or so seats decided the formation of government; in 1992, the Conservative Parliamentary majority rested on 21 seats won with a majority of less than 2.5 per cent. The 2 per cent or so of the vote that can be gained by an MP's personality, vigorous campaigning or record of constituency service may therefore make a significant difference overall.

Campaign Learning

Campaigners may learn something from their own previous successes and failures, from those of other parties and from elections abroad. By 1962 Labour was sufficiently impressed by the Conservative success in 1959 to call upon the skills of professional public relations experts and its decision to employ an advertising agency in 1983 was influenced by the impact of Saatchi & Saatchi on the Conservatives in 1979. Although that experience was not a success the party set up a Shadow Communications Agency of volunteers to ensure that the party used modern communication methods in subsequent campaigns. After 1992 the post-Kinnock party leadership decided that the Agency had exercised too much initiative and appointed an advertising agency again. Conservative Central Office was so impressed with Labour's use of private polls in 1964 that it embarked on an ambitious polling exercise of its own (see p. 131). Post-mortems on the Conservative victory in 1987 concluded that the party had not conducted a good media operation, particularly on television, and that it should learn from Labour. The mood was summed up by the words of one official: 'We are determined not to be out-Mandelsoned next time'. In 1992 the biographical election broadcast of John Major was partly inspired by the success of the Kinnock film in 1987, and the 'Meet John Major' question and answer sessions followed Neil Kinnock's use of the format in 1987. One of Major's most powerful election speeches was a parody of Neil Kinnock's warning in 1983 not to be unemployed, sick, homeless or elderly, for a Tory government would make life harder on them. He warned an audience in Manchester against a Labour victory: 'I warn you not to be qualified. I warn you not to be successful. I warn you not to buy shares . . . I warn you not to accept promotion . . . I warn you not to own a house'.

Conclusion

Democratic election campaigns have many functions. They are a means of choosing government, a choice that encompasses the voter's retrospective verdict on the parties' records in office and an anticipatory one on their promises; an opportunity for popular participation which in turn may confer a mandate and legitimacy on the government, and a means of promoting political learning and citizenship. It is this last function that is causing some concern today. To what extent do modern elections contribute to informed choice and have the trends discussed earlier in this book promoted or hindered the making of such a choice?

In several respects there are potential gains from the modern communications. Opinion polls provide feedback to the elite and inform voters of the views of others. Direct mail and more specialized media outlets allow parties to target their messages more precisely to voters. Television enables politicians to communicate directly with voters and the latter to see political leaders in the flesh, so to speak. The fairly continuous media coverage of election campaigns should also facilitate gains in information and opportunities to make informed judgements.

What are the results? Figures on the level of public interest are ambiguous. Interest in politics is heightened at election time and three-quarters of the electorate believe that holding an election makes politicians pay attention to the public (Butler and Stokes 1969: 32–3). But this positive feature co-exists with a good deal of voter indifference and cynicism. Membership and activity in political parties has been declining for some years and is now at a postwar low. The new media techniques, with their packaged politics, have, according to one writer, weakened direct political debate and meant that 'voters have become spectators rather than participants in debate' (Franklin 1994: 23). Some two-thirds of voters believe that parties are 'only interested in people's votes, not their opinions', that MPs lose touch with people pretty quickly once they are elected and that people like themselves have no say in what government does (Jowell and Topf 1988; Bovell, McGregor and Weber 1992: 165). Many also complain about excessive media coverage of the election – understandable in as much as many voters resent the displacement of their favourite programmes for political coverage; in 1992 some two-thirds claimed that there was 'much too much' or 'too much' television coverage of the election (Butler and Kavanagh 1992: 179).

Critics sometimes mourn the use which the campaign managers have made of the new techniques. It is undeniable that campaign managers in Britain are now much more inclined to provide photo-opportunities and stage pseudo-events in the hope that these will gain media coverage. Has television – by emphasizing pictures over argument and image over substance, and greater use of soundbites, 'buzz words' and 'nine-word sentences' – undermined the intellectual content of what is presented to the voters? It has certainly led to a demise of oratory and the elaboration of political arguments or discussion of complex problems; leaders today give far fewer major speeches compared to even twenty or thirty years ago (Atkinson 1984). The importance of personal appearance on television means that it is doubtful that, for example, a President Truman or a Clement Attlee would get to the top today. Modern electioneering, under the influence of television, has also limited direct personal contact between party leaders and voters. One thoughtful critique of the 1992 campaign claims that the trends are undermining the democratic process. Joe Rogaly, in the *Financial Times*, complained about issues ignored by the campaign, and 'The big set-piece press conferences – on recession, recovery, health, education, foreign affairs, crime and housing – have all begun with the reading out of short, easily digestible statements and concluded with the TV cameras watching journalists ask limited questions' (9 April 1992).

The growth of more negative political advertising in the US has, according to Kern and Just (1994), increased popular alienation from the electoral process. In turn media journalists are more inclined to expose, in disdainful terms, the parties' attempts at agenda management and the result is likely to be greater cynicism among voters. The circle is a vicious one, for 'Negative advertisements are believed because politicians are increasingly distrusted by people who believe negative advertisements' (Kern and Just 1994: 13).

Few can doubt the potential usefulness of opinion polls as a reading of public mood and source of feedback to the politicians. But the media fascination with predictions and the horse race means that immense coverage is devoted to them at the cost of more substantial news. The constant year-round polling also contributes to an electioneering atmosphere and perhaps to an undue concern with the short term.

Weekly and monthly opinion polls, by-elections and annual local government elections (all hyped by the mass media) create an impression of a permanent election campaign. The bitter resignation speech of Norman Lamont to the House of Commons in 1993 was not devoid of special pleading. But it was interesting that he complained that his former colleagues' excessive interest in opinion polls affected policy decisions – 'Far too many important decisions are made for 36 hours' publicity'. To what extent do the opinion polls' readings of public opinion induce a greater homogeneity in the political communications offered by vote-seeking parties and therefore to a limitation of choice? In 1992 it was noticeable that the major differences between the Labour and Conservative parties were very few – disputes over marginal rates of direct taxation, whether Britain should adopt the EC's Social Charter and changes in constitutional arrangements – and voters perceived a marked narrowing of differences between the parties (Heath and Jowell 1994).

In the United States much concern has been expressed about the effects of these trends on the vitality of the parties, quality of candidates and conduct of politicians. David Mayhew (1974) found that electoral pressures and the growing electronic media coverage of the US Congress encouraged Congressmen to concentrate on local vote-winning and media-interesting activities rather than broader policy and legislative roles. The permanent electioneering detracts from the quality of legislative oversight and initiatives. Indeed, the communications techniques and discipline of political campaigning are not intrinsically different from those found in 'peacetime' politics. Increasingly politicians and policies are packaged for the mass media and parties have become more sophisticated, even relentless, in their attempts to manage news (Franklin 1994; Cockerell, Hennessy and Walker 1984). Local government, Whitehall departments and party organizations make growing use of public relations, marketing consultants and media advisers in an effort to shape the agenda.

Britain has not travelled as far down this road as the United States. But it would be difficult to argue that the new techniques have actually promoted the quality of public debate, clarified the choice for voters at elections or have much relevance to the post-election tasks facing governments. In the 1987 election campaign, for example, a number of issues which proved crucial in the new Parliament – the poll tax, membership of the Exchange Rate Mechanism (ERM) and reforms in the health service – were hardly discussed at all. In 1992 the impact on

Britain of developments in the European Community was virtually ignored by the party leaders and media. No major party was prepared to address the post-election problems of Britain remaining within the ERM, funding existing social programmes and balancing the looming budget deficit; these were lost among Conservative warnings that a Labour government would lead to a bigger budget deficit, increased public spending, larger tax increases and imperil Britain's membership of the ERM. As a preparation for what actually happened after the election the warnings were vindicated but they occurred under a Conservative government. Within less than two years of the election victory public approval in the opinion polls for John Major and the government had sunk to record lows.

The new techniques have certainly added to the armoury of political campaigners. Assessing whether they are a good or a bad thing – for voters, for politicians, for the political process – is of limited usefulness. Defenders of the new communications may fairly claim that their primary concern is to help politicians persuade people and win votes – not to promote civic education or the quality of government. They cannot be blamed for the strategic choices made by campaigning politicians. One judgement is that 'political marketing has improved the extent, quality and efficiency of communication between voters and parties' and that it is unrealistic to assume that without political marketing campaigns 'would become real debates about issues' (Harrop 1990: 290). It is also unrealistic to expect that political parties will ignore the communicative techniques used in commerce and which voters are familiar with.

The new specialists are certainly more influential *vis-à-vis* the parties than was the case before 1959. This has concerned some commentators, for example those who attributed the Conservative victories in 1959 and 1979 to the party's greater investment in public relations than Labour; they feared that wealth could buy public relations expertise and with it political power. Such judgements, however, ignore the effect of free party-election broadcasts in reducing the impact of the parties' different financial strengths. The prohibition of political advertising on television also reduces the impact of money in that medium. The third and minor parties, who make less use of these techniques, have seen their support reach postwar highs in the past twenty years. It also ignores the importance of politics. In 1959 and 1979 the political context was overwhelmingly favourable for the Conservatives and unfavourable for Labour. Much the same could be said about the leadership, policies and records of the parties in the 1983 and 1987 elections. As Harrop tersely observes, 'Strategy matters far more than promotion' (1990: 288). Labour's skilful communications campaigns in 1987 and 1992 could not overcome underlying doubts about the party's competence.

This study lends little support to the notion that a group of media and public relations maestros manipulates voters and politicians. Senior politicians never lack for political advice – from the media, colleagues, special advisers, party activists, party officials, think tanks and, in government, civil servants. Some of these sources will also give advice about electoral strategy. The party's communications professionals are highly specialized in one area – reporting on the mood of voters and suggesting the most effective ways of communicating with voters. But this advice competes with alternative suggestions from other advisers and sometimes the professionals struggle to gain the attention of the politicians, particularly when the latter are in government.

Leading politicians are usually more concerned with more immediate problems of party management, Parliament, policy development and gaining a good press than in preparing strategy for an election a year or two hence. As noted in chapters 6 and 7, political leaders not only reject key recommendations from the communicators – which is their right – but also often keep the latter at arm's length. Party officials and the party leaders' private staffs, who work full time, guard their turf against outsiders.

It is difficult to point to the outcome of any recent general election campaign which was decided, even to a significant degree, by the contributions of opinion pollsters, advertising agencies or other communicators. In a closely run campaign, as in 1964 and 1992, their interventions could have been decisive, but in an election decided by a slim margin that could be said about virtually any factor. Opinion polling and communications advice about strategy is more likely to be accepted when it reinforces the existing predispositions of politicians, e.g. Labour's concentration on Harold Wilson in 1964 and 1970; emphasis on rising prices, rather than the miners' strike, in February 1974; on the social agenda in 1987; on health in 1992. The same is true of the Conservative advocacy of national unity in October 1974, promotion of Mrs Thatcher's resolute leadership in 1983 and 1987, reliance on tax and leadership in 1992. In all these cases it was the leading politicians who made strategic decisions.

LIST OF
INTERVIEWEES

Interviews, which are cited in the text, were held with the following:

Bartle, John: Managing Director, Bartle, Bogle and Hegarty advertising agency.

Bell, Sir Tim: Chairman, Lowe, Bell Communications since 1987. Previously with CPV and Saatchi & Saatchi, agencies which worked for the Conservative party in general elections. Handled Conservative party account in 1979 and 1983. Continued to advise Mrs Thatcher informally in the 1987 campaign.

Booth-Clibborn, Edward: Chairman, DAD. Organized Labour communications campaign for 1979 general election.

Butterfield, Les: Managing Director, Butterfield, Day, Devito, Hockney, appointed as advertising agency for Labour in 1993.

Carroll, Roger: Public relations. Formerly leader writer on *Sun* newspaper. Worked in No. 10 for Labour's 1979 election campaign as speechwriter to Mr Callaghan, and as communications adviser to SDP 1983.

Day, Barry: Creative Director, McCann Erickson. Speechwriter for Mr Heath for 1970 and 1974 elections. Now Director, Worldwide Lintas.

Delaney, Barry: Managing Director, DFSD Bozell. Labour party communications adviser.

Delaney, Tim: Creative Director, Leagas Delaney. Worked on Labour party election broadcasts in 1979.

Douglas, James: Member Conservative Research Department 1950–76. Director of Research Department 1970–4.

Fletcher, Winston: Chairman, DFSD Bozell. Writer of books on advertising and public relations. Communications adviser to SDP.

Gould, Philip: Coordinator Labour party Shadow Communications Agency (1986–92), Communications adviser to European socialist parties for European elections, 1994, and for Labour party under Tony Blair.

Harris, Lord: Journalist, then personal assistant to Hugh Gaitskell 1959–62. Director of Publicity Labour party 1962–4. Special adviser to Roy Jenkins 1965–70. Minister in Labour government 1975–9.

Hill, David: Special adviser to Roy Hattersley. Campaigns and Communications Director for Labour party 1991–3. Press secretary for the leader of the Labour party since 1993.

Hollick, Lord: Managing Director, MAI Company and Chairman, Meridian Television. Member of Labour's Shadow Communications Agency.

Kingsley, David: Founded KMP advertising agency 1964. Communications adviser to Labour party 1962–70. Communications adviser to SDP 1981–7. Since 1987 consultant in management marketing and communications.

Kinnock, Neil: Leader, Labour party 1983–92.

Lansley, Andrew: Civil servant, policy director for Association of British Chambers of Commerce. Director, Conservative Research Department, 1990–5.

Lindsey, John: Head of Broadcasting, Conservative Central Office 1960–79.

Lovell-Davis, Lord: Managing Director, Central Press Features, 1952–70. Communications adviser to Labour party 1962–76. Junior minister in Labour government 1975–6.

Mandelson, Peter: Television producer. Labour Campaigns and Communications Director 1985–90. Labour MP since 1992.

Patten, Chris: Director, Conservative Research Department 1970–4. Conservative MP, 1979–92 and Conservative Cabinet minister, 1989–92. Chairman of Conservative party 1990–2. Governor, Hong Kong 1992–.

Powell, Chris: Managing Director, BMP. Communications adviser to Labour party and member of Shadow Communications Agency.

Reece, Sir Gordon: Formerly television producer. Adviser to Mrs Thatcher. Director of Publicity, Conservative party 1978–80. Now public affairs consultant.

Saatchi, Maurice: Co-founder Saatchi & Saatchi advertising agency 1970. Managing Director since 1984.

Sharkey, John: Deputy Chairman and Director, Saatchi & Saatchi 1984–7. Handled account for Conservative party in 1987 general election. Now Joint Chairman BDDP Holdings (UK) Ltd.

Sherbourne, Stephen: Conservative Research Department 1970–5. Special adviser to Patrick Jenkin, Cabinet minister, 1982–3. Political Secretary to Mrs Thatcher 1983–8. Managing Director Lowe-Bell consultancy from 1988.

Sinclair, Jeremy: Worldwide Creative Director Saatchi & Saatchi until 1994. Worked for Saatchi's on all Conservative election campaigns 1979–92.

Tebbit, Norman: Conservative Cabinet minister 1981–5, and Chairman of Conservative Central Office 1985–7.

Tucker, Geoffrey: Worked for CPV agency on Conservative account for 1959 election. Managing Director, Young & Rubicam. Director of Publicity, Conservative party 1968–70. Manager, Geoffrey Tucker Ltd.

Waller, Robert: Research Director, Harris Opinion Research. Private pollster for the Conservative party.

White, Michael: Political editor, the *Guardian*.

Woodward, Shaun: Television producer and editor. Conservative Director of Communications 1991–2.

Worcester, Robert: Managing Director, MORI. Private pollster for Labour party 1970–89.

REFERENCES

Abrams, M. (1963) 'Public Opinion Polls and Political Parties', *Public Opinion Quarterly* 27 (1), 9–18.

Abrams, M. and Rose, R. (1960) *Must Labour Lose?* Harmondsworth, Penguin.

Alt, J. (1978) *The Politics of Economic Decline*, Cambridge, Cambridge University Press.

Ansolab, S., Iyengar, S., Adam S. and Valentino, N. (1994) 'Does Attack Advertising Demobilize the Electorate?' *American Political Science Review* 88 (4), 829–38.

Arterton, C. (1984) *Media Politics*, Lexington, Mass., D. C. Heath.

Atkinson, M. (1984) *Our Masters' Voices*, London, Methuen.

Barker, A. and Rush, M. (1970) *The Member of Parliament and his Information*, London, Allen & Unwin.

Bauman, S. and Herbst, S. (1994) 'Managing Perceptions of Public Opinion: Candidates' and Journalists' Reactions to 1992 Polls', *Political Communications* 11 (2), 133–44.

Beith, A. (1965) 'The Press' in D. Butler and A. King, *The British General Election of 1966*, London, Macmillan, 185–283.

Bell, T. (1982) 'The Conservatives' Advertising Campaign' in R. Worcester and M. Harrop (eds) *Political Communications*, London, Allen & Unwin, 11–26.

Bennett, W. Lance (1992) *The Governing Crisis*, New York, St Martin's Press.

Berrington, H. (1992) 'Dialogue of the Deaf? The Elite and the Electorate in mid-century Britain' in D. Kavanagh (ed.) *Electoral Politics*, Oxford, Oxford University Press, 71–96.

Berry, S. (1992) 'Labour's Strategy and the Media', *Parliamentary Affairs* 45 (4), 565–81.

Blumenthal, R. (1985) *The Permanent Campaign*, Boston, Beacon Press.

Blumler, J. (1974) 'Mass Media and Reactions in the February Election' in H. Penniman (ed.) *Britain at the Polls*, Washington DC, American Enterprise Institute, 131–62.

Blumler, J. and Gurevitch, P. (1981) 'Politicians and the Press: An Essay on Role Relationships' in D. Nimmo and K. Sanders (eds) *Handbook of Political Communications*, London and Beverly Hills, Sage, 467–93.

Blumler, J. and McQuail, D. (1968) *Television in Politics*, London, Faber.

Blumler, J., Gurevitch, M. and Nossiter, T. (1989) 'The Earnest vs The Determined: Election Newsmaking at the BBC' in I. Crewe and M. Harrop (eds) *Political Communications: The General Election Campaign of 1987*, Cambridge, Cambridge University Press, 157–74.

Blumler, J., Gurevitch, M. and Nossiter, T. (1995) 'Struggles for Meaningful Election Communication' in I. Crewe and B. Gosschalk (eds) *Political Communications: The General Election Campaign of 1992*, Cambridge, Cambridge University Press.

Blumler, J., Kavanagh, D. and Nossiter, T. (1995) 'Modern Communications versus Traditional Politics in Britain: Unstable Marriage of Convenience' in P. Mancini and D. Swanson (eds) *Politics, Media and Modern Democracy*, New York, Praeger.

Bogdanor, V. (ed.) (1984) *Parties and Democracy in Britain and America*, New York, Praeger.

Bovell, M., McGregor, R. and Weber, M. (1992) 'Audience Reactions to Parliamentary Television' in B. Franklin (ed.) *Televising Democracies*, London, Routledge, 149–70.

Briggs, A. (1970) *The History of Broadcasting in the United Kingdom* Vol. 3, Oxford, Oxford University Press.

Broadbent, S. (1981) *How Advertising Works*, London, Holt, Rinehart Winston.

Bruce, B. (1992) *Images of Power*, London, Kogan Page.

Budge, I. and Fairlie, D. (1983) *Explaining and Predicting Elections*, London, Allen & Unwin.

Butler, D. and Kavanagh, D. (1974) *The British General Election of February 1974*, London, Macmillan.

Butler, D. and Kavanagh, D. (1980) *The British General Election of 1979*, London, Macmillan.

Butler, D. and Kavanagh, D. (1984) *The British General Election of 1983*, London, Macmillan.

Butler, D. and Kavanagh, D. (1987) *The British General Election of 1987*, London, Macmillan.

Butler, D. and Kavanagh, D. (1988) *The British General Election of 1987*, London, Macmillan.

Butler, D. and Kavanagh, D. (1992) *The British General Election of 1992*, London, Macmillan.

Butler, D. and King, A. (1966) *The British General Election of 1966*, London, Macmillan.

Butler, D. and King, A. (1965) *The British General Election of 1964*, London, Macmillan.

Butler, D. and Pinto-Duschinsky, M. (1971) *The British General Election of 1970*, London, Macmillan.

Butler, D. and Ranney, A. (1984) 'Parties and Media in the United States and Britain' in V. Bogdanor (ed.) *Parties and Democracy in Britain and America*, New York, Praeger.

Butler, D. and Ranney, A. (eds) (1992) *Electioneering: A Comparative Study of Continuity and Change*, Oxford, Oxford University Press.

Butler, D. and Rose, R. (1960) *The British General Election of 1959*, London, Macmillan.

Butler, D. and Stokes, D. (1969) *Political Change in Britain*, London, Macmillan.

Butler, P. and Collins, N. (1993) 'Campaigns, Candidates and Marketing in Ireland', *Politics* 13 (1), 3–8.

Butler File, Oxford, Nuffield College.

Cain, B., Ferejohn, J. and Fiorina, M. (1987) *The Personal Vote: Constituency Service and Electoral Independence*, Cambridge, Mass., Harvard University Press.

Campbell, J. (1993) *Edward Heath: A Biography*, London, Cape.

Carroll, R. (1989) 'The Alliance's Non-advertising Campaign' in I. Crewe and M. Harrop (eds) *Political Communications: The General Election Campaign of 1987*, Cambridge, Cambridge University Press, 87–92.

Cockerell, M. (1988) *Live From Number 10*, London, Faber.

Cockerell, M., Hennessy, P. and Walker, D. (1984) *Sources Close to the Prime Minister*, London, Macmillan.

Cockett, R. (1994) 'Party, Publicity and the Media' in A. Seldon and S. Ball (eds) *The Conservative Century*, Oxford, Oxford University Press, 547–77.

Crewe, I. (1982) 'Improving but Could Do Better: The Media and the Polls in the 1979 General Election' in R. Worcester and M. Harrop (eds) *Political Communications*, London, Allen & Unwin, 115–25.

Crewe, I. (1992) 'A Nation of Liars? Opinion Polls and the Election', *Parliamentary Affairs* 45 (4), 475–95.

Crewe, I. (1993) 'Voting and the Electorate' in P. Dunleavy et al. (eds) *Developments in British Politics*, London, Macmillan, 92–122.

Crewe, I. and Gosschalk, B. (eds) (1995) *Political Communications: The General Election Campaign of 1992*, Cambridge, Cambridge University Press.

Crewe, I. and Harrop, M. (eds) (1986) *Political Communications: The General Election Campaign of 1983*, Cambridge, Cambridge University Press.

Crewe, I. and Harrop, M. (1989) *Political Communications: The General Election of 1987*, Cambridge, Cambridge University Press.

Crewe, I., Alt, J. and Sarlvik, B. (1977) 'Partisan Dealignment in Britain 1964–74', *British Journal of Political Science* 7, 129–90.

Crossman, R. (1960) *Labour in the Affluent Society*, London, Fabian Society Tract No. 325.

Crouse, T. (1972) *The Boys on the Bus*, New York, Ballantine Books.

Curtice, J. and Semetko, H. (1994) 'Does it Matter what the Papers Say?' in A. Heath, R. Jowell, and J. Curtice (eds) *Labour's Last Chance*, Aldershot, Dartmouth, 43–63.

Day, B. (1982) 'The Politics of Communications, or the Communication of Politics' in R. Worcester and M. Harrop (eds) *Political Communications*, London, Allen & Unwin, 3–10.

Delaney, T. (1982) 'Labour's Advertising Campaign' in R. Worcester and M. Harrop (eds) *Political Communications*, London, Allen & Unwin, 27–31.

Denver, D. and Hands, G. (1992) 'Constituency Campaigning', *Parliamentary Affairs* 45 (4), 528–44.

Donoughue, B. (1987) *Prime Minister*, London, Jonathan Cape.

Dunleavy, P. and Husbands, C. (1985) *Democracy at the Crossroads*, Cambridge, Cambridge University Press.

Falkender, M. (1983) *Downing Street in Perspective*, London, Weidenfeld & Nicolson.

Fletcher, W. (1990) 'Muddle of the SDP Message', the *Guardian* 4 June.

Foley, M. (1993) *The Rise of the British Presidency*, Manchester, Manchester University Press.

Foster, J. and Muste, C. (1992) 'The United States' in D. Butler and A. Ranney (eds) *Electioneering*, Oxford, Oxford University Press, 11–42.

Franklin, B. (1992) *Televising Democracies*, London, Routledge.

Franklin, B. (1994) *Packaging Politics*, London, Edward Arnold.

Glasgow University Media Group (1976) *Bad News*, London, Routledge.

Glasgow University Media Group (1980) *More Bad News*, London, Routledge.

Gold, P. (1986) *Advertising, Politics and American Culture: From Salesmanship to Therapy*, New York, Paragon House.

Gould, P., Herd, P. and Powell, C. (1989) 'The Labour Party's Campaign Communications' in I. Crewe and M. Harrop (eds) *Political Communications: The General Election of 1987*, Cambridge, Cambridge University Press, 72–86.

Graber, D. (1987) *Processing the News: How People Tame the Information Tide*, New York, Longman.

Graber, D. (1989) *Mass Media and American Politics*, Washington DC, C. Q. Press.

Grossman, M. and Kumar, M. *Portraying the President*, Baltimore, Johns Hopkins University Press.

Hare, D. (1992) *Asking Around*, London, Fontana.

Harris, R. (1992) 'We are a Nation of Liars', *Sunday Times* 12 April.

Harrison, M. (1974) 'Television and Radio' in D. Butler and D. Kavanagh, *The British General Election of February 1974*, London, Macmillan, 146–69.

Harrison, M. (1992) 'Politics on the Air' in D. Butler and D. Kavanagh, *The British General Election of 1992*, London, Macmillan, 155–79.

Harrop, M. (1984) 'Press' in D. Butler and D. Kavanagh, *The British General Election of 1983*, London, Macmillan, 175–218.

Harrop, M. (1986) 'The Press and Post-war Elections' in I. Crewe and M. Harrop (eds) *Political Communications: The General Election Campaign of 1983*, Cambridge, Cambridge University Press, 137–49.

Harrop, M. (1988) 'Press' in D. Butler and D. Kavanagh, *The British General Election of 1987*, London, Macmillan, 163–90.

Harrop, M. (1990) 'Political Marketing', *Parliamentary Affairs* 43 (2), 277–91.

Harrop, M. and Scammell, M. (1992) 'A Tabloid War' in D. Butler and D. Kavanagh, *The British General Election of 1992*, London, Macmillan, 180–210.

Harrop, M. and Shaw, A. (1989) *Can Labour Win?* London, Unwin.

Heath, A. and Jowell, R. (1994) 'Labour's Policy Review' in A. Heath, R. Jowell and J. Curtice (eds) *Labour's Last Chance*, Aldershot, Dartmouth, 191–211.

Heath, A., Jowell, R. and Curtice, J. (1991) *Understanding Political Change*, Oxford, Pergamon.

Heath, A., Jowell, R. and Curtice, J. (eds) (1994) *Labour's Last Chance*, Aldershot, Dartmouth.

Heffernan, R. and Marquesee, M. (1992) *Defeat from the Jaws of Victory: Inside Neil Kinnock's Labour Party*, London, Verso.

Hennessy, D. (1961) 'The Communication of Conservative Policy', *Political Quarterly* 32 (3), 238–56.

Hennessy, P. (1986) *Cabinet*, Oxford, Blackwell.

Hershey, M. (1989) 'The Campaign and the Media' in G. Pomper (ed.) *The Election of 1988*, Chatham, NJ, Chatham House, 73–102.

Hertsgaard, M. (1988) *On Bended Knee: The Press and the Reagan Presidency*, New York, Farrar, Straus and Giroux.

Hughes, C. and Wintour, P. (1990) *Labour Rebuilt*, London, Fourth Estate.

Hurd, D. (1979) *An End To Promises*, London, Collins.

Jamieson, K. H. (1992a) *Eloquence in an Electronic Age: The Transformation of Political Speech-making*, New York, Oxford University Press.

Jamieson, K. H. (1992b) *Dirty Politics: Deception, Distraction and Democracy*, New York, Oxford University Press.

Jones, B. (1992) 'Broadcasters, Politicians and the Political Interview' in B. Jones and L. Robins (eds) *Two Decades of British Politics*, Manchester, Manchester University Press, 53–78.

Jones, N. (1992) *Election '92*, London, BBC Books.

Jowell, R. and Topf, R. (1988) 'Trust in the Establishment' in R. Jowell, S. Witherspoon and L. Brook (eds) *British Social Attitudes: 5th Report*, Aldershot, Gower.

Jowell, R., Witherspoon, S. and Brook, L. (eds) (1988) *British Social Attitudes: 5th Report*, Aldershot, Gower.

Jowell, R. et al. (1993) 'The 1992 British General Election: The Failure of the Polls', *Public Opinion Quarterly* 57, 238–63.

Kavanagh, D. (1970) *Constituency Electioneering in Britain*, London, Longman.

Kavanagh, D. (1981) 'The Politics of Manifestos', *Parliamentary Affairs* 34 (1), 7–27.

Kavanagh, D. (1985) 'Power in British Parties: Iron Law or Special Pleading?' *West European Politics* 8 (i), 5–20.

Kavanagh, D. (1989) 'The Timing of Elections: The British Case' in I. Crewe and M. Harrop (eds) *Political Communications: The General Election of 1987*, Cambridge, Cambridge University Press, 3–14.

Kavanagh, D. (ed.) (1992) *Electoral Politics*, Oxford, Oxford University Press.

Kavanagh, D. and Gosschalk, B. (1995) 'Failing to Set the Agenda' in I. Crewe and B. Gosschalk (eds) *Political Communications: The General Election Campaign of 1992*, Cambridge, Cambridge University Press.

Kelley, S. (1956) *Professional Public Relations and Political Power*, Baltimore, Johns Hopkins Press.

Kern, M. and Just, M. (1994) *How Voters Construct Images of Political Candidates: The Role of Political Advertising and Televised News*, Cambridge, Mass., Harvard University, John F. Kennedy School of Government Research Paper, R-10.

Kernell, S. (1986) *Going Public: New Strategies of Presidential Leadership*, Washington DC, C. Q. Press.

Kirchheimer, O. (1966) 'The Transformation of Western European Party Systems' in J. La Palombara and M. Wiener (eds) *Political Parties and Political Development*, Princeton, NJ, Princeton University Press, 177–200.

Koss, S. (1984) *The Rise and Fall of the Political Press in Britain*, Vol. 2, London, Hamish Hamilton.

Lamb, K. and Smith, P. (1968) *Campaign Decision-Making: The Presidential Election of 1964*, Belmont, California, Wadsworth.

Lawson, N. (1992) *The View From No. 11: Memoirs of a Tory Radical*, London, Bantam Press.

Levine, P. (1974) 'Consultants and American Political Culture', *Philosophy and Public Policy* 14 (3–4), 1–6.

Levy, M. (1981) 'Disdaining the News', *Journal of Communications* 31 (3), 24–31.

Lippman, W. (1922) *Public Opinion*, New York, Macmillan.

Luntz, F. (1988) *Candidates, Consultants and Campaigns: The Style and Substance of American Electioneering*, Oxford, Blackwell.

MacArthur, B. (1989) 'The National Press' in I. Crewe and M. Harrop (eds) *Political Communications: The General Election of 1987*, Cambridge, Cambridge University Press, 95–107.

Mackintosh, J. (1962) *The British Cabinet*, London, Stevens.

McClure, T. and Patterson, T. (1976) *The Unseeing Eye: The Myth of Television Power in National Politics*, New York, Putnams.

McGinniss, J. (1970) *The Selling of the President*, Harmondsworth, Penguin.

McKenzie, R. (1963) *The British Political Parties*, London, Heinemann.

McKenzie, R. and Silver, A. (1968) *Angels in Marble*, London, McGibbon & Kee.

Mancini, P. and Swanson, D. (1995) (eds) *Politics, Media and Modern Democracy*, New York, Praeger.

Margach, J. (1978) *The Abuse of Power*, London, W. H. Allen.

Marquand, D. (1977) *Ramsay MacDonald*, London, Cape.

Mayhew, D. (1974) *Congress: The Electoral Connection*, New Haven, Conn., Yale University Press.

Michels, R. (1962) *Political Parties*, New York, Anchor Books.

Miliband, R. (1961) *Parliamentary Socialism*, London, Merlin.

Miller, W. (1991) *Media and Voters*, Oxford, Clarendon Press.

Miller, W., Clarke, H., Harrop, M., Le Duc, L. and Whiteley, P. (1990) *How Voters Change: The 1987 British General Election in Perspective*, Oxford, Clarendon Press.

Minkin, L. (1980) *The Labour Party Conference*, Manchester, Manchester University Press.

Nimmo, D. (1970) *The Political Persuaders*, Englewood Cliffs, NJ, Prentice Hall.

Nimmo, D. and Sanders, K. (eds) (1981) *Handbook of Political Communications*, London and Beverley Hills, Sage.

Nixon, R. (1978) *Memoirs of Richard Nixon*, New York, Grosset and Dunlap.

Noonan, P. (1990) 'What I saw at the Revolution', New York, Random House.

O'Shaughnessy, N. (1990) *The Phenomenon of Political Marketing*, London, Macmillan.

Panebianco, A. (1988) *Political Parties: Organization and Power*, Cambridge, Cambridge University Press.

Pardoe, J. (1989) 'The Alliance Campaign' in I. Crewe and M. Harrop (eds) *Political Communications: The General Election of 1987*, Cambridge, Cambridge University Press, 55–60.

Patterson, T. (1993) *Out of Order*, New York, Knopf.

Pattie, C., Whiteley, P., Johnstone, R. and Seyd, P. (1994) 'Measuring Local Campaign Effects: Labour Party Constituency Campaigning at the 1987 General Election', *Political Studies* 42 (3), 469–79.

Pearson, J. and Turner, G. (1965) *The Persuasion Industry*, London, Eyre & Spottiswoode.

Penniman, H. (ed.) (1974) *Britain at the Polls*, Washington DC, American Enterprise Institute.

Petracca, M. (1989) 'Political Consultants and Democratic Governments', *PS* 22 (1), 11–14.

Phillips, M. (1992) 'The Siege of our Screens', the *Guardian* 17 February.

Pinto-Duschinsky, M. (1974) 'The Conservative Campaign: New Techniques versus Old' in H. Penniman (ed.) *Britain at the Polls*, Washington DC, American Enterprise Institute, 85–108.

Pinto-Duschinsky, M. (1982) *British Political Finance 1830–1980*, London, American Enterprise Institute.

Pinto-Duschinsky, M. (1991) 'The Funding of Political Parties since 1945' in A. Seldon (ed.) *UK Party Politics since 1945*, Oxford, Philip Allan, 95–109.

Pomper, G. (1989) (ed.) *The Election of 1988: Reports and Interpretations*, Chatham, NJ, Chatham House.

Ramsden, J. (1980) *The Making of Conservative Policy*, London, Longman.

Ranney, A. (1983) *Channels of Power*, New York, Basic Books/Urbana, Ill., University of Illinois Press.

Ranney, A. (1954) *The Doctrine of Responsible Party Government*, Urbana, Ill., University of Illinois Press.

Rhodes-James, R. (1969) *Memoirs of a Conservative: J. C. C. Davidson Memoirs and Papers 1910–37*, London, Weidenfeld & Nicolson.

Robertson, D. (1971) 'The Content of Election Addresses and Leaders' Speeches' in D. Butler and M. Pinto-Duschinsky, *The British General Election of 1970*, London, Macmillan, 437–45.

Rose, R. (1965) 'Pre-Election Public Relations and Advertising' in D. Butler and A. King, *The British General Election of 1964*, London, Macmillan, 369–80.

Rose, R. (1967) *Influencing Voters*, London, Faber.

Rose, R. (1974) *The Problem of Party Government*, London, Macmillan.

Rose, R. (1980) *Do Parties Make a Difference?* Chatham, NJ, Chatham House.

Rose, R. (1988) *The Post-Modern President: The President Meets the World*, Chatham, NJ, Chatham House.

Rose, R. (1992) 'Structural Change or Cyclical Fluctuation', *Parliamentary Affairs* 45 (4), 451–65.

Rose, R. and McAllister, I. (1990) *The Loyalties of Voters*, London, Sage.

Saalvik, B. and Crewe, I. (1983) *The Decade of Dealignment*, Cambridge, Cambridge University Press.

Sabato, L. (1981) *The Rise of Political Consultants*, New York, Basic Books.

Sabato, L. (1991) *Feeding Frenzy: How Attack Journalism has Transformed American Politics*, New York, Free Press.

Sackman, A. (1994) 'Labour's Problems and the Changing Values of the United Kingdom Electorate', *Contemporary Political Studies* x, 465–79.

Salmore, S. and Salmore, B. (1985) *Candidates, Parties and Campaigns: Electoral Politics in America*, Washington DC, C. Q. Press.

Schnudson, M. (1984) *Advertising: The Uneasy Persuasion*, New York, Basic Books.

Schumpeter, J. (1976) *Capitalism, Socialism and Democracy*, London, Allen & Unwin.

Seldon, A. (ed.) (1991) *UK Party Politics Since 1945*, Oxford, Philip Allan.

Seldon, A. and Ball, S. (eds) (1994) *The Conservative Century*, Oxford, Oxford University Press.

Semetko, H., Blumler, J., Gurevitch, M. and Weaver, D. (1991) *The Formation of Campaign Agendas*, Hillsdale, NJ, Lawrence Erlbaum.

Seyd, P. and Whiteley, P. (1992) *Labour's Grass-Roots*, Oxford, Oxford University Press.

Seymour-Ure, C. (1968) *The Press, Politics and the Public*, London, Methuen.

Seymour-Ure, C. (1974) *The Political Impact of the Mass Media*, London, Constable.

Seymour-Ure, C. (1991) *The British Press and Broadcasting Since 1945*, Oxford, Blackwell.

Seymour-Ure, C. (1992) 'Press, Partisanship: Into the 1990s' in D. Kavanagh (ed.) *Electoral Politics*, Oxford, Oxford University Press, 51–70.

Seymour-Ure, C. (1993) 'The Polls and the 1992 Election', paper presented at the 1992 Conference on Elections and Media, Colchester, Essex University.

Shaw, E. (1992) 'Labour's Campaigning and Communications Strategy 1987–92', unpublished paper.

Sieb, L. (1987) *Who's in Charge? How the Media Shape News and Politicians Win Votes*, Dallas, Texas, Taylor.

Simpson, J. (1992) 'A Nasty and Menacing Election', *Spectator* 20 March.

Spero, R. (1980) *The Duping of the American Voter*, New York, Lippincott.

Tebbit, N. (1988) *Upwardly Mobile*, London, Weidenfeld & Nicolson.

Thatcher, M. (1993) *The Downing Street Years*, London, HarperCollins.

University of Loughborough (1992) 'Election Study for the *Guardian*', University of Loughborough Communications Research Centre.

Wallas, G. (1948) *Human Nature in Politics*, London, Constable.

Waller, R. (1992) 'The Polls in 1992' in I. Crewe and B. Gosschalk (eds) *Political Communications: The General Election Campaign of 1992*, Cambridge, Cambridge University Press.

Webb, P. (1992) 'Election Campaigning, Organizational Transformation and the Professionalization of the British Labour Party', *British Journal of Political Research* 21 (3), 267–88.

Whiteley, P., Seyd, P. and Richardson, J. (1994) *True Blues: The Politics of Conservative Party Membership*, Oxford, Oxford University Press.

Wilson, H. (1971) *The Labour Government 1964–70*, London, Weidenfeld & Nicolson.

Windlesham, Lord (1965) ' The Communication of Conservative Policy 1963–64', *Political Quarterly* 36 (2), 164–80.

Wober, M. (1989) 'Party Political and Election Broadcasts, 1985–1987' in I. Crewe and M. Harrop (eds) *Political Communications: The General Election Campaign of 1987*, Cambridge, Cambridge University Press, 139–46.

Wober, M., Svennevig, M. and Gunter, B. (1986) 'The Television Audience and the 1983 Election' in I. Crewe and M. Harrop (eds) *Political Communications: The General Election Campaign of 1983*, Cambridge, Cambridge University Press, 95–103.

Worcester, R. (1977) 'Rasmussen interview with Robert Worcester' in *British Politics Newsletter*, spring 1977.

Worcester, R. (1991) *British Public Opinion: A Guide to the History and Methodology of Political Opinion Polling*, Oxford, Blackwell.

Worcester, R. and Harrop, M. (eds) (1982) *Political Communications: The General Election Campaign of 1979*, London, Allen & Unwin.

Young, Lord (1990) *The Enterprise Years*, London, Weidenfeld.

INDEX